Wii For Dummies®

Common Wii Remote Shortcuts

Press This	To Do This
+/– buttons	Zoom in or out on text or zoom the camera view
+/– buttons (on menus)	Change page
Directional pad	Scroll through pages or views
A+B buttons (hold and move pointer)	Pick up and move Mii or object
A button	Select option
B button	Go back in menus
B button (hold and move pointer)	Quick scroll
+ button (in games)	Pause
HOME button	Pause/edit controller options or return to Wii Menu

Wii Menu Shortcuts

Press This	To Do This
+/– buttons	Change page
A+B buttons (hold and move pointer)	Pick up or move Channel
A button	Bring up preview screen or start Channel

Mii Channel, Mii Plaza, and the Check Mii Out Channel Shortcuts

Press This	To Do This
+/– buttons	Zoom view in/out
A button	Display Mii name and details
Directional pad	Scroll view
B button (hold and move pointer)	Scroll view
A+B buttons (hold and move pointer)	Pick up and move Mii to menu item or new location

Photo Channel Shortcuts

Press This	To Do This
+/– buttons	Zoom in/out
A button	View picture
Directional pad	Scroll view
1 button (when viewing video)	Advance three seconds
2 button (when viewing video)	Rewind three seconds

For Dummies: Bestselling Book Series for Beginners

Wii For Dummies®

Cheat Sheet

Internet Channel Shortcuts

Press This	To Do This
A button	Follow link
+/− buttons	Zoom in/out
Directional pad	Scroll through page
B button (hold and move pointer)	Quick scroll
2 button	Toggle single-column mode
B+ − (minus) buttons	Go back to last page
B++ (plus) buttons	Go to next page
B+↑ on the directional pad	Reload current page
B+↓ on the directional pad	Open Favorites menu
B+← on the directional pad	Search the Web
B+→ on the directional pad	Enter Web address

News or Forecast Channel Global View Shortcuts

Press This	To Do This
+/− buttons	Zoom in/out
A button	View news stories or forecast for city
A button (hold and move pointer)	Spin globe
↑/↓ on the directional pad	Raise/lower viewing angle
←/→ on the directional pad (in Forecast Channel)	Change displayed weather information

For Dummies: Bestselling Book Series for Beginners

Wii™ FOR DUMMIES®

by Kyle Orland

WILEY

Wiley Publishing, Inc.

Wii™ For Dummies®

Published by
Wiley Publishing, Inc.
111 River Street
Hoboken, NJ 07030-5774
www.wiley.com

Copyright © 2008 by Wiley Publishing, Inc., Indianapolis, Indiana

Published by Wiley Publishing, Inc., Indianapolis, Indiana

Published simultaneously in Canada

For general information on our other products and services, please contact our Customer Care Department within the U.S. at 800-762-2974, outside the U.S. at 317-572-3993, or fax 317-572-4002.

For technical support, please visit www.wiley.com/techsupport.

Wiley also publishes its books in a variety of electronic formats. Some content that appears in print may not be available in electronic books.

Library of Congress Control Number: 2008935265

ISBN: 978-0-470-40297-9

Manufactured in the United States of America

10 9 8 7 6 5 4 3 2

WILEY

About the Author

Kyle Orland has been playing video games pretty much nonstop since just before he got a Nintendo Entertainment System for his seventh birthday. At age 14, he started writing about those games professionally when he set up a fansite for *Super Mario Bros. HQ* on the free Web space provided by his parents' America Online account. Twelve years later, Super Mario Bros. HQ is still up and running at a more professional-looking home at `www.smbhq.com`.

From that humble beginning, Kyle has gone on to become a successful freelance journalist specializing in video games. He writes regular news posts and features for popular gaming weblog Joystiq.com, and he writes a variety of columns and reviews for CrispyGamer.com, including Games for Lunch (`http://gamesforlunch.blogspot.com`), a daily, one-hour playlog. Kyle's work has also appeared in *Electronic Gaming Monthly, Paste Magazine, Gamasutra, GameDaily,* and *The Escapist,* among other outlets. He has been quoted as a gaming expert in *The New York Times, The Washington Post,* G4TV, and TheStreet.com, among other outlets.

This is Kyle's second book. He co-wrote *The Video Game Style Guide and Reference Manual* with David Thomas and Scott Steinberg in 2007 (published by Lulu.com). His favorite game of all time is *Super Mario 64*.

Dedication

To my wife, Michelle, who never lets me think I can't do anything I put my mind to.

To my parents, who bought me my first Nintendo Entertainment System and held their tongues when I threw away a nice, secure, decently paying desk job to follow my dream of becoming an underpaid game journalist.

To all the friends, family, and colleagues who wouldn't let me go crazy while writing nearly 300 pages of reference material about a single game system.

Author's Acknowledgments

Thanks to Gateway for making a solid laptop that stood up to hours and hours of typing and editing for the making of this book. Thanks to Pinnacle for making the Dazzle, a device that made taking the screenshots for the in-book figures a painless process. Thanks to Sony for making a nice little camera that I used to take many pictures of their competitor's system. Thanks to Nadeo for making *TrackMania*, a game that helped keep me sane during many a writing break.

Thanks to Nintendo for providing the hardware and much of the software used in the making of this book (not to mention the decades of gaming enjoyment they've provided me through their products). Thanks to my editors at Wiley, including Amy Fandrei, Steven Hayes, Jean Nelson, and Barry Childs-Helton, for making me look good. Thanks to Alexander Sliwinski for making sure you can actually *do* everything I say you can do in the book. Thanks to the team at Joystiq that helped me get this gig and understood when I went on a functional leave of absence for two months to actually write it.

Thanks to my sister, Paige, for not letting me distract myself from writing by talking to her on Instant Messenger. Thanks to my friend Mike for loaning me a Wii Remote Jacket to use in some figures. Last but not least, thanks to Michelle for forcing me to get out of the house occasionally during the whirlwind writing process.

Publisher's Acknowledgments

We're proud of this book; please send us your comments through our online registration form located at www.dummies.com/register/.

Some of the people who helped bring this book to market include the following:

Acquisitions, Editorial

Project Editor: Jean Nelson

Acquisitions Editor: Amy Fandrei, Steven Hayes

Senior Copy Editor: Barry Childs-Helton

Technical Editor: Alexander Sliwinski

Editorial Manager: Kevin Kirschner

Editorial Assistant: Amanda Foxworth

Sr. Editorial Assistant: Cherie Case

Cartoons: Rich Tennant (www.the5thwave.com)

Composition Services

Project Coordinator: Patrick Redmond

Layout and Graphics: Ana Carrillo, Reuben W. Davis, Nikki Gately, Melissa K. Jester, Christin Swinford, Christine Williams

Proofreaders: Debbye Butler, Jessica Kramer

Indexer: Potomac Indexing, LLC

Publishing and Editorial for Technology Dummies

Richard Swadley, Vice President and Executive Group Publisher

Andy Cummings, Vice President and Publisher

Mary Bednarek, Executive Acquisitions Director

Mary C. Corder, Editorial Director

Publishing for Consumer Dummies

Diane Graves Steele, Vice President and Publisher

Composition Services

Gerry Fahey, Vice President of Production Services

Debbie Stailey, Director of Composition Services

Contents at a Glance

Table of Contents

Introduction

● ●

*I*f you're actually reading this Introduction, you're probably a customer in a bookstore, trying to decide whether or not you should buy this book. To help you out, I've made up a simple quiz:

1. Do you own a Wii?

2. Do you intend to own a Wii soon?

If you answered yes to either question, then congratulations, you are one of the millions of people worldwide who should buy this book! If you answered "No," please feel free to go out and buy a Wii and then retake the quiz (refer to Chapter 1 for some tips on how to find one). Thank you.

About This Book

Think of this book as the unabridged edition of those tiny user manuals that come with the Wii itself. While those manuals are all right for getting started, this book gives you much more detail on the inevitable issues that come up when using the Wii. From setting the Wii system up with your entertainment center to using the Wii's many unique controllers; from connecting the system to the Internet to playing games, this book has the detailed instructions and troubleshooting you need to get it done.

This book isn't meant to be read from front to back. Treat it more like a reference that you can consult whenever you find something confusing or difficult when using the Wii. The book is divided into chapters and sections by topic, so you can easily find what you're looking for by perusing the table of contents. Failing that, please consult the index for the specific issue you need to know more about.

Conventions Used in This Book

I know that doing something the same way over and over again can be boring, but sometimes consistency can be a good thing. For one thing, it makes stuff easier to understand. In this book, those consistent elements are *conventions*. In fact, I use italics to identify and define the new terms.

Like all game systems, the Wii comes with a controller. The *Wii Remote* is the white, wireless, handheld controller that comes with the system and is the main means for interacting with the Wii. The book makes frequent mention of pressing *buttons* on this Remote. These buttons are clearly labeled on the Wii Remote itself, or you can consult Chapter 3 for more on the Remote's button layout.

The Remote can also be used to control an on-screen *pointer* using infrared technology. Moving this pointer over an on-screen option and pressing the A button is referred to in the book as *clicking.* You may also have to hold down a button on the Remote and *drag* the pointer to another location on the screen at times. See Chapter 3 for more on using the Wii Remote as a pointer.

In general the Wii can run two types of programs, disc-based games, which are discussed in Part III, and *Channels,* which are discussed in Part II. Channels are simply applications that are stored on the Wii's internal memory and don't require a separate disc to run. See Chapter 5 for more on using the Wii Menu to access Channels and start disc-based games.

When I provide URLs (Web addresses) within a paragraph, they are in a monospace font and look like this: www.dummies.com.

What You Don't Have to Read

While the bulk of this book is reference material that relates directly to getting the most out of your Wii, some sections simply provide supplemental information that some readers might find interesting. This extra information is placed in sidebars that are broken out in separate shaded boxes.

Any section labeled with the Technical Stuff icon (see the "Icons Used in This Book" section, farther along) is meant for advanced users, and won't be necessary for the majority of Wii owners.

Foolish Assumptions

I've written this book with inexperienced Wii owners in mind — the new gamers who've never owned a video-game system before, or the lapsed gamers who last played games on their Atari 2600 or home *Pong* units. Those with more gaming experience will find shortcuts, tips, and tricks they may not have discovered on their own.

I'm assuming you have a basic familiarity with your television and your specific home-entertainment setup. If you don't, you may want to consult the documentation for your home-entertainment equipment before you connect the Wii to your entertainment center (described in Chapter 2).

If you're planning to hook your Wii up to the Internet, I assume you currently have a broadband Internet connection hooked up in your home and understand the basic functionality of your high-speed modem and/or router. A complete tutorial on setting up a home Internet network is beyond the scope of this book — for help there, check out *Home Networking For Dummies,* 4th Edition, by Kathy Ivens (Wiley Publishing, Inc.).

How This Book Is Organized

I divided this book into parts, organized by topic. Each part deals with one important aspect of the Wii experience. If you're looking for information on a specific topic, check the headings in the table of contents, or skim the index.

By design, this book enables you to get as much (or as little) information as you need at any particular moment. For example, if you just need guidance setting up the system, refer to Chapter 3; if you're just looking to use the Photo Channel, look up Chapter 8. By design, *Wii For Dummies* is a reference that you'll reach for again and again whenever some new question about the Wii comes up.

Part 1: The Basics

After some brief background about the history of Nintendo and the new Wii system, Part I tells you what to do with your new Wii after you get it from the store into your house. This includes information on hooking up the system to your TV or home entertainment setup, taking control of the system with the included and optional controllers, and connecting the system to your high-speed Internet connection.

Part II: The Channels

Video game systems aren't just about games anymore, and the Wii is no exception. The Wii Menu lets you access other functions through built-in applications called Channels. These Channels open the Wii up to functions that used to be limited to a computer, such as a full-featured Web browser and digital photo viewer. You can also use Channels to create and share cartoon-like digital avatars called Miis and download new games and Channels directly from the Wii Shop Channel. You also discover the News, Weather, and other miscellaneous Channels.

Part III: The Games

Despite the added functionality of the Channels, the Wii is still a game system, and so it's meant to play video games. Part III details some basic information on how to pick games that are right for you and your family before diving in to a detailed description of two of the most popular games for the system: *Wii Sports,* which comes packaged with every Wii system, and *Wii Fit,* the revolutionary personal trainer in a box that uses your entire body as a controller. You can also find some recommendations of games to buy from your local gaming or electronics store.

Part IV: The Part of Tens

I've remained true to *For Dummies* style by including a Part of Tens. The chapters in this part can help you find ten games to download from the Wii Shop Channel, as well as ten optional Wii accessories that can help spice up your Wii experience.

Icons Used in This Book

To make your experience with the book easier, I use various icons in the margins of the book to indicate particular points of interest.

Whenever I give you a hint or a tip that makes an aspect of the Wii easier to use, I mark it with this little Tip thingamabob — it's my way of sharing what I've figured out the hard way — so you don't have to.

This icon is a friendly reminder or a marker for something that you want to make sure that you keep in mind. Usually this stuff is discussed elsewhere in the book, but who knows if you've read that part yet?

Ouch! This icon warns you about potential pitfalls or problems that you could run into, and gives advice on avoiding or fixing the issue. Be sure to read the whole paragraph before you even think of doing anything discussed next to this little guy.

The Wii is specifically designed not to require a lot of arcane, technical knowledge from its users, so this icon isn't used too often in this book. When it is used, it means this portion discusses some advanced stuff that most users won't need to worry themselves with. For the most part, if you don't understand anything next to one of these icons, just ignore it.

Where to Go from Here

Now you're ready to use this book. Look over the table of contents and find something that catches your attention, or a topic that you think can help you solve a problem.

Do you have any questions about this book? How about comments? Bitter invective? You can contact me online through my personal Web site, www. kyleorland.com.

Part I
The Basics

"I don't see the nunchucks, but I've got a set of throwing stars we can use instead."

In this part . . .

Welcome to the wonderful world of Wii! This part of the book is for new Wii owners just getting to know their new systems. First, you get a little background about the history of Nintendo and the Wii's historic launch. Then it's time to get busy hooking the Wii up to your entertainment center — and figuring out how to use the Wii Remote and other controllers that work with the Wii. Finally, you discover how to hook the Wii up to your high-speed Internet connection to access a world of new features.

So wander this way, and wade waist-deep into the Wii waters (okay . . . I promise that's the last time I'll do that).

Chapter 1

How the Wii Came to Be

In This Chapter

▶ Reliving the Wii's secretive development

▶ Finding a system in stores

*1*f you're like a lot of new Wii owners, you probably don't know much about your new purchase or the story behind it. Sure, you may have heard a snippet on the local news about how the system was almost impossible to find after its initial release in late 2006. You even may have read a newspaper story about how the system is catching on with all sorts of unlikely groups of new gamers.

These factoids are just a part of the story behind the Wii. This chapter covers the hundred-plus year history of Nintendo leading up to the launch of the Wii and beyond.

Nintendo's early years

Nintendo wasn't always the electronic-entertainment powerhouse it is today. The company was originally founded in 1889 as a producer of traditional handmade Japanese playing cards called *hanafuda*. The name "Nintendo" roughly translates to "Leave luck to heaven." Company founder Fusajiro Yamauchi had plenty of luck when the Yakuza (the Japanese mafia) took a liking to Nintendo's cards for their illegal gambling halls. This interest helped the company expand to American-style playing cards by 1907, and build a wide-ranging distribution network of Japanese retailers by 1927. In 1947, Nintendo opened a three-story factory next door to the simple, one-room office that had once served as its headquarters.

By the 1950s, control of Nintendo had transferred to Hiroshi Yamauchi, Fusajiro's grandson. He expanded the company's card business by introducing plastic-coated cards in 1953 and, in 1959, signed on with Walt Disney Co. to sell cards printed with popular Disney characters. The new Disney-branded cards took the Japanese playing-card market out of the illegal gambling dens and expanded it to the family home. Nintendo sold a record 600,000 packs of cards of the year the Disney printings were introduced.

(continued)

(continued)

Despite this continued success, Yamauchi wasn't satisfied managing a playing-card company. In the 1960s, Nintendo experimented with marketing and selling a variety of different products, eventually expanding into the toy business. Plastic toys like the Ultra Hand (an extendable grabber), the Ultra Machine (an indoor ping-pong-ball-pitching machine), and the Ultra Scope (a toy periscope) were marketed heavily on TV, and sold through Nintendo's already established network of retailers.

Nintendo jumped to electronic toys in the early '70s with the Nintendo Beam Gun, a light-emitting rifle that activated small, light-sensitive cells which caused a set of plastic barrels to explode. Nintendo used this same essential technology to convert a series of abandoned bowling alleys into virtual skeet-shooting ranges. When these light-gun ranges fell out of style, Nintendo headed back to the home market, selling a licensed version of a Magnavox-made, *Pong*-style game in Japan in 1977. Nintendo had finally entered the video-game business.

This chapter also gives you some advice on hunting down your very own Wii (or helping a friend hunt down a Wii, if you already own one).

I learned much of the history in the sidebars in this chapter from David Sheff's excellent book *Game Over: How Nintendo Zapped an American Industry, Captured Your Dollars and Enslaved Your Children* (published by Random House). Check it out for a much more thorough account of Nintendo's early history.

Wii Development and Unveiling

Even while releasing the GameCube system in 2001, Nintendo was already beginning the planning for its follow-up system, then codenamed Revolution. From the outset, Nintendo wanted the Revolution to take the video game market in a new direction. Instead of trying to make a system with the most powerful technology or the most realistic graphics, Nintendo was going to attempt to change the fundamental way people played games. "The consensus was that power isn't everything for a console," said legendary Nintendo game designer Shigeru Miyamoto, the man behind *Donkey Kong* and *Super Mario Bros.*, in a 2007 interview with *BusinessWeek*. "Too many powerful consoles can't coexist. It's like having only ferocious dinosaurs. They might fight and hasten their own extinction."

Nintendo president Satoru Iwata confirmed this new direction for the company when he announced the existence of the Revolution project to the world at a 2004 press conference. "Today's consoles already offer fairly realistic expressions, so simply beefing up the graphics will not let most of us see a difference," he said. "The definition for a new machine must be different. I want you to know that Nintendo is working on our next system and that system will create a gaming revolution. Internal development is underway."

The rise and fall of a video-game giant

In 1981, Nintendo caught the crest of the huge arcade-gaming wave with *Donkey Kong*. The game was notable for its basic story (told through animated cut scenes), run-and-jump gameplay, and one of the first identifiable human characters in a game (who would eventually be known as Mario the plumber). The game sold hundreds of thousands of units to arcades in Japan and the United States. Nintendo had further success with a few follow-up arcade games, and with a popular line of miniature, handheld games known as *Game* and *Watch*.

This early success in the arcade game market was all a drop in the bucket, though, compared to the overwhelming reaction to Nintendo's Family Computer, or Famicom. First released in Japan in 1983, the home system became a hit — thanks, in part, to *Super Mario Bros.,* one of the first action games to feature a smooth-scrolling background. Nintendo brought the Famicom to the United States in 1985 as the Nintendo Entertainment System (NES). The American market was initially wary of the Japanese-made system, but the system slowly built up momentum and eventually took over 90 percent of the American video-game market, By the early '90s, there was a NES in nearly one in three American households. The name "Nintendo" was synonymous with "video games."

Nintendo followed up the phenomenal success of the NES with the even more phenomenal success of the Game Boy in 1989. One of the first portable systems to support interchangeable games stored on plastic cartridges, the Game Boy fended off competition from more powerful portables thanks to a lower price, longer battery life, and exclusive rights to the addictive puzzle game *Tetris*. The Game Boy line sold over a hundred million units worldwide over the next two decades.

Nintendo's success on the home-gaming front was not as consistent. After achieving market dominance with the NES, Nintendo was slow to react when Sega's more powerful Genesis system started to find some success in the early '90s. By the time the new Super Nintendo Entertainment System was released, Sega had enough of a foothold to gain control of nearly half the home gaming market.

In the mid-90s, Nintendo's market position eroded further in the face of the Sony PlayStation, whose compact-disc-based games made similar games on the new Nintendo 64 system look like relics from long ago. By the dawn of the new millennium, Nintendo's GameCube and Microsoft's new Xbox system were fighting over the market scraps left behind by Sony's PlayStation 2, which was becoming nearly as dominant in the marketplace then as the NES had been almost 20 years prior. Two decades after the NES launched in America, "PlayStation" was now synonymous with "video games" to an entire generation of players. Nintendo needed something big to turn its market position around. That "something big" turned out to be the Wii.

Among avid gamers, rumors started flying about what, exactly, Nintendo had planned for its mysterious Revolution. Some speculated that the system would include a controller with a built-in touch screen, similar to the company's recently released Nintendo DS handheld. Others thought the controller might include a built-in microphone for voice-controlled gaming, or a modular design with specialized, snap-off sections. There were a few gamers who even envisioned fanciful concepts for three-dimensional virtual reality helmets or projection systems that transformed the entire living room into a magical play space.

It wasn't until the Tokyo Game Show in September 2005 that Nintendo finally halted the speculation by revealing a prototype of its unique new remote controller. Selected members of the gaming press got to try out the controller on a series of specially designed demos that showed off the Remote's ability to sense the movement of the player's hand. Initial reactions among the press were cautiously optimistic. A writer at 1UP.com said the Remote initially made his arms and hands tired, "but once I sat down and relaxed, resting my hands on my legs as I would with a normal controller, everything clicked." A writer from gaming website IGN said it was "easy to imagine why Nintendo is so heavily invested in the idea. There is such great potential to do so many unique things."

This initial enthusiasm turned to confusion, though, when Nintendo revealed the final name for its new system in early May 2006. From then on, what had been known as Project Revolution would officially be known as the Wii. Nintendo explained the new name in a press release, saying in part that, "Wii sounds like 'we,' which emphasizes that the console is for everyone. Wii can easily be remembered by people around the world, no matter what language they speak. No confusion. No need to abbreviate. Just Wii."

The press wasn't so understanding. Journalists, developers and gamers around the world made fun of the system's name with less-than-wholesome homonyms. Some in the industry thought it was a joke, intended to get some free press from the marketing world. A few gamers even tried to boycott the name, continuing to call the system Revolution long after that name was officially dead. Over time, though, the initial shock seems to have worn off, and today most gamers can talk about their Nintendo Wii with a completely straight face.

By the end of May 2006, Nintendo was ready to let a wider audience of industry insiders try out the Wii for the first time at the Electronic Entertainment Expo, an annual game industry trade show. Crowds flocked to Nintendo's booth throughout the three-day event, snaking around the Los Angeles Convention Center and waiting up to four hours to get into the small demonstration area. The long wait was worth it, to be among the first gamers anywhere to try demos of games like *Wii Sports, Super Mario Galaxy,* and *The Legend of Zelda: Twilight Princess.*

On September 14, 2006, Nintendo finally revealed that the Wii would launch in the United States just two months later, on November 19, at a price of $250. This put the system's launch just two days after that of Sony's PlayStation 3, the $500-to-$600 follow-up to the then-dominant PlayStation 2. Both new systems also had to contend with Microsoft's Xbox 360, which had launched to great fanfare nearly a year before. The Wii was heavily outclassed in terms of processing power and the support of many prominent game developers.

When November 19 finally came around, eager Nintendo fans lined up outside their favorite gaming stores to be the first to own the long-awaited system. The entire stock was sold out within hours, and new shipments were hard to come by for the remainder of 2006 — meaning gamers who didn't plan ahead missed out on the holiday season. Early reviewers were generally impressed with the Wii's unique controller and its prospects of getting game players off the couch, but some were underwhelmed by the system's decidedly last-generation graphics and (initially) thin library of games. Some predicted the system would be a flash in the pan — a gimmicky impulse buy that would get a lot of attention initially before being relegated to the back of America's collective closet.

As the months went by, though, this proved not to be the case. While the Xbox 360 and PlayStation 3 eventually recovered from the holiday rush and became widely available at retailers nationwide, stocks of the Nintendo Wii remained sparse well into 2007. A combination of a lower price and a growing public fascination with the system's unique controller led to shortages across the country. Some suspected Nintendo of purposely creating a false shortage, but consumers were simply buying up everything Nintendo's revamped production line could produce — the system routinely outsold the competition month after month. The problem only got worse as the 2007 holiday season came around and the Wii was still hard to come by. To this day, potential Wii owners have to be a little bit lucky to find a Wii on the shelves (see the next section).

Game publishers that had been wary of Nintendo in years past flocked to the successful Wii, increasing the system's game library to over 200 games as of this writing. Nintendo continued development as well, releasing new games and Channels, as well as innovative new controllers such as the Balance Board that comes with *Wii Fit*. In early 2008, Nintendo surpassed the ten-million-unit threshold in worldwide sales. In the summer of 2008, Nintendo overcame Microsoft's year-long head start to become the best-selling system in North America. Upcoming peripherals like Wii MotionPlus and games like *Wii Music* seem set to continue Nintendo's now successful video game revolution.

Finding a Wii

If you're reading this book, you probably already have a Wii. Even so, you may have a friend, or a neighbor, or a jealous cousin who just can't seem to find the system in his or her local store. Take pity on your fellow gamers by sharing these handy tips for finding the extremely hard-to-find Wii out in the retail wild:

- ✔ **Visit your local stores constantly:** Most game and electronics stores don't know when exactly their next shipment of Wiis will come in; the inventory of new systems tends to disappear within hours (or even minutes) after they arrive. This means that finding a Wii in stock at your local store is largely a matter of luck. You can increase your chances by stopping by frequently to ask about the store's inventory.

  You can also call local stores to ask about inventory, but be warned: By the time you get in the car and drive to the store, the systems might be out of stock yet again. . . .

- ✔ **Keep an eye on Sundays:** While there's no precise schedule to when stores receive their shipments of Wiis, some stores stockpile systems and make them available on Sundays, to coincide with newspaper circulars. It couldn't hurt to make yet another trip out first thing Sunday morning.

- ✔ **Use the Web:** Sites like `www.WiiTracker.com` and `www.NowInStock.net/wii` keep track of Wii availability at a variety of online stores. These sites aren't 100-percent reliable, but they're a good way to find out which Web sites might have a Wii to sell you at any given moment.

- ✔ **Buy a bundle:** With the Wii shortage still in full swing, many online and brick-and-mortar retailers only sell Wiis in bundles, together with various games and accessories. These bundles may have some items you don't necessarily want, and they cost more than a system by itself. That said, bundles tend to remain in stock much longer than unadorned systems, so you'll probably have better luck finding one.

- ✔ **Use eBay:** New Wii systems are generally plentiful on this popular auction site. The only catch: You usually have to pay a slight premium over the suggested retail price of $250 to compete with your fellow potential buyers. See *eBay For Dummies,* 5th Edition, by Marsha Collier (Wiley Publishing, Inc.) for more on finding good deals in online auctions.

- ✔ **Recruit family:** When my sister wanted a Wii, she recruited me to climb out of bed early on a frigid Sunday morning in January to scope out my local stores. She ended up finding a system before I actually had to leave the house, but her theory was sound — increase your chances by increasing the number of searchers.

Chapter 2

Getting to Know the Wii

In This Chapter

▶ Identifying the items that come in the Wii box

▶ Picking out the accessories that aren't included in the box

▶ Hooking the Wii up to your TV and/or entertainment center

▶ Calibrating the Wii to your personal preferences and setting up parental controls

*Y*ou finally got it. It took weeks of searching through online ads, two hours in line on a frigid Sunday morning, and a $20 bribe to the manager at your local toy store, but it all paid off now that you have that bright white box in your hands. Congratulations, you're the proud owner of a brand new Nintendo Wii.

Now what?

In this chapter, you find out how to assemble the myriad pieces that come in the Wii box into a fully functioning gaming and entertainment system. You discover how to plug everything in, how to adjust the system settings to your personal tastes, and how to keep young children from getting at the stuff they aren't supposed to. The setup and calibration aren't just going to happen by themselves, so jump right in. . . .

Opening the Box

Inside that sleek white box, the Wii and its components are encased in cardboard, Styrofoam, plastic bags, and tape. Remove all this detritus and lay everything out as shown in Figure 2-1. Use the following list to make sure you have every piece:

✔ **Wii console:** The white rectangle with a slot for inserting discs. Be careful when handling the console because it contains sensitive electronics (see the "Caring for your Wii" sidebar).

- ✔ **Wii console stand:** This comes in two parts: a rectangular gray stand and a clear, flat plastic Wii stand plate. Make sure you have both handy.

- ✔ **Wii Remote:** The hand-held white rectangle with buttons on it. This is your primary controller. Make sure you also unpack the two included AA batteries and the clear plastic Wii Remote sleeve. See Chapter 3 for more on how to use the Wii Remote.

- ✔ **Nunchuk:** The rounded white hand unit with a thumbstick sticking up from the top and a wire hanging down from the bottom. Named after the nunchaku, the martial arts weapon it resembles when plugged into the Wii Remote. See Chapter 3 for more on how to use the Nunchuk with the Wii Remote.

- ✔ **Sensor Bar:** The thin black bar with a long, thin wire running from the back. Make sure you also unpacked the clear plastic pedestal and included sticky tape to affix the bar to your TV.

- ✔ **Wii AC adapter:** The thick, rectangular gray block with power cords coming out both sides.

- ✔ **Wii Audio/Video cable:** A standard composite A/V cable with red, yellow, and white inputs for your TV. Your home entertainment setup may require or support other cables to hook up to the Wii. See the later section, "Getting the Rest of What You Need."

- ✔ ***Wii Sports* game disc:** The disc is in a labeled paper sleeve. (See Chapter 12 for more playing on *Wii Sports*.)

- ✔ **Manuals:** The box includes two Wii Operations Manuals: System Setup and Channels and Settings; plus a Quick Setup foldout card and a Wii extended warranty pamphlet.

Caring for your Wii

Although the white plastic exterior might make it look like a toy, the Wii is actually a complicated piece of electronics. As such, it's susceptible to damage if you don't treat it gently. Here's some general advice for making sure your Wii continues to work properly for a long, long time:

- ✔ Don't expose the system to extreme temperatures.

- ✔ Don't drop the system or jostle it violently.

- ✔ Don't spill water or other liquids on the system.

- ✔ Don't obstruct the air intakes on the back and bottom of the system.

- ✔ Don't stand the system up vertically without the included Wii System Stand.

- ✔ Don't pull or bend the attached cables at sharp angles.

- ✔ Keep the system out of humid environments.

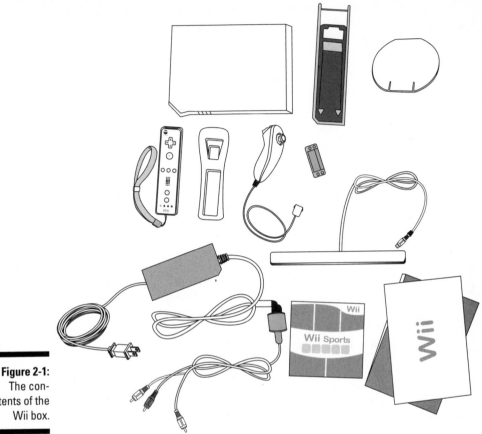

Figure 2-1:
The con-
tents of the
Wii box.

TIP

While the preceding list covers everything included in the basic Wii packaging, some retailers sell the Wii as part of a bundle with extra games, remotes, and possibly other accessories. Check the packaging and manuals to make sure you have all the items that *should* be included.

Getting the Rest of What You Need

Although the Wii box technically has everything you need to start enjoying your new system immediately, there are a few other items that you might want to look in to in order to get the most out of your Wii experience. These include:

✔ **Broadband modem and/or wireless router:** These are required to connect the Wii to the Internet and enjoy the system's online functions. You also need to subscribe to a high-speed Internet service through an Internet service provider (See Chapter 4 for more on getting the Wii onto the Internet).

✔ **SmartDigital (SD) card:** These portable, miniature memory cards can be used to back up saved game data, transfer data between Wiis, and transfer photos and music onto your system. (See Chapter 8 for more on using SD cards for photos and music and Chapter 16 for more on how to choose an SD card.)

✔ **GameCube memory card:** These are necessary to save data for GameCube games played on the Wii. (See Chapter 16 for more on GameCube memory cards.)

✔ **Component cables:** These cables provide a higher-quality image on enhanced-definition and high-definition TVs. You can purchase official Wii-compatible component cables for $29.95 from Nintendo by visiting `http://store.nintendo.com/componentvideocable` or by calling 1-800-255-3700. Third-party cables are also available from many electronics and gaming retailers for about $10 to $20. (See the later section, "Setting Up Your System," for information on calibrating the system to work with component cables.)

✔ **Additional controllers:** To play most multiplayer games (including many of those included on the included *Wii Sports* disc), you need to buy extra controllers. Wii Remotes generally retail for $40 and Nunchuks run you $20 each at major retailers. Additionally, you may need a GameCube controller or Wii Classic Controller to play certain games. See Chapters 3 and 6 for more advice on which controllers you need for which games.

✔ **Additional games:** Although the packaged *Wii Sports* disc is great, the Wii can play a library of hundreds of games — including classic discs designed for the Nintendo GameCube. (See Part III for recommendations on which games are right for you and your family.)

✔ **Accessories:** Since the Wii was released, many companies have released optional accessories to increase the functionality and style of your system. (See Chapter 16 for more on which accessories to look for and which to avoid.)

Hooking Up Your System

All right, you've got everything out of the box and you know how to tell a Sensor Bar from a Wii Remote. Now you need to hook it all up. The following steps show you how to hook up the Wii so you'll be playing with your system before you know it:

1. **Choose a location for the Wii.**

   Pick a space in your entertainment center or TV area where the Wii can rest level and comfortably. Note that the Wii can sit either horizontally or vertically, depending on the layout of your entertainment center. Make sure the location you choose has plenty of ventilation and that the air vents on the back of the system won't be blocked. Also make sure you have easy access to the back of the system because you need to plug in a variety of components back there in the next steps.

   a. If you're setting the system up vertically, you need to place it in the Wii System Stand to make sure it's stable and properly ventilated. First, slide the clear plastic Wii Stand Plate into the slots on the bottom of the stand. (This process is shown in greater detail in Figure 2-2.) Then lower the console into the top of the stand so the front is pointing toward the elevated side.

   b. If you're setting the system up horizontally, you do not need to use the Wii System Stand — simply put the system in place so the disc slot is located above the buttons on the face of the system. Set the two pieces of the System Stand aside and proceed to Step 2.

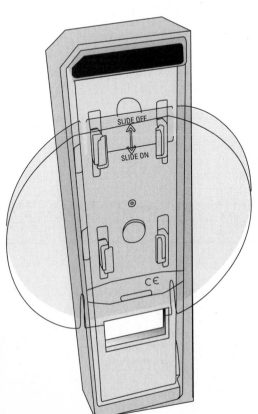

Figure 2-2:
Assembling
the Wii
System
Stand.

2. Connect the A/V cable to the system and TV.

Connect the rectangular gray end of the Wii A/V cable to the back of the Wii in the slot labeled AV Multi Out (see Figure 2-3). Connect the red, yellow, and white prongs on the other end of the cable to the appropriate inputs on your TV. Note that some home entertainment setups may require you to plug the Wii into a VCR or cable box instead of directly into your TV — consult the documentation for these devices for more information.

Some older TVs don't have the standard yellow, red, and white A/V input ports needed for the Wii A/V cables. Don't fret — you might be able to connect the system to your TV using a generic radio-frequency (RF) modulator. This device converts the Wii A/V cables into an RF input that can be plugged into a TV's coaxial cable input. These generally sell for $5 to $20 and can be found at any specialty electronics retailer.

3. Connect the Sensor Bar.

The Sensor Bar is used by the Wii Remote to detect its position relative to your TV. As such, it's very important that the Sensor Bar sits near the TV with an unobstructed view of the area where people will be controlling the Wii.

First, decide whether you want the Sensor Bar to sit on the top of your TV or on the bottom. Either way, align it so the center of the Sensor Bar is lined up with the center of the TV. Make sure the Sensor Bar sits parallel to the screen and roughly level with the ground, with the shiny, black side pointing directly out from the TV. See Figure 2-4 for an example of correct placement.

Use the included plastic stand and double-sided tape to secure the Sensor Bar in place, if necessary. When the bar is placed, thread the cable behind the TV and plug it into the orange Sensor Bar slot on the back of the system (refer to Figure 2-3).

Figure 2-3: The Wii's rear connections.

Sensor bar

Figure 2-4:
Correct
placement
of the Wii
Sensor Bar
on the top
of a TV.

With some entertainment-center setups (such as those using a rear projector) it's possible that the Sensor Bar cable won't be long enough to reach to the system. Don't panic; independent accessory makers have made wireless sensor bars that can be placed independently of the Wii system itself. No special setup is required for these sensor bars — just place them as described in the preceding paragraphs and continue setup as normal. Wireless sensor bars are available for $20 at many major retailers.

4. **Plug in the AC adapter.**

   The end with the electrical plug goes into a standard 120 V AC wall outlet. The rectangular end goes into the slot labeled 12V=IN on the back of the system (refer to Figure 2-3). After you plug in the AC adapter, a small red light should appear on the power button on the front of the Wii.

5. **Put the batteries in the Wii Remote.**

   Remove the battery cover from the back of the Wii Remote and place the two AA batteries in the indentation. Make sure the positive and negative sides of the batteries line up with the instructions printed on the inside of the Remote. Replace the battery cover.

The Wii Remote goes through regular alkaline batteries like a child tearing through wrapping paper on Christmas morning. Consider investing in some rechargeable batteries to keep your Remote going through extended play sessions. See Chapter 16 for more on rechargeable battery packs and chargers designed specifically for the Wii Remote.

If you're using a Wii Remote other than the one that came packaged with your system, it may need to be synchronized with the Wii before use. See Chapter 3 for more information on synchronizing Remotes to your system.

6. **Turn on your TV and then your Wii.**

   Turn on the TV and choose the appropriate input setting for the slot you plugged the Wii in to (consult your TV or VCR manual for more information on selecting the correct input). Push the Power button on the front of the Wii. If everything is set up correctly, the light on the power button should turn green and a generic safety message should appear on your TV. If you don't see the message, double check all wire connections and make sure the TV input is set correctly.

   Push the A button on the Wii Remote and you see the Wii Channel menu, shown in Figure 2-5. Congratulations! Your Wii is on and working!

Figure 2-5: The Wii Channel menu, a sign of successful Wii installation.

Now that your system is on, you need to know how to turn it off. You also need to know how to use the other various buttons on the system itself. These are shown in Figure 2-6 and detailed in the following list:

✔ **Power button:** Turns the system on and off. Press the button briefly to send the system to standby mode, where the WiiConnect24 Internet service will continue to work (see Chapter 4 for more on WiiConnect24). Hold down the button for three seconds to turn the system off completely.

✔ **Power LED:** This light shows the current status of the Wii. It has three settings.

   • **Green:** The system is on.

   • **Orange:** The system is in Standby mode and able to receive data from WiiConnect24. See Chapter 4 for more on WiiConnect24.

   • **Red:** The system is completely off and not receiving data from WiiConnect24. To force the system to this state when WiiConnect24 is on, hold down the power button for three seconds.

✔ **Reset:** Press this button to restart the system.

✔ **SYNCHRO button:** Used to synchronize the Wii with new Wii Remotes so they can be recognized by the system. Note that this button is hidden behind a small white cover. See Chapter 3 for more on synchronizing Remotes.

✔ **SmartDigital card slot:** Used for memory-expanding SD cards. Note this slot is hidden by a protective white cover. See Chapter 8 for more on inserting and using SD cards with the Wii and Chapter 16 for how to pick out an SD card.

✔ **Eject:** Press this button to remove the disc currently in the disc slot.

✔ **Game disc slot:** This is where both Wii and GameCube game discs are inserted. Make sure the shiny side of the disc is facing down (if the system is in its horizontal position) or to the left (if the system is standing vertically).

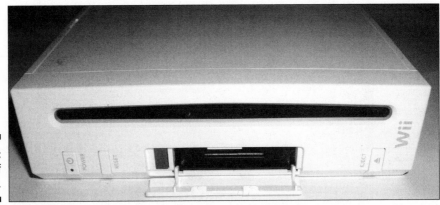

Figure 2-6:
The front of the Wii.

Setting Up Your System

When your Wii is hooked up and blasting audio and video out of your TV, the next thing to do is calibrate it to your exact specifications using the Wii Settings menu. In this section, I walk you through the menu's many options and help you decide which settings to use.

Before moving on, you need to have a basic familiarity with using the Wii Remote to move the on-screen pointer and clicking on-screen options with the A button. (Chapter 3 provides more details on using the Wii Remote.)

To calibrate your Wii, follow these steps:

1. **Open the Wii Settings menu by clicking the Wii icon in the lower-left corner of the Wii Channel menu (see Figure 2-5).**

2. **Click Wii Settings to bring up the menu shown in Figure 2-7.**

3. **Click the arrows on the left and right sides of the screen to scroll through the various pages of menu items.**

   Pressing the + and – buttons on the Wii Remote has the same effect.

4. **Click the on-screen menu options to bring up the submenus described in the list shown in the next step.**

5. **When you're done adjusting a specific setting, click OK or Confirm to save your settings, or click Back to return to the Wii Settings menu without saving your changes.**

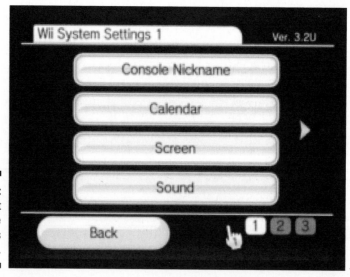

Figure 2-7:
The first page of the Wii Settings menu.

The Wii Settings menu contains the following options:

- ✔ **Console Nickname:** This is pretty straightforward — a nickname your Wii will use to identify itself when it connects to other Wiis via the Internet. Click the white text-entry area, and then use the on-screen keyboard to enter your desired nickname (see Chapter 4 for more on the on-screen keyboard). Your console nickname can have up to ten characters.

- ✔ **Calendar:** Set the Wii's internal date and time via this menu option. Click either Date or Time on the submenu, and then click the arrows to adjust the appropriate numbers up and down. Note that the Wii uses a 24-hour clock, so 6:00 p.m. reads as 18:00.

  The Wii doesn't support any dates past Dec. 31, 2035. (If you're reading this book in 2036 for some reason, may I suggest upgrading your video game system already? I'm sure gaming has advanced quite a bit since the Wii came out.)

- ✔ **Screen:** The four submenu options on this screen let you adjust how the Wii's video signal displays on your TV:

  - • **Screen Position:** On some TVs, the image output by the Wii may appear slightly off center. The Screen Position option lets you fix this problem by clicking the blue arrows until the red box is centered on your screen.

  - • **Widescreen Settings:** If you're playing the Wii on a widescreen TV (one with a 16:9 aspect ratio), you can use this menu option to adjust the Wii's output to stretch across the entire screen. If you choose the widescreen option, the Wii reminds you to make sure your TV is set to widescreen mode. Heed the Wii's advice. The Wii is wise and all-knowing.

  - • **TV Resolution:** If you're using the optional Wii component cables (see the earlier section, "Getting the Rest of What You Need"), you can use this option to set the Wii's output to 480p enhanced definition. If you are using the included composite A/V cables, this option is inaccessible.

  - • **Screen Burn-in Reduction:** This function helps prevent damaging burn-in on some TV models. When this option is turned on, the on-screen image fades out when a Wii game is paused for five or more minutes; push any button on the Wii Remote to return to full brightness and resume play. Note that this feature does not work when playing GameCube games on the Wii.

- ✔ **Sound:** Toggle between Monaural, Stereo, or Surround sound, depending on your entertainment setup.

✔ **Parental Controls:** This submenu is a little bit complicated, but important to set up if you want to prevent children from accessing restricted content on the Wii.

The first time you enter the Parental Controls submenu, you're asked to enter a four-digit PIN code by clicking the white box and using the on-screen numeric pad. You need this code later if you want to access restricted content or edit the parental control settings, so it's important you don't forget it. (You may want to use the same PIN you use at your local bank ATM.)

After you enter the code a second time for confirmation, you're asked to choose a secret question that you'll be asked if you forget your PIN. Be sure to pick a question that your child or children (or any kids who may visit) won't know the answer to — and, more importantly, one that *you'll* remember the answer to if and when you need it. Click on the white box and use the on-screen keyboard to type in your answer (See Chapter 4 for more on using the on-screen keyboard).

If you forget your PIN, your answer has to match the one you enter here *exactly*. Spelling and capitalization count, so be careful.

After this initial setup, you can access two further submenus, Game Settings and PIN and Other Settings. Also note that the Clear Settings button, at the bottom of the menu, can be used to reset and turn off the system's parental controls.

• **Game Settings and PIN:** This option lets you edit your PIN and secret question after the initial setup. You can also choose which games are playable by players who don't know your PIN (such as your children) by clicking the Highest Game Rating Allowed button, as shown in Figure 2-8.

Games are grouped according to ratings assigned by the Entertainment Software Ratings Board, each of which is described on the screen as you scroll using the on-screen arrows. Choose the highest rating that you're comfortable with your children playing and click OK. For even more about what each rating means, see Chapter 11.

Wii Parental Control settings will not work with GameCube games played on the Wii.

• **Other Settings:** When you choose this option, the Wii asks you a series of questions about what sorts of online content should be available to your children. See Chapter 4 and the channel descriptions in Part II for more about the Wii's online functions and which ones might not be suitable for children.

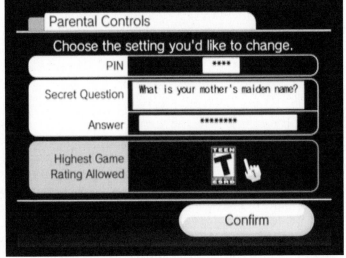

Parental Controls

Choose the setting you'd like to change.

PIN   ****

Secret Question   What is your mother's maiden name?

Answer   ********

Highest Game Rating Allowed

Confirm

Figure 2-8:
The Wii
Parental
Controls
Game
Settings and
PIN menu.

✔ **Sensor Bar:** This submenu allows you to adjust two different settings relating to the Wii Sensor Bar:

• **Sensor Bar Position:** Use this option to tell the Wii where the Sensor Bar is situated in relation to your TV. This helps the Wii determine where your Remote is pointing in relation to the television and makes pointing the Remote at the TV screen itself feel more natural. The Wii Remote still works if the wrong option is chosen, but the pointer may seem misaligned when the Wii Remote is pointed at the screen.

• **Sensitivity:** Use this option to control how the Wii Remote finds the Sensor Bar. After reading the on-screen messages, click OK twice to bring up a gray box with a sensitivity slider at the bottom, as shown in Figure 2-9. Point the Wii Remote at the Sensor Bar and two blinking white dots should appear in the gray box. These dots should move as you move the Wii Remote relative to the Sensor Bar.

If you see more than two dots, push the – button on the Wii Remote to lower the sensitivity until only two dots remain. You might also want to remove any other sources of bright light and any reflective surfaces near the Sensor Bar; these could interfere with the Remote's operation.

If you see no white dots, push the + button on the Wii Remote to increase the sensitivity until they do appear. If the sensitivity level is set to 5 and you still don't see the dots, make sure the Remote is located the recommended three to eight feet from the Sensor Bar and that there's nothing between the Sensor Bar and Wii Remote.

Also make sure that the Remote is on and that the Sensor Bar is plugged in correctly.

When the sensitivity is set correctly and the two white dots are blinking steadily and holding their position, press A to exit the calibration screen.

Bright lights or highly reflective materials near the Sensor Bar can affect the functioning of the Wii Remote.

✔ **Internet:** The options in this submenu are for setting up the Wii to talk to the Internet. (For much greater detail about configuring the Wii to work with the Internet, see Chapter 4.)

✔ **WiiConnect24:** This submenu controls the Wii's ability to access the Internet automatically to download certain messages and updates. (See Chapter 4 for more about these options.)

✔ **Language:** Use this option to change the default language used by the Wii menus and games. Be careful playing around with this menu — if you set the menus to a language you don't understand, it might be hard to get your Wii back to normal.

✔ **Country:** Select the country the system is being used in from the 42 options listed. This setting determines what content you get on certain channels, including the Wii Shop Channel and the Everybody Votes Channel. Click the blue arrows on-screen to scroll through the list. Note that if you are using a Wii in a different region than it was bought from (among North America, Europe, and Asia), your country might not be available.

✔ **Wii System Update:** If you've connected your Wii to the Internet (see Chapter 4), you can use this option to update the Wii's internal software with new features and bug fixes. Click Yes and then click I Accept to start the download process. If there's a new update available, the Wii downloads and installs it automatically (this may take a few minutes). If your software is up to date already, the system tells you so. Either way, you're returned to the Wii Channel menu when the process is done.

It's a good idea to attempt to download a system update as soon as possible after you first take your system out of the box, just to make sure that your Wii system software is up to date. Other than that, the system sends you a Message Board message or gives you an on-screen warning when a new system update is available or necessary; don't worry about remembering to check for updates on your own. (See Chapter 5 for more about the Wii Message Board.)

✔ **Format Wii System Memory:** Be *very* careful when selecting this option — because *it will delete all downloaded channels and all saved data currently stored on the system.* In general, the only reason you should even consider using this option is to erase your personal data if and when you're planning on selling the system or returning it to the store. A Nintendo technical support representative might also tell you to use this option if your Wii is not working correctly. Otherwise, just stay away from it!

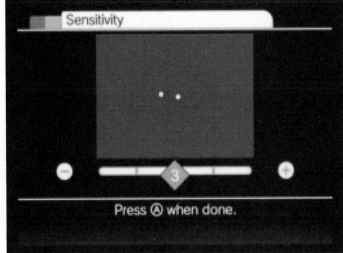

Figure 2-9:
The Sensor
Bar sen-
sitivity
adjustment
screen.

Chapter 3

Know Your Controllers

*F*or at least the past decade, most video-game controllers have seemed designed specifically to scare off newcomers. With their confusing arrangements of buttons, joysticks, and directional pads, it can be hard for a beginner to figure out how to *hold* many game controllers, much less use them effectively. Luckily, Nintendo eschewed this confusing convention with the Wii Remote — a simple, motion-based controller that resembles a TV remote more than a video-game controller.

Still, unlocking the full power of the Wii Remote takes some know-how (and a little practice). In this chapter you discover the ins and outs of the Wii Remote and how to use it effectively to control your Wii experience. You find out about the optional Nunchuk attachment that's used to control some games. You also figure out how to choose which additional controllers you actually need from amongst the dizzying array of other Wii-compatible controllers.

Bonding with Your Wii Remote

The Wii Remote is different from standard console game controllers and joysticks — it's easier and more intuitive to use, and it's lots of fun, too!

The following sections get you familiar with your Wii Remote, from the placement of the buttons to using it with the Wii Menu to describing the different motions you can make to control games.

Finding the buttons

Throughout this book, I refer to the buttons and indicators on the Wii Remote. These buttons are labeled on the controller itself (as shown in Figure 3-1) and described further in the following sections. While the specific function of each button depends on the menu and/or game being controlled, some buttons are often used consistently for the same function from game to game and Channel to Channel.

Front buttons

The following is a list of the buttons and other items on the front of the Wii Remote (see Figure 3-1):

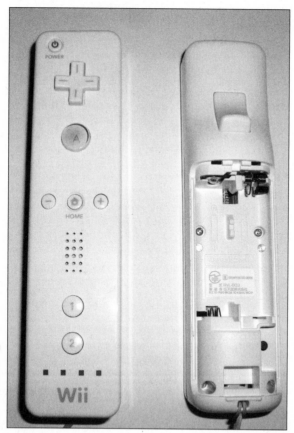

Figure 3-1:
The Wii
Remote and
its buttons.

- **Power:** Hold this button down for two seconds to turn the system on or off.

  Do not use this button if you want to turn off the Remote independently of the Wii system itself. (See "The Wii Remote Settings Menu" section later in this chapter for more on turning off the Remote by itself.)

- **Directional pad:** Used to scroll quickly through many menus and for directional input in many games. The directional pad is sometimes called the *d-pad* for short.

- **A button:** The *A button* is an all-purpose button used to make selections on many menus and perform the most frequent actions in many games.

  When this book refers to "clicking" an on-screen option, it means pointing at the option and pushing the A button.

- **Home button:** Pressing this button at any time pauses whatever you're doing and brings up the Home Menu, as shown in Figure 3-2. From this menu you can click the on-screen buttons to return to the Wii Channel menu (see Chapter 5) to restart the current game or enter the Wii Remote Settings menu. When you're playing downloaded WiiWare of Virtual Console games, you can use the Home menu to access the on-screen Operations Guide. (See Chapter 6 for more on this.)

- **– and + (minus and plus) buttons:** In general, these buttons adjust sliders and scroll through pages on many menus. Many games also use the + button as a Pause button.

- **Speaker:** The Wii Remote is the first video-game controller that can actually talk to you through this built-in speaker. The speaker volume can be adjusted or muted using the Wii Remote Settings menu (as described in the later section, "The Wii Remote Settings Menu").

- **1 and 2 buttons:** Used primarily in games to control various in-game functions, especially in games that use the Remote's horizontal configuration. (See the later section, "Getting the right grip.")

- **Player LEDs:** Used to indicate which controller is assigned to which in-game player number, starting with Player 1 on the left and going through Player 4 on the right.

When you turn on a Wii Remote, you might notice that some of the player LEDs blink as the controller connects to the system (see the later section, "Connecting Additional Remotes to the Wii"). The number of blinking lights corresponds roughly to the amount of charge left in that Remote's batteries. All four lights blinking means a nearly full battery, three lights blinking means 75% charge, two lights blinking means 50% charge, and so on. (This information is also available on the Home menu, but it's handy to know from the moment you turn on the controller.)

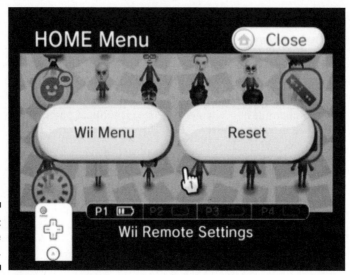

Figure 3-2:
The Home
Menu.

Rear buttons

The following buttons and other items can be found on the bottom or back
of the Wii Remote (refer to Figure 3-1):

✔ **B button:** Push this button with your index finger to back out from
many menus or perform secondary functions in games.

In many Channels and games, you can push the A and B buttons
together to virtually pick up an object with the on-screen pointer.

✔ **Battery cover:** As you probably guessed, this covers the battery
housing. Remove it to insert the batteries and reach the SYNCRO
button.

✔ **SYNCRO button:** Used to connect a new Wii Remote to the system for
the first time. (See the later section, "Connecting Additional Remotes to
the Wii," for more about synchronizing a new remote.)

✔ **Wrist strap:** Wrap this around your wrist to keep the Remote from flying
out of your hand and into your brand new 70-inch plasma screen TV
during heated play. (See the later section, "Safety first.")

✔ **External extension connector:** Use this to hook up optional controller
accessories such as the Nunchuk and Wii Classic Controller (more about
these controllers later in this chapter).

Safety first

If you pay attention to the news, you may have heard some stories about the rash of property damage caused by Wii Remotes flying out of players' over-enthusiastic hands soon after the system launched. How can you avoid being featured in such an awful episode? Well, you could coat your entire house in a protective layer of bubble wrap. Or you could take advantage of the extensive safety features Nintendo has devised for the Wii Remote, as detailed in the following subsections.

The wrist strap

Attached to the bottom of every Wii Remote, the Wrist strap is the main method for preventing massive damage from flying controllers. It ensures that if the Remote slips out from your sweaty hands, it won't get very far before dangling harmlessly from your arm.

To put the wrist strap on, slide the adjustment strap up toward the remote, stick your hand through the loop, then tighten the adjustment strap around your wrist, as shown in Figure 3-3. The fit should be snug, but it doesn't have to be too tight — there's no need to cut off your circulation!

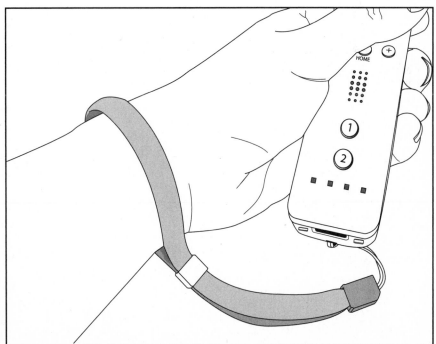

Figure 3-3:
The Wii
wrist strap.

Soon after the Wii was released, many users reported their wrist straps broke as the Remote flew from their hands, eliminating the entire point of the safety strap. Nintendo responded to these claims by recalling the original straps and replacing them with thicker, sturdier straps in December 2006, less than one month after the system's North American launch. All Remotes made after December 2006 (including those currently sold in stores and included with new Wiis) have these new, stronger straps. If you have an old Remote with a weaker strap, you can request a replacement from Nintendo by using the online form at www.nintendo.com/consumer/strapreplace.jsp.

The Wii Remote Jacket

For a few months, Nintendo relied on the new, beefed-up wrist straps to save plasma screens and drywall from flying Remotes. Then, in October 2007, Nintendo beefed up the protection even further with a springy, clear plastic jacket. The appropriately named Wii Remote Jacket ensconces the Remote in a cushioned, protective field while still leaving all the buttons exposed, as shown in Figure 3-4. It also makes the Remote easier to grip through a series of textured grooves. It may look a little silly and feel like overkill, but trust me, you'll be glad it's there when a Remote inevitably flies out of your hand and bonks you or your friend on the head.

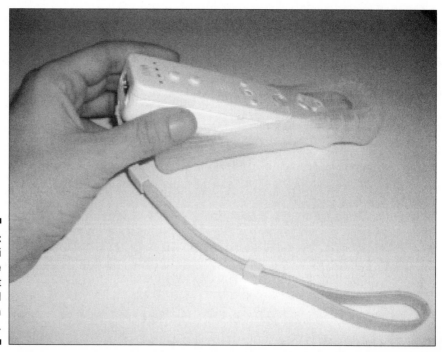

Figure 3-4:
The Wii
Remote
Jacket
wrapped
around a
Wii Remote.

A Remote Jacket is packaged with the Wii itself, and with all Wii Remotes currently sold in stores. If you need extra jackets for Remotes bought before October 2007, you can request them from Nintendo by using the online form at www.nintendo.com/consumer/jacket/jacketrequest.jsp.

Getting the right grip

In video-game controllers, as in golf, the correct grip is everything. There are two primary ways to hold the Wii Remote by itself. The first (shown in Figure 3-5) is the vertical position. This one-handed position is the basic grip used to navigate most Wii menus and channels, as well as to control many Wii games.

Notice how your thumb rests naturally on the large A button — you can also move your thumb to reach the other buttons on the face of the controller. Also notice how your index finger tucks into the indentation for the B button on the underside of the Remote. This position works just as well in either hand, making it perfect for both left- and right-handed gamers. Unless otherwise noted in the text, this is the position used to navigate all menus discussed in this book.

The second configuration, shown in Figure 3-6, is called the horizontal position. This two-handed configuration is similar to the way you would hold a GameCube or Xbox video-game controller, with the left thumb resting on the directional pad and the right thumb hovering above the 1 and 2 buttons. This configuration is primarily used to control certain classic games that require a more traditional control scheme. Note that you can use your left index finger to press the B button on the underside of the Remote, and that you can use your left thumb to reach over to press the central face buttons.

In either configuration, don't forget to use the wrist strap and Wii Remote Jacket to protect the controller and the room from each other.

Basic Wii Remote actions

With most game controllers, pushing buttons is the only way the controller can talk to the system. With the Wii Remote, though, that's only the beginning. The Wii Remote is motion-sensitive; you can use it as a virtual pointer and as a moving analogue for real-world actions. These unique Remote features are described in the following subsections.

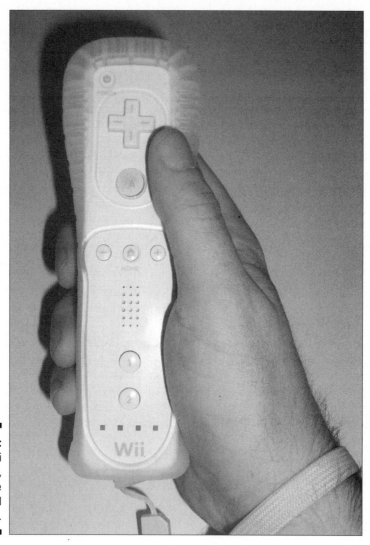

Figure 3-5:
The Wii
Remote,
held in the
vertical
position.

Using the Remote as a pointer

Remember that Sensor Bar you set up near the TV (described in Chapter 2)?
That little black bar lets you use the Wii Remote like a laser pointer to directly
interact with menus and games. It couldn't be simpler — just point the tip
of the Remote at the Sensor Bar and a hand-shaped pointer appears on the
screen. Move the remote slightly side to side or up and down and the on-
screen pointer moves along with it. You don't need grand sweeping gestures to
move the pointer around — small flicks of the wrist are enough to move from
one corner of the screen to another.

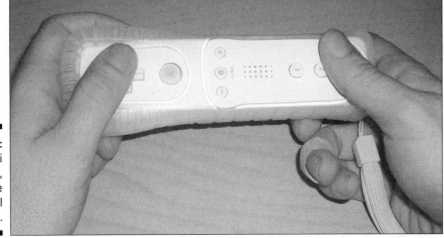

Figure 3-6:
The Wii
Remote,
held in the
horizontal
position.

If the pointer isn't showing up or is jumping around, here are a few things to keep in mind:

- ✔ Make sure the Remote is turned on and synced with the system, as described in the later section, "Connecting Additional Remotes to the Wii."

- ✔ Make sure the Sensor Bar is positioned and plugged in correctly, as discussed in Chapter 2.

- ✔ Make sure the Sensor Bar sensitivity is set correctly. (See Chapter 2 for more on this.)

- ✔ Make sure there are no other strong light sources or reflective materials around the Sensor Bar or screen area.

- ✔ Make sure there's nothing blocking the path from the Wii Remote to the Sensor Bar.

- ✔ Make sure you're approximately 3 to 8 feet from the Sensor Bar, as shown in Figure 3-7.

- ✔ Make sure you're actually pointing the remote *at* the Sensor Bar. Try jiggling the Remote around quickly to see if the pointer shows up.

While pointing at the screen, you can also use the Wii Remote buttons to interact with on-screen objects. Specific button functions depend on the context, but there are a few general rules. You can usually push the A button to select on-screen items, for instance, while pushing and holding the A and B buttons together can pick up objects in games or Channels. Note that the Wii can also sense how close the Remote is to the screen; some games and channels use that function to let you push and pull on-screen objects (more about that shortly).

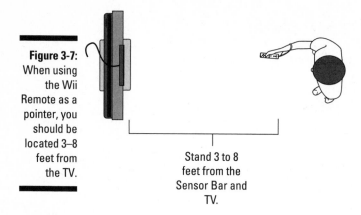

Figure 3-7: When using the Wii Remote as a pointer, you should be located 3–8 feet from the TV.

Stand 3 to 8 feet from the Sensor Bar and TV.

Feeling the motion

In addition to the pointer functionality, the Wii can also be used as a sort of magic wand that detects how it's about in 3-D space. These motions can be quick and sharp or large and sweeping, depending on the game. Each game is different, so experiment with different motions until you get a feel for them.

While different games each have different motion controls, a few basic motions get used frequently. Note that the Wii detects these motions regardless of whether the Remote is pointed at the screen.

- ✔ **Waving:** Sweep the controller back and forth in a large arc. The Wii can detect a variety of different types of waves — up and down, side to side, a golf swing, and so on.

- ✔ **Shaking:** Shake the Wii Remote quickly in place. This is used to activate special moves or effects in many games.

- ✔ **Tilting:** Gently lean the controller up and down. This is often used in games to tilt an on-screen object or a piece of scenery.

- ✔ **Twisting:** Turn the Wii remote in your hand like a key. This is used to rotate objects in many games and channels.

Don't start swinging the Wii Remote around without first putting on the wrist strap and Wii Remote Jacket. Make sure that you're standing in a clear space when you're playing, too — it's really easy to bump into or knock over objects when you're swinging the Remote. You don't want to break an antique vase or knock a glass of grape juice onto the carpet.

Connecting Additional Remotes to the Wii

With most video-game systems, connecting the controller to the system is as simple as plugging it in. Because the Wii Remote is wireless, however, getting the system to recognize additional controllers takes a few more (fortunately simple) steps.

Using the Remote that comes packaged with your Wii couldn't be simpler — just turn on the system and press the A button on the Remote. Connecting further Remotes to your system for the first time involves a process known as *syncing,* which the upcoming steps walk you through.

Note that this process only has to be performed once for every new Remote used on a particular system. After a Remote is synced to a system, simply pressing the A button turns on the Remote and connect it to the system. A Remote stays synced to a specific system until it is synced to another system.

To synchronize a new Wii Remote to your Wii, follow these steps:

1. **Turn on the Wii.**

   Use the power button on the system itself, not the one on the Wii Remote.

2. **Push the SYNCRO button on the Wii Remote.**

   This button can be found beneath the battery cover, as shown in Figure 3-8. Make sure there are batteries in the Remote. The Player LED lights on the front of the Remote start blinking.

3. **Push the SYNCRO button on the Wii itself.**

   This button is found under the protective flap on the front of the system, as shown in Figure 3-8.

4. **Watch for the lights on the Wii Remote to stop blinking.**

   After a few seconds, the Player LEDs on the Remote stops blinking and a single light stays on consistently. The Remote is now synced with the system. The solid light on the Remote indicates which player number is assigned to the Remote, from Player 1 on the left to Player 4 on the right.

Figure 3-8:
Syncing
your Wii
Remote.

The Wii Remote Settings Menu

Looking to turn off those annoying rumbling and speaker functions on your Remote? Trying to turn off a controller without turning off the system? Look no further than the Wii Remote Settings menu. This menu is accessible at any time by simply pressing the Home button on an active Wii Remote, and then clicking the Wii Remote Settings panel on the bottom of the screen (as shown in Figure 3-2). To leave the menu, click the Close Wii Remote Setting panel at the bottom of the screen, or simply push the Home button on the connected Remote.

From the Remote Settings menu, you can alter the following settings:

- ✔ **Volume:** Click the on-screen + and – buttons to adjust the volume of the noise coming from the Wii Remote speakers. You can also use the + and – buttons on the Remote itself to make this adjustment. As you adjust the volume, the Remote emits a short tone at the currently selected volume level, to give you an idea of what to expect.

    All Wii Remotes connected to the system must share the same volume setting.

- ✔ **Rumble:** This option controls whether the Wii Remote vibrates to indicate certain on-screen or in-game actions. The Remote rumbles slightly when the player clicks the On button on-screen.

    All Wii Remotes connected to the system must share the same rumble setting.

- ✔ **Connection:** Use this option to disconnect Remotes from the system without turning the system off.

    1. **Click the Reconnect button to temporarily disconnect all currently connected Remotes from the system.**

        This turns off the Remotes.

    2. **Press the 1 and 2 buttons simultaneously on each Remote you want to reactivate.**

        The Player LED lights blink for a few seconds, and then stabilize on a specific player light based on the order in which the Remote was reconnected.

    This method for connecting Remotes even works with controllers not formally synced to the system. This temporary syncing goes away when the system is turned off, though — making it most suitable for Remotes brought over temporarily from a friend's house.

Whipping Out the Nunchuk

The preceding sections should make it clear how revolutionary the Wii Remote is, and how much it changes the way video-game systems are controlled. For some games, however, a traditional thumb joystick is just more appropriate. For these games, you need to break out the Wii Nunchuk.

Plugging it in

Unlike the Wii Remote, the Nunchuk (yes, it really is spelled that way) is not wireless. Fortunately, you don't have to tether the optional controller to the system itself — you just have to plug it in to the bottom of the wireless Wii Remote, as shown in Figure 3-9. If the Wii Remote is on and connected to the system, the Nunchuk is detected automatically as soon as it's plugged in.

Note that there is a clear plastic tab on the back of the Nunchuk connector, used to thread the thin portion of the Wii Remote wrist strap. I personally find this thread hard to use and of limited use for holding the Nunchuk onto the Remote, but some people might find the Nunchuk feels more secure with it threaded in. Use your own discretion.

For those who just can't abide that dangling Nunchuk wire, Nyko makes a wireless Nunchuk that's available at most gaming retailers for $35.

The Nunchuk and Wii Remote are both designed to be used in either hand. This means you can hold the Remote in your right hand and the Nunchuk in your left, or vice versa. Both configurations work equally well — use whichever one feels more natural.

Nunchuk functions

The Nunchuk is a bit simpler than the Wii Remote, having only three major control functions, as shown in Figure 3-10.

- **The analog stick:** Like the directional pad on the Remote, this thumb-stick is used mainly for directional input. Unlike the d-pad, the analog stick is sensitive enough to detect a wide variety of directions and intensities. Tilting the stick slightly might cause an in-game character to walk, for instance, while pushing it all the way causes the character to sprint. The analog stick is controlled with the tip of the thumb, as shown in Figure 3-10.

- **The C and Z buttons:** The functions of the C button (the small, round one on the top) and the Z button (the large square one on the bottom) vary from game to game — consult the instruction manual to figure out what they're used for in each game. These buttons should be pressed with the index or middle finger, as shown in Figure 3-10.

As the infomercial salesman might say, "But wait — there's more!" The Nunchuk also has a motion sensor, much like the one in the Wii Remote, that can detect basic movement in all three dimensions. Games often ask you to flick, tilt, or twist the Nunchuk to activate additional in-game moves. The Nunchuk can't be used as a pointer, though — which is why most Wii menus and Channels use the Remote by itself.

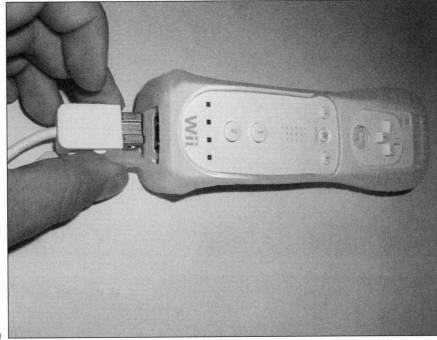

Figure 3-9:
Connect-
ing the
Nunchuk
to the Wii
Remote.

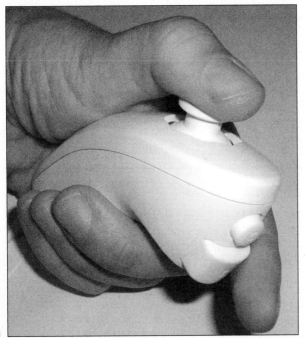

Figure 3-10:
The proper
Nunchuk
grip.

How many Nunchuks do you need?

While the Wii box comes packaged with a Nunchuk to go along with your first Remote, additional Remotes and Nunchuks are sold separately in stores. This can lead to some confusion when it comes time to go to the cash register. The question at hand: Is the $40 Remote enough, or do you need to add on a $20 Nunchuk for each Remote you have?

The answer depends largely on what kinds of games you're playing. The packaging for all Wii games contains a logo on the back of the box indicating whether the gameplay supports the Nunchuk. Games that support the Nunchuk tend to be action-oriented and/or first-person games that require quick reflexes and precise controls. Some games, such as the boxing portion of *Wii Sports,* also use the Nunchuk to detect motion by the players second hand (in

fact, the *Wii Sports* boxing game requires the purchase of a second Remote *and* Nunchuk for two-player bouts).

Be careful, though — some games with the Nunchuk logo on the box don't really require the Nunchuk to play the game. Games like *Super Smash Bros. Brawl* and *Mario Kart Wii* can be controlled with or without the Nunchuk, meaning the number of Nunchuks you need depends largely on the control preferences of each player.

So what's the answer? In short, I recommend holding off on the additional Nunchuks until you find an absolute need for them. Very few multi-player games require multiple Nunchuks, and the add-ons will still be available in stores if and when you run into a game that requires them.

Going Retro with the Wii Classic and GameCube Controllers

Even with the Nunchuk attached, the Wii Remote is still a pretty poor approximation of the traditional controllers found on classic Nintendo systems. There's something about the button orientation and general feel of those older controllers that makes it awkward playing certain games with the Wii Remote and Nunchuk. Don't fret: The Wii offers even more control options for the traditional gamer.

The Wii Classic Controller

With the wide variety of downloadable classic games available on the Wii's Virtual Console (see Chapter 6), Nintendo needed a Wii controller that could mimic the layout and functionality of the Nintendo 64, Super Nintendo Entertainment System, Sega Genesis, Nintendo Entertainment System, and more. Their best effort at this is the Wii Classic Controller, shown in Figure 3-11.

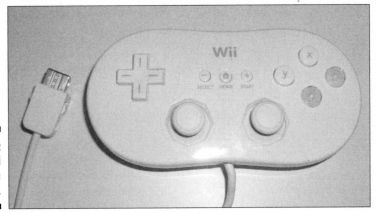

Figure 3-11:
The Wii
Classic
Controller.

The Classic Controller plugs into the bottom of the Wii Remote with a connection similar to the one used for the Nunchuk (refer to Figure 3-9). As long as the Remote is on and connected to the system, the Wii automatically recognizes the Classic Controller — no extra setup is necessary.

The Wii Classic Controller may look intimidating, but it's nothing to be afraid of. It's held with two hands, much like the Wii Remote in its horizontal position, with one thumb resting on each side. The left thumb is used for the directional pad and the left thumbstick, while the right thumb operates the four face buttons and the right thumbstick. The controller also has four "shoulder" buttons on the thin top edge which you can press with your index fingers. The functions of all these various buttons differ by game; they're explained in the on-screen instructions for all Virtual Console downloads (see Chapter 6). The +, –, and Home buttons share the same functions as the similar buttons on the Wii Remote itself.

In addition to the standard buttons on the Classic Controller, you might also notice a small switch on the top edge of the controller. This switch opens and closes a small clamp on the back of the controller. While Nintendo hasn't announced any official use for this clamp, peripheral maker Nyko utilizes it for its Classic Controller Grip, shown in Figure 3-12. This accessory snaps to the back of the Classic Controller and provides a more comfortable, molded grip for your palms. It also provides a place where you can wrap the Classic Controller Cord and hold the Wii Remote it's attached to. This grip is available for $5 to $10 at most game retailers, and really improves the Classic Controller experience.

Note that the Classic Controller isn't *required* to play Virtual Console games — some can be played with the Wii Remote and/or GameCube Controller. Also note that the classic controller can be used to control some disc-based Wii games, such as *Super Smash Bros. Brawl* and *Mario Kart Wii*. See Chapter 6 for more on which controllers work with which games.

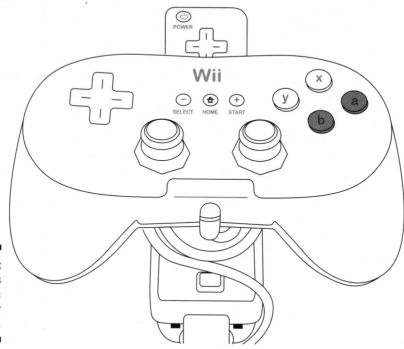

Figure 3-12:
Nyko's
Classic
Controller
Grip.

The GameCube controller

You might already know that the Nintendo Wii comes with the added bonus of being able to play the hundreds of games designed for Nintendo's previous system, the GameCube (see Chapter 5). But did you know that the Wii also lets you plug in classic GameCube controllers (see Figure 3-13) to use with those and other games? Well, now you know.

Besides being required for any GameCube game played on the Wii, the GameCube controller can also be used to control some Virtual Console titles (but not all: See Chapter 6). Some disc-based Wii games are also specifically designed to use the GameCube controller. These games can be identified by the small GameCube controller logo on the game's packaging.

Unlike the Wii Remote, most GameCube controllers have wires and actually have to be plugged into the system to be used (but not all: see the sidebar "Wireless GameCube controls: The WaveBird"). The Wii does, in fact, have built-in ports to connect these controllers, but they're not exactly easy to find when you're staring at the Wii's sleek, white exterior.

Figure 3-13:
The
GameCube
controller.

As shown in Figure 3-14, the GameCube controller ports are hidden under a small flap on the top of the system (or on the left of the system, if it's sitting horizontally). Open up the flap and you can plug in up to four GameCube controllers at once. Each port has small indented dots above it corresponding to the player number for that port (Player 1 is toward the front of the system, the Player 2 port is behind it, and so on). Figure 3-14 also shows the secondary flap used to protect the slots for GameCube memory cards — see Chapter 5 for more on using these.

Wireless GameCube controls: The WaveBird

Wii owners who are just obsessed with wirelessness should know that Nintendo has also made a wireless version of the GameCube controller. The WaveBird has the same button-and-joystick layout as the traditional GameCube controller, only it doesn't have any wires (it also doesn't support the vibration function of the traditional controller). The battery-powered controller communicates with the system using a small receiver that plugs into the appropriate controller slot on the GameCube or Wii. While Nintendo no longer makes the WaveBird, the controller is still available from many online and brick-and-mortar retailers for about $30.

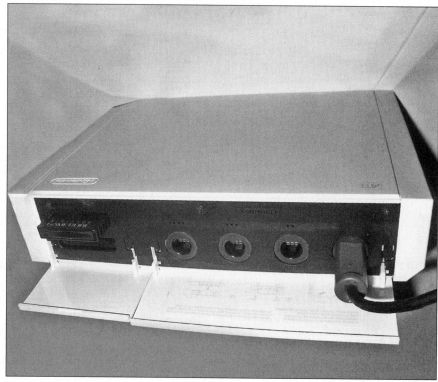

Figure 3-14:
The Wii's
GameCube
controller
and
memory-
card slots.

Flipping up these protective flaps does tend to ruin the simple aesthetic of the Wii. Luckily, you can easily remove the flaps to maintain the integrity of the Wii's look when using GameCube accessories. Simply open the flap and push gently toward the system right above the hinges. You hear a small click, and you can then lift the flap right up off the system. If you want to replace the flap, simply slide it back into place in the same manner.

Using Other Controllers

As if the four control options discussed previously weren't enough, even more controllers and controller add-ons can be used to change up the Wii gameplay experience. Some of these controllers only work with specific games while others simply change the way the standard Wii Remote and Nunchuk are held in your hands. The major controllers and controller add-ons available as I write are listed in the following sections. Who knows how many more there will be as the Wii continues to mature?

Wii Balance Board

The next step in motion-based controls, the Wii Balance Board (shown in Figure 3-15) gets the whole body involved in the game. The board itself acts sort of like a fancy bathroom scale, detecting how much weight is being placed on it — and, more importantly, how that weight is distributed across the surface of the board. By shifting your weight back and forth and left to right, you can control specially designed games such as the fitness simulator *Wii Fit* (which comes packaged with the board), and others that use the board to simulate everything from skiing to skateboarding. See Chapter 13 for more on *Wii Fit* and setting up the Balance Board with the Wii.

Wii Wheel

Not exactly a controller in and of itself, the Wii Wheel is a plastic, steering-wheel shaped shell for the Wii Remote, as shown in Figure 3-16. While the Wii Wheel doesn't add any specific functionality to the Wii Remote, it does make the controller feel more balanced and natural — more like a tiltable steering wheel for many racing games. The Wii Wheel comes packaged with *Mario Kart Wii* and can also be purchased on its own for $15 from many game retailers.

Figure 3-15:
The Balance Board.

Figure 3-16:
The Wii
Wheel.

Wii Zapper

Much like the Wii Wheel, the Wii Zapper doesn't add any functionality to
the standard Wii Remote and Nunchuk. (See Figure 3-17.) It does, however,
create a fun new way to control many shooting-based games. The Wii Zapper
is designed to be held with two hands and aimed at the screen from waist
height. An on-screen reticle shows where you're aiming in certain games, like
Link's Crossbow Training, which is packaged with the $20 accessory. Other
accessory makers make similar products to make the Wii Remote resemble a
gun — see Chapter 16 for more on these options.

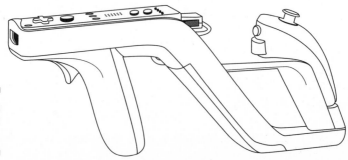

Figure 3-17:
The Wii
Zapper.

Wii Guitar Controller

This wireless Gibson Les Paul-shaped controller is (unsurprisingly) used to control Activision's guitar simulator *Guitar Hero 3,* which it comes packaged with. (See Figure 3-18.) A similar controller also comes with *Rock Band,* a competing game from Electronic Arts that also uses included drum and microphone controllers (see Chapter 14 for more on *Rock Band*). Note that the *Guitar Hero* controller works with *Rock Band,* but the *Rock Band* guitar controller won't work with *Guitar Hero III.*

Figure 3-18:
The Guitar
Controller.

With either controller, you hold down the fret buttons on one end and strum the strummer on the other in time with the music and the on-screen instructions. The Wii remote slides into a slot in the back of the shell to provide motion-sensing and rumble functionality to the guitar. It's not quite as rewarding as playing a real guitar, but it's a lot easier, and almost as much fun.

Nintendo DS

The Wii's Wi-Fi capabilities mean it can connect wirelessly with Nintendo's other Wi-Fi equipped system, the portable Nintendo DS, shown in Figure 3-19. The latter can even be used as a controller for specially designed games like *Pokemon Battle Revolution*. The Nintendo DS can also be used to download demos of portable games offered from the Nintendo Channel, as discussed in Chapter 10.

Figure 3-19:
The
Nintendo
DS.

Chapter 4

Getting the System Online

. . . .

. . . .

*B*ack in the day, computers and video-game systems sat alone in an electronic void. They were connected to their users by keyboards and controllers, but they weren't connected to their fellow computers in any way. It seems like ancient history today, when even a low-cost computer can easily connect to the Internet, enabling people to communicate easily, worldwide.

Video-game console makers in general (and Nintendo specifically) have been a little slower than their computer-making brethren in embracing the Internet, but they've dived online in a big way in the last few years. The Wii is a prime example of this trend, allowing users to not only play games online with competitors from around the world, but also to send messages and photos to their friends, surf the Web, and even download entire games (discussed more in Part III). This chapter shows you how to get the Wii connected to the Internet so you can unlock all these great features.

What You Need to Connect the Wii to the Internet

A discussion of how to set up a home network is beyond the scope of this book — for details, check out *Home Networking For Dummies,* 4th Edition, by Kathy Ivens (Wiley). Instead, this section outlines the basic items you need to get your Wii online.

To start with, getting the Wii online means having a high-speed Internet connection of some sort in your home. For most people, this means signing up for Internet service through your local cable or DSL provider. Dial-up Internet service through basic phone lines will not work with the Wii.

In addition to your high-speed Internet connection, you need *one* of the following Internet appliances to connect the Wii to your Internet connection:

- ✔ **A wireless access point:** Also known as an *802.11 wireless router,* this device converts your wired Internet signal to a wireless signal that can be recognized by the Wii's internal Wi-Fi antenna. To simplify the setup with your Wii, look for an access point with AirStation One-Touch Secure System (AOSS) support (it should be highlighted on the packaging). You may also want to choose an access point that supports WEP or WPA security so your neighbors can't steal your wireless signal.

- ✔ **The Nintendo Wi-Fi USB Connector:** This small USB fob (shown in Figure 4-1) plugs into a personal computer with a wired high-speed Internet connection and broadcasts a Wi-Fi Internet signal recognizable by the Wii.

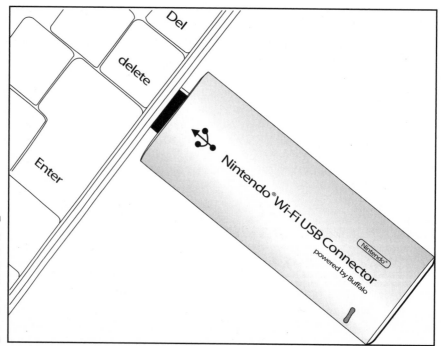

Figure 4-1:
The Nintendo Wi-Fi USB Connector, plugged into a PC.

Nintendo discontinued manufacture of the Wi-Fi USB connector in November 2007, but the ones they did make are still available from many online and brick-and-mortar retailers for about $30. This option is cheaper and easier to set up than a full-fledged wireless access point, but offers less utility for other wireless networking applications (such as connecting a laptop to your home network).

The Wi-Fi USB Connector only works with computers running Windows XP.

✔ **The Wii LAN Adapter:** This compact device (shown in Figure 4-2) converts a wired Ethernet cable into a USB connection that can plug into one of the USB slots in the back of the Wii. Note that using this option means the Wii needs to be physically close to your high-speed modem or router. The adapter can be purchased directly from Nintendo online at `http://store.nintendo.com` or at many major retailers for about $25.

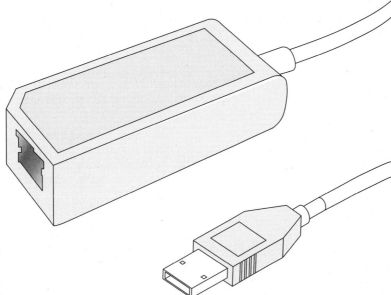

Figure 4-2:
How to connect the Wii LAN Adapter.

Configuring the Wii's Internet Options

After you have your home network set up, you need to tell the Wii how it's going to talk to the Internet. You do this through the Wii's Internet Settings menu (shown in Figure 4-3). To get there, open the Wii Settings menu (as described in Chapter 2) and choose the Internet submenu on the second page of options.

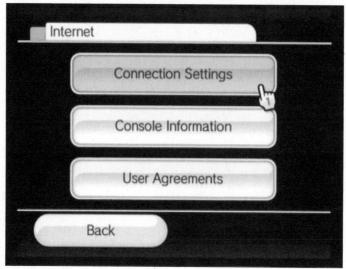

I address the Console Information and User Agreements options later in
the chapter. For now, click Connection Settings to bring up the Connection
Settings menu shown in Figure 4-4. From there, follow these steps to configure your Wii to work with your Internet connection:

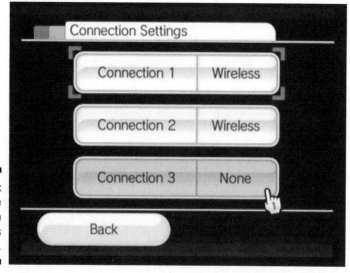

1. **Choose an open connection.**

   The Wii can save up to three sets of Internet configuration data. Any connection labeled "None" is currently free and ready to be configured. It doesn't matter which connection number you choose, although Connection 1 seems the natural first choice for most users.

2. **Choose your connection type.**

   If you are using the Wii LAN Adapter (as described in the "What You Need to Connect the Wii to the Internet" section, earlier in this chapter) choose Wired Connection. Make sure the LAN adapter is plugged into your modem or router through an Ethernet cable and into the Wii through the rear USB ports (refer to Figure 4-2). Skip ahead to Step 4.

   If you're using a wireless access point or the Nintendo Wi-Fi USB Connection, choose Wireless Connection and continue to Step 3.

3. **Choose your wireless connection type.**

   If you're using a wireless Internet connection, choose the option that applies and go through the specific instructions that follow. (Note that the Manual Setup option is reserved for advanced users and shouldn't be necessary for basic setup.)

   a. If your wireless access point supports the AirStation One-Touch Secure System, the AOSS menu option is the easiest way to configure the Wii to use your access point. Click AOSS and the Wii tells you to "press the AOSS button on the access point until the AOSS lamp flashes." Do this and the Wii quickly detects the access point and automatically configures itself to your Internet connection. Simple!

   b. If you're using a wireless access point that doesn't support AOSS, choose Search for an Access Point. The Wii spends a few seconds searching for nearby networks, and then displays a list of all those in range, along with their relative strength and security status. If your wireless network doesn't show up, make sure your router is set to broadcast its SSID (consult your router documentation for more on how to do this). If you've enabled security on your wireless network, choose the type of security and enter the password, using the on-screen keyboard (remember, passwords are case-sensitive). Click OK to save the settings.

   c. If you're using the Nintendo Wi-Fi USB Connector, the system asks you to make sure you've installed the software included with the Connector on your PC, and that the Connector is plugged into a USB slot on your computer. After you've confirmed both of these facts, click Next and move over to your PC. A Wi-Fi USB icon appears in the Windows task bar. Double-click this icon, and then select your Wii system from the menu (the system shows up with the nickname you gave it when you set up the Wii). Choose Grant Permission to Connect and go back to the Wii, which confirms that the "Nintendo Wi-Fi USB Connector setup is complete."

4. Click OK to begin the connection test.

The Wii tries to communicate with the Internet, using the settings you configured. If the test is successful, then congratulations — your Wii is officially part of the Internet!

You're asked if you want to perform a Wii system update. You should probably take the Wii up on this offer — it's generally a good idea when connecting your Wii to the Internet for the first time — but it's by no means required. You can always perform the update later by choosing the option from the Wii Settings menu (see Chapter 2 for more on this). If you do decide to download an update, be patient — the process can take a few minutes. If the connection test fails, see the "Troubleshooting" section for possible fixes.

Thankfully, you only have to perform this setup process the first time you connect your Wii to the Internet. The Wii saves your settings, and in the future uses them to connect automatically to the Internet when necessary.

To edit your Internet connection settings later, go back to the Connection Settings menu and choose a configured connection. From here you can also re-test the connection or clear its setting from the system. If you've defined multiple Internet configurations, you can also choose which one you want the Wii to use by choosing Use This Connection from this menu.

Troubleshooting

If your connection test doesn't work after the initial setup, a few simple things could be wrong. The following list describes the most common fixes for connection problems:

 ✔ Confirm that all the pieces of your Internet connection setup are plugged in and working correctly.

 ✔ If possible, move the wireless access point or Nintendo USB Wi-Fi Connector closer to the Wii itself. This improves the wireless signal strength.

 ✔ Make sure that the wireless router's MAC filtering function is off, or that the Wii's MAC address is included on the approved devices list. You can find the Wii's MAC Address by choosing Console Information in the Internet Settings Menu (refer to Figure 4-3).

WiiConnect24

Did you ever feel like your "always-on" high-speed Internet connection is being wasted when you aren't actively using the Internet? Nintendo apparently feels the same way. That's why they created the WiiConnect24 service to make use of that Internet connection even when the system isn't being used. The always-on WiiConnect24 service downloads data for the Wii Message Board and certain Channels (like the Forecast and News Channels) even when the system is sitting idly in standby mode.

For the Wii to do this, though, you have to first set up the WiiConnect24 service through the Wii Settings menu. Access the Settings menu by clicking the Wii icon in the lower-right corner of the Wii Channel menu, and then open the WiiConnect24 submenu on the second page of options. You can then toggle the following submenu options:

- ✔ **WiiConnect24:** This option lets you turn the WiiConnect24 service on or off. I highly recommend leaving this feature on; it allows for a lot of neat features. If you really don't want the Wii sending and receiving data without your input, turn it off.

- ✔ **Standby Connection:** This setting determines whether the WiiConnect24 feature operates when the system is sitting in standby mode. If this option is switched off, WiiConnect24 only connects to the Internet when the system is on and being used.

    I recommend activating the standby connection, as it allows the Wii to alert you when you receive Message Board messages (see the following bullet) and allows for automatic download of other data. Don't worry about the Wii sucking up all your Internet bandwidth — the service isn't very demanding and shouldn't interfere with other uses of your Internet services.

- ✔ **Slot Illumination:** When WiiConnect24 detects that you've received a message on your Wii Message Board, a blue light illuminates from behind the system's disc slot to alert you. You can use this menu to turn this feature off or turn down the brightness of the light by choosing the Dim option.

Connecting to Your Friends: The Wii Message Board

Okay, so your Wii is online. Now what? Well, much like an Internet-connected computer, your Wii can now be used to send messages and photos to other users through the Wii Message Board. Unfortunately, connecting to your friends through the Wii isn't quite as simple as jotting down an e-mail address and typing a quick message. This section navigates you through the somewhat cumbersome process of registering Wii Friends and sending them messages and photos.

To start with, you access the Message Board itself by going to the Wii Channel menu and clicking on the envelope icon in the bottom-right corner.

This brings up the Message Board screen, as shown in Figure 4-5. From this screen you can register Wii friends on your system and send and receive messages and photos, using these options:

✔ **Message envelopes:** These represent messages you've received from Wii Friends or from the Wii itself. Click an envelope icon to read the message and view any attached photos. (You can enlarge an image by clicking on it.) The dot above the message blinks if the message is less than six hours old. You can move a message around the screen by holding down the A and B buttons and dragging the message into its new position.

✔ **Change Days buttons:** The Message Board only displays messages one day at a time, based on the day they were received. Click the arrow buttons on the right and left sides of the screen to scroll to adjacent days. Pressing the + and – buttons on the Wii Remote has the same effect.

✔ **Calendar:** Opens up the calendar screen as shown in Figure 4-6. Days on which you received messages are noted with an envelope icon. Click on a day to display that day's messages. Use the blue arrows on the sides of the screen to scroll through the months. Pressing the + and – buttons on the Wii Remote has the same effect.

✔ **Create message:** Click this button to bring up the submenu shown in Figure 4-7. The options on this menu aren't labeled, but they're described here in left to right order:

• **Create Memo:** Write a personal note to be posted on your Wii's Message Board. This is useful for leaving messages for your family or reminders for yourself. See the later section, "Sending Message Board messages," for more on this.

Figure 4-5:
The Wii
Message
Board
screen.

- **Create Message:** Create a message to send to a registered Wii Friend. See the later section, "Sending Message Board messages."

- **Address Book:** Register Wii Friends you'd like to send messages to. You can also check your Wii's individual Wii Number. See the later section, "Registering Wii Friends."

Figure 4-6:
The Wii Message Board Calendar.

Sun	Mon	Tue	Wed	Thu	Fri	Sat
27	28	29	30	1	2	3
4	5	6	7	8	9	10
11	12	13	14	15	16	17
18	19	20	21	22	23	24
25	26	27	28	29	30	31

Back

May 2008

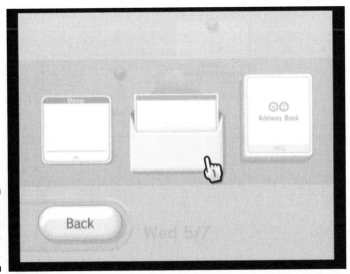

Figure 4-7:
The Create Message submenu.

Back

Address Book

Registering Wii Friends

Just like you need your friends' phone numbers before you can call them on the phone, you need your friends' 16-digit Wii Numbers before you can send them a message using the Wii. Not only that, but your friends also have to have your Wii Number registered in their Wii before you can talk to each other. This registering is done through the Wii's Address Book, and it goes a little something like this:

1. **Open the Wii Address Book by navigating to the Wii Message Board menu, clicking the Create Message icon, and clicking the Address Book icon.**

   This brings up the Address Book, as shown in Figure 4-8.

2. **Click Register.**

3. **Choose the type of friend you want to register.**

   Choose Wii if you want to send messages directly to a friend's Wii. Choose Others if you want to send e-mail messages to a computer or cell phone user.

4. **Enter the Wii number or e-mail address.**

   Use the on-screen keypad or keyboard to enter your friend's Wii Number (for friends using a Wii) or e-mail address (for friends using a computer or cell phone). If your friends don't know their Wii Number, tell them they can find it on the front page of their Wii Address book (use the preceding instructions if you need to walk them through how to get there). Click OK to continue.

Figure 4-8: The front page of the Wii Address Book, which includes your personal Wii Number.

5. **Enter a nickname for your friend.**

   This nickname is how your friend is identified in your address book. No one else sees this name — it's just a personal reminder of who this Wii Number or e-mail address belongs to. Nicknames can have up to ten characters. Click OK to continue.

6. **Attach a Mii (optional).**

   If you want, you can attach a Mii to each person in your address book as a visual reminder of who the person is. You can add a Mii later by editing the Address Book entry, as described later in this section. For more on Miis, see Chapter 7.

7. **Click OK to complete the registration.**

8. **Get your friend to confirm your registration.**

   Even though your friends' information is now in your address book, you won't be able to send them a message until they confirm that they actually know you. For friends using a Wii, this means they have to enter your Wii Number into their address books. You can find your Wii Number on the front page of your Address Book, as shown in Figure 4-8.

   When you register Wii Friends using an e-mail address, they receive a message in their inbox asking them to confirm that they know you. This message comes from an e-mail address that includes your Wii Number and a `nintendo.com` domain name. Make sure your friend receives the e-mail and replies to it to confirm the registration.

   Even after this confirmation takes place, it still might take a little while for Nintendo's servers to register the connection and allow communications between you and your friends through the Wii. Be patient. When your friends have been confirmed, their names in your address book changes from a light gray to a dark black and you can send messages to each other, as described in the following section.

You can edit entries in your Address Book after the fact by opening the Address Book and finding the name you'd like to edit. As usual, you can scroll through the pages of the address book by clicking the arrows on the sides of the screen or using the + and – buttons on the Wii Remote. Clicking a name brings up the menu shown in Figure 4-9, from which you can send a message, change a nickname, or remove a person from your Address Book entirely.

You can only have 100 Wii Friends registered at one time. If you have more than that, you have to delete some before adding more. On a more personal note, can I ask how you got so incredibly popular?

Figure 4-9:
The Wii
Address
Book infor-
mation
page.

Sending Message Board messages

After you have your Wii Friends registered and confirmed, you can send them messages directly from your Wii Message Board. Even if you don't have any Wii Friends, you can still leave personal memos on your local Message Board for family members or as personal reminders. Follow these steps to complete either of these tasks:

1. **Go to the Wii Message Board.**

2. **Enter the Send Message submenu by clicking the Create Message envelope icon.**

   See Figure 4-7.

3. **Choose to send a memo or a message.**

   Choose the icon on the left to create a personal memo that stays on your local Wii Message Board. Choose the icon in the middle to create a message that is sent to one of your registered Wii Friends via the Internet.

4. **Choose your Wii Friend (for Internet messages only).**

   If you're sending a message to a Wii Friend, your Address Book pops up. Navigate the pages by clicking the on-screen arrows or the + or – buttons on your Remote, and then click the name for the Wii Friend you want to send the message to. Note that if a name shows up in gray, it means that your Wii Friend hasn't confirmed your registration yet.

5. **Enter your text.**

Click the text area and use the on-screen keyboard to enter your message. For more on using the on-screen keyboard, see the following section.

6. **Attach a Mii (optional).**

If you'd like to include an identifying Mii with your message, click the Mii icon in the upper left and choose from among the Miis in your Mii Plaza.

7. **Click Post.**

In addition to creating posts from whole cloth, you can also reply to messages you receive in a similar fashion. Simply click Reply when reading a Message Board message, and then follow the preceding instructions starting from Step 5.

You can also use the Message Board to send digital pictures to your Wii Friends. (See Chapter 8 for more on how to do this.)

The on-screen keyboard

Since the Wii doesn't have a built-in keyboard, typing in memos and messages usually means using the on-screen keyboard shown in Figure 4-10. The on-screen keyboard is also used to enter text into many menus.

Predicted word area

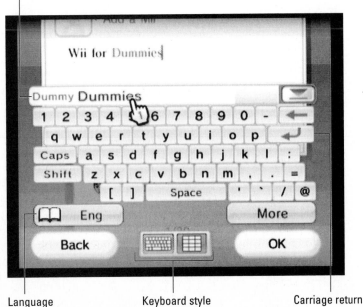

Figure 4-10:
The Wii's
on-screen
QWERTY
keyboard.

Language   Keyboard style   Carriage return

If you don't like using the on-screen keyboard, the Wii also supports any number of standard USB keyboards that you can plug into the USB ports on the back of the system. It's a little inconvenient having a keyboard in the living room, but if you're writing a lot of messages, the faster typing speed might be worth it.

The on-screen keyboard itself is largely self-explanatory — simply point at and click a letter to enter it into the message — but there are a few buttons and displays on the keyboard that might be a little confusing. They're labeled in Figure 4-10 and described further in the following list:

- ✔ **Predicted word area:** This area can help speed up your typing on Wii Message Board messages and memos by predicting the whole word based on the first few letters. For instance, if you type in "d-u-m-m" the words "dummy" and "dummies" appears in this area as suggestions for the word you may be typing. If either of these is the word you're going for, you can click on the word itself to save a few virtual keystrokes.

- ✔ **Carriage return:** Advances the text down to the next line.

- ✔ **More:** Brings up a menu with additional punctuation marks and special characters not shown on the keyboard.

- ✔ **Language:** Change the language used by the predicted word area. Choose between English, French, and Spanish.

- ✔ **Shift:** The next letter you type is uppercase. You can also use this key to access further punctuation and symbols on certain keys; it works just like the Shift key on a regular computer keyboard.

- ✔ **Caps:** Letters you type appear in uppercase until you click the Caps button again.

- ✔ **Keyboard style:** Click the number pad icon to switch from the QWERTY keyboard to one that resembles a cell phone texting keypad, as shown in Figure 4-11. This works a bit differently from a regular keyboard, as any experienced cell phone text messenger knows. You have to click on a specific button multiple times to cycle to your desired letter. For instance, clicking the button labeled "def" twice would enter the letter E, as it does on a cell phone. Note that if you want to enter another letter from the same button (a D to follow the E, for instance), first you have to move the pointer off the button briefly to advance the cursor. Use the buttons on the left to switch among the capital-, lowercase-, and number-entry modes.

  The predictive text area also works a little differently for the cell phone-style keyboard: Instead of entering the first few letters of the word you want to type, you only have to click the applicable buttons once. For instance, if you want to enter the word "dummy," you'd click the "def" button, the "tuv" button, then the "mno" button twice. The word shows up in the predictive text area, along with other words you could have typed using those same buttons (such as "funny" or "dunno").

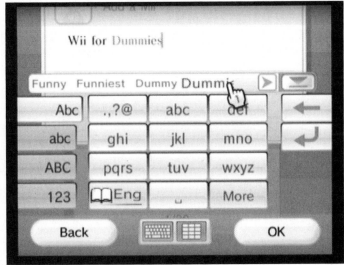

Figure 4-11:
The Wii's
on-screen
cell phone-
style
keyboard.

In addition to the on-screen buttons, the buttons on the Wii Remote itself can be used for certain shortcuts. For instance, the – button can be used to delete a character, and the directional pad can be used to move the cursor to a different point in the message (though this only works if the predictive text feature is turned off). You can also move the cursor around simply by pointing to the desired position in the message and pushing the A button on the Remote.

Part II
The Channels

By Rich Tennant

"You can go to the Wii News Channel and select national news, international news, or just use the pointing finger cursor to pick Brian Williams' nose."

In this part . . .

It's pretty obvious that Nintendo's latest system was influenced by the universal simplicity of the common TV set. Not only does the Wii have a controller that resembles a TV remote control, but the system's basic interface also is broken into units called Channels. Just like their TV counterparts, each Channel has a different focus. Flipping through the list lets you do everything from downloading new games to creating cute characters called Miis, viewing digital photos and Web pages, and much more. There's even an on-screen guide, the Wii Menu, that lets you jump directly to what you want. All this, and you don't even need to install an antenna or satellite dish on your roof. Isn't technology grand?

Chapter 5

Wii Channel Basics

Most people prefer a piece of electronics with more features to a similar device with fewer features. Just as important in such a comparison, though, is how easy those features are to access and use. As any tech-head knows, accessing the advanced functions on some electronic devices like cell phones can be a baffling experience.

Luckily, the Nintendo Wii doesn't hide its features in a confusing maze of menus. Instead, all the myriad functions of the Wii can be accessed from the Wii Menu (sometimes called the Wii Channel menu). The Wii Menu is the first menu you see when you turn on the system, so knowing your way around it is pretty important to successfully using the system. In this chapter, I show you how to navigate the Wii Menu to access the various Wii Channels, including the game-playing Disc Channel. You also find out how to organize the icons on the Wii Menu to your liking, as well as how to back up and clean out your Wii's internal system memory.

Navigating the Wii Channel Menu

The first time you turn on the Wii, the Wii Menu looks much the way it does in Figure 5-1. Each colored square represents a *Channel,* which is a distinct game or application you can start with just a few clicks of the Remote. The grayed-out squares are empty for now, but they can be filled in with other Channels and games in the future.

You can set the time and date at the bottom of the Wii Menu using the Settings menu, as described in Chapter 2. You can also access the Wii Message Board by clicking the envelope icon in the bottom-right corner. (Using the Message Board is described in more detail in Chapter 4.)

Figure 5-1:
The Wii
Channel
menu, full of
Channels.

If your Wii is hooked up to the Internet, some of the Channel icons may be periodically updated with new information. The Wii Shop Channel, for instance, automatically downloads a list of the latest games and Channels available for download, and scrolls this list on the icon visible right there on the Wii Menu. You can use this information to save yourself the trouble of starting the Channel to see if it has been updated. Note that WiiConnect24 service must be turned on for this feature to do its thing. See Chapter 4 for more on configuring the Wii to work with the Internet and WiiConnect24.

If you twist the Remote in your hand while pointing at the Wii Menu, the on-screen pointer rotates to match its angle. Rotating the pointer isn't good for anything per se, but it *is* fun.

Changing the Channel

Navigating the Wii Menu is a simple, point-and-click affair. Simply point the Wii Remote at the Sensor Bar and hover the on-screen pointer over your desired Channel. (See Chapter 3 for more on using the Wii Remote as a pointer.) The Channel is highlighted in blue and its name appears below the pointer. Press the A button at this point and you bring up the Channel Preview screen for that Channel, as shown in Figure 5-2.

Figure 5-2:
The Channel
Preview
screen.

The Remote gives a slight rumble as you move it over the various Channels on the Wii Menu. (You can turn this rumbling off by using the Wii Remote Settings screen in the Wii's Home menu, as described in Chapter 3.)

From the Channel Preview screen, click the Start button to start that Channel, or click the Wii Menu button to go back. You can also use the arrows on the left and right sides of the screen to jump to other Channel preview screens without returning to the Wii Menu (the + and − buttons on the Wii Remote have the same effect). Which Channel Preview comes up next in the scrolling depends on the arrangement of Channels on the Wii Menu itself (see the "Reorganizing the Wii Menu" section, later in this chapter).

If your Wii is hooked up the Internet, some Channel Preview screens can also provide updated information about a Channel, much like the Wii Menu icons discussed previously. The Forecast Channel, for instance, can be calibrated to show local weather conditions and temperature on the Preview Screen, without the need to load the Channel itself. (See Chapter 10 for more on the Forecast Channel.)

Playing games with the Disc Channel

As an example of how to start Channels with the Wii Menu, this section describes the process for playing disc-based games on the Wii using the Disc Channel. Older systems let you play a game just by putting it in the system; Wii owners have to use the Disc Channel manually to start the game.

First, you have to put the disc in the system, as shown in Figure 5-3.

After the disc is in the system, the Disc Channel icon changes to a small preview of the game (or to a GameCube logo, in the case of GameCube games). If the system is having problems detecting the disc, make sure it's inserted correctly — with the shiny, blank side of the disc pointing toward the buttons on the face of the system. (This means the shiny side should point to the left if the system is standing upright, and point downward if the system is lying horizontally.)

When the disc is inserted correctly and detected, click the Disc Channel icon to bring up the preview screen. Figure 5-4 shows the preview screen as it looks for *Wii Sports.* Click the Start button and your game starts.

Figure 5-3:
Putting a
game disc
into the Wii.

Even after you've started a game or Channel, you're never more than a few button presses from returning to the Wii Menu. Just press the Home button on the Wii Remote to bring up the Home Menu (as shown in Figure 5-5). Then click the Wii Menu button to get back to your Channel list.

Figure 5-4:
The *Wii Sports* Preview screen.

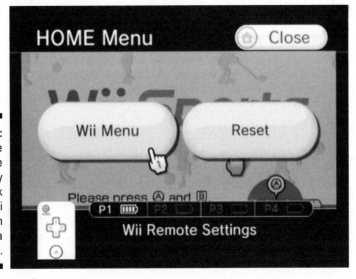

Figure 5-5:
The Home Menu, the easiest way to get back to the Wii Menu from inside a Channel.

Adding new Channels

The Wii Menu might look a little barren when you first pull the system out of the box, but you can fill in those blank spaces in one of two ways:

- **The Wii Shop Channel:** If your Wii is hooked up to the Internet, you can use the Wii Shop Channel to download new games and Channels. These downloadable games and Channels appear automatically in an open slot on your Wii Menu as soon as they've been downloaded. Some of these Channels are free to download, so if you have an Internet connection, there's really no reason not to start to fill up your Wii Menu. See Chapter 6 for more on downloading games and Channels from the Wii Shop Channel.

- **Install Channels from a game disc:** Some games let you install a game-specific Channel to your Wii Menu straight from the game disc. These Channels let you perform some of that game's functions even if you don't have the game disc in the system. (See Chapter 10 for more on installing and using these game-specific Channels.)

Turning the page

After you install downloadable games and Channels on your Wii, you might start running out of room on the 12 slots on the front page of the Wii Menu. Don't fret — the Wii Menu can actually hold up to 48 Channels on its four pages.

To access the other pages of the Wii Menu, simply click the arrow on the right side of the screen, as shown in Figure 5-6. To go back to the first page, use the similar arrow that appear on the left side of the screen. If you don't feel like pointing, you can use the + and − buttons on the Wii Remote to scroll quickly through the menu's pages.

Reorganizing the Wii Menu

As your Wii Menu starts filling up, you might find that some icons aren't arranged as conveniently as you might like. Maybe some Channels you use all the time are hiding on the back pages, while rarely used Channels are clogging up the front page. Maybe you want all your Virtual Console games to be next to each other, rather than scattered all over the place. Maybe you want all the Channels that require the Internet on the third page, just because that's where they have the best Feng Shui. All these situations can be easily fixed by rearranging the Channel icons on the Wii Menu itself as follows:

✔ **To move a Wii Menu icon to a new slot,** simply hover the pointer over the icon you wish to move and pick it up by pressing the A and B buttons together. Picture this as holding the icon between your thumb and forefinger with a pinching grip. The pointer changes to a clenched fist carrying the Channel icon, as shown in Figure 5-7.

✔ **To place the Channel in its new location** after picking it up, simply move the pointer over an empty space on the Wii Menu and let go of A or B (the new location should be highlighted in blue before the drop). The Channel icon disappears from its old location and reappears in the new one.

Note that you can't move a Channel to a slot that already has an icon on it. If you want to have two icons switch places, you have to use an empty slot as a temporary holding space for one of them. If there are absolutely no empty slots on any of the Wii Menu's four pages, consult the "Cleaning Out the Cobwebs: Wii Memory Management" section for information on how to clear some space for your reorganizing.

Figure 5-6:
Turning pages on the Wii Menu.

Figure 5-7:
Moving a
Channel
icon to a
new
location
on the Wii
Menu.

> ✔ **To move a Channel to an open slot on a different page,** simply pick it up as normal then hover over the page-turning arrow (refer to Figure 5-4). The Wii Menu scrolls to the next page, allowing you to place the icon where you want it.

One Channel can't be moved using the methods discussed here: The Disc Channel. This game-playing Channel is so important that it's impossible to move away from the upper-left corner of the Wii Menu's front page. This is probably for the best — after all, do you really want to go searching through the Wii Menu every time you want to play a disc-based game?

Cleaning Out the Cobwebs: Wii Memory Management

Those icons on your Wii Menu don't just represent downloaded games and Channels — they also represent files stored in the 1,840 or so "blocks" of internal system memory on the Wii. This internal memory is where everything that makes your Wii unique is stored — from the Channels on the Wii Menu to the saved game data that keeps track of your in-game progress to the messages stored on the Wii Message Board.

For the most part, you don't have to concern yourself with the arrangement and management of this internal memory — the Wii handles all your files automatically. In a few situations, though, you may want to back up, delete, or move files out of the Wii's internal memory. The following sections describe how to handle these situations.

Backing up files

If you've ever lost a term paper at 11:30 p.m. the night before it was due because your computer crashed, you know how important it can be to back up files on your computer. But not many people think of how important it is to back up the files on their game systems. Aren't the 40 hours you've put into *The Legend of Zelda: Twilight Princess* just as important as the 40 hours you put into that term paper?

Files stored on the Wii's Internal Memory — including game saves, Channels, and games downloaded from the Wii Shop Channel — can be backed up to a SmartDigital (SD) card by following these steps:

1. **Insert an SD card with some free space into the slot on the front of the system.**

   More details on how to do this can be found in Chapter 8.

2. **Go to the Wii Menu and click the Wii icon in the lower-left corner (refer to Figure 5-1).**

3. **Click Data Management.**

4. **To back up Channels or downloaded games, click Channels. To back up saved game progress, click Save Data, and then click Wii.**

   At this point, you see a grid view showing all the files you've requested represented as icons, as shown in Figure 5-8. Hovering the pointer over an icon on this menu gives you the name of the file. Note that this screen also displays how many of the roughly 1,840 blocks of free space are left on the system's internal memory. As this number gets lower and lower, the need to back up and delete unneeded data becomes more urgent.

5. **Click the icon for the file you want to back up.**

   This brings up a menu screen asking whether you want to copy or erase the file. Note that this screen also tells you how many of the Wii's 1,840 blocks of memory are being used by the file you've selected. This information can be handy when you're choosing which files to erase when pruning your Wii's memory banks. (See the following section, "Deleting data").

Figure 5-8:
A grid view of the Wii save data.

 Data for some games, such as Nintendo's *Super Smash Bros. Brawl,* is protected and can't be copied to an SD card. A message saying that this file can't be copied pops up for these games. Unfortunately, there is no way to back up this data.

6. Click Copy, and then click Yes when asked for confirmation.

The Wii begins to copy the selected file to the SD card. (The data-copying process may take a few minutes, so be patient.)

 Do not remove the SD card or turn off the system during the copying process, because this might corrupt the data and make the entire SD card unusable.

 You can only have one copy of a certain file saved on an SD card at any one time. If you already have a copy of that file on the SD card, the Wii won't let you make the new copy. You have to remove the old file from the SD card before copying the new data over (see the later section, "Restoring files," for more on how to do this).

Deleting data

After a file has been backed up on an SD card, that file can be safely deleted from the Wii's internal memory.

You can also delete files that haven't been backed up, but be warned: There's no way to recover these files later.

The process for deleting files from the Wii's system memory is very similar to the process for backing up the files:

1. **Repeat steps 1 through 5 in the "Backing up files" section.**

2. **Click Erase, and then click Yes when asked for confirmation.**

Before you do this, make sure you've either backed up the file or that you're really, *really* sure you want to get rid of this file permanently. After you click Yes, the file is gone. There's no getting it back. Channels and downloaded games deleted in this manner disappear from the Wii Menu, although they can be downloaded again through the Wii Shop Channel at any time. Games with saved data deleted in this way have to be restarted from the beginning.

Restoring files

Having a file backed up on an SD card is all well and good, but it doesn't really do anyone any good just sitting all alone on that card. To actually use the file again, it has to first be restored onto the system's internal memory. It's a relatively simple process that's performed like this:

1. **Repeat Steps 1 through 4 of the "Backing up files" section earlier in this chapter.**

2. **Click the SD Card tab at the upper-right corner of the screen.**

    This brings up a list of all the Wii files you've copied onto the SD card. Notice that the amount of free space on the SD card is shown in the Blocks Open area at lower right.

3. **Click the icon for the file you want to copy to the Wii System.**

4. **Click Copy, and then click Yes when asked for confirmation.**

    The file is copied from the SD card back to the Wii System Memory. Note that you can only have one copy of a particular file on your system at any time. If a copy of the backed up file is already on the system, the Wii tells you that "this data already exists in the Wii System Memory." You have to delete the older version from the Wii system memory before you can copy the desired data from the SD card.

Note that if you want to free up some space on your SD card for some reason, you can delete files from the SD card in much the same fashion. Simply complete Steps 1 through 3 as above, and then click the Erase option instead of Copy.

Remember that clicking Erase removes the file from the SD card permanently, so be careful if you're toying around with your only backup.

Moving files to another Wii

The SD card isn't just handy for backing up personal files on your Wii; it's also the only way to transfer files from one Wii to another. The process for moving files from one system to another is exactly the same as that outlined in the earlier sections, "Backing up files" and "Restoring files," only in this case you're restoring the files to a system other than the one you backed them up from. This is a great way to share saved game data with friends who might not be as amazingly awesome at a certain game as you are.

Wii Channels and games downloaded from the Wii Shop Channel can't be transferred from system to system in this manner. These Channels and games are tied to the system they're first downloaded to — meaning they won't work on any other system. If you want to share a new Channel or downloaded game, you have to take your entire Wii system over to your friend's house. No biggie. The system is pretty portable, after all.

Handling GameCube data

GameCube saved data can't be copied to an SD card or to the Wii system memory, but it can be copied between GameCube memory cards, using the two GameCube card slots located on the top of the system (see Chapter 2 for more on this feature). This backup process is similar to the method described earlier in this chapter:

1. **Make sure there are GameCube memory cards in both card slots.**

2. **Go to the Data Management screen (as described in Steps 1–3 in the earlier section, "Backing up files").**

3. **Choose Save Data, and then GameCube.**

   This brings up the GameCube Save Data menu, as shown in Figure 5-9. Note the tab at the top of the screen that allows you to toggle the view between Slot A and Slot B.

4. **Select the data you want to copy, and then choose Copy to copy it over to the other card. Or you can simply choose Erase to erase the data from the card completely.**

Figure 5-9:
The
GameCube
Save Data
menu.

Chapter 6

The Wii Shop Channel

There are two ways to get software for your Wii. The first involves getting up, getting in your car, driving to the store, finding a game on the shelf, waiting in line, purchasing (or renting) the game, getting back in the car, driving home, opening the case, putting the game in the system, and playing.

The second involves sitting on your couch, using the Wii Remote and an on-screen menu to download the game, and playing.

Which method sounds better to you?

Not surprisingly, many Wii owners are thrilled with the Wii Shop Channel, which lets them download new and classic games directly to their Wii consoles from the comfort of the couch. While the games on the Shop Channel tend to be older and/or less technically advanced than their disc-based brethren, they can be just as much fun and, just as importantly, a lot cheaper.

What's more, the Wii Shop Channel also lets Wii owners download fun and functional Channels to increase the versatility of their systems. Many of these Channels are offered for free, meaning there's really no reason not to take advantage of them. This chapter tells you how to download and use these games and channels.

Setting Things Up

Before you get going with the Wii Shop Channel, make sure that your Wii is connected to the Internet (see Chapter 4 for instructions if your Wii isn't online yet).

Fire up the Wii Menu and click the Wii Shop Channel. If your Internet connection is set up correctly, you get a white screen with the Wii logo and a rotating blue circle to indicate that the Channel is loading. The loading process can take anywhere from 30 seconds to a few minutes, depending on your connection speed, so be patient. Eventually, you see the Wii Shop Channel's main menu, as shown in Figure 6-1.

Figure 6-1:
The Wii Shop Channel main menu.

Clicking one of the game names at the top of this menu brings up the information page for that game. Clicking one of the headlines under Important Info brings up the details of the announcement. (You can scroll through these news stories using the up and down arrows on the Wii Remote's directional pad.) The specific games and headlines shown on this page change from week to week, generally updating every Monday.

After browsing the new games and headlines to your heart's content, click Start Shopping to dive right into the Wii's full catalog of downloadable games and Channels, as described in the following section.

When browsing the Wii Shop Channel, don't be alarmed if the page doesn't change immediately as soon as you click a button. After you click your selection, there may be a few seconds' pause while the Wii downloads the requested data from the Nintendo servers. You can make sure the Wii is still working by looking for a rotating gray circle in the upper-left corner of the screen. If the gray circle stops spinning (or if it remains spinning for a full minute or more), restart the system, check your Internet connection setup, and try again.

Browsing the Virtual Aisles

After you click the Start Shopping button, you see the Shopping menu shown in Figure 6-2. Consider this the main hallway in a virtual mall filled with downloadable content for your Wii. This hallway has a lot of potential doors to go through, and what's behind each one is explained in the following list:

Figure 6-2:
The Wii
Shop
Channels
Shopping
menu.

- ✔ **Virtual Console:** Browse, purchase, and download games originally designed for classic video-game systems, now downloadable and playable on the Wii.

- ✔ **WiiWare:** Browse, purchase, and download original software created specifically for the Wii.

- ✔ **Wii Channels:** Browse, purchase, and download fun and functional non-game applications for the Wii.

✔ **Add Wii Points:** Purchase Wii Points, the currency used to purchase games and Channels through the Wii Shop Channel.

✔ **Account Activity:** View a summary of your Wii Point and download activity, as shown in Figure 6-3. This menu provides a good way to monitor your account to keep track of the Wii Shop Channel purchases you and your family have been making. Scroll through the pages of the list using the blue arrows on the bottom right, or click on a Channel or game name to view details about that Channel or game purchase. Click Back to return to the Shopping menu.

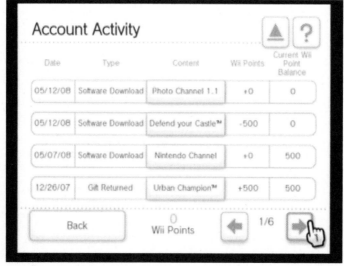

Figure 6-3:
The
Account
Activity
page.

✔ **Titles You've Downloaded:** View a list of all the games and Channels you've downloaded so far. This is handy if you have to download a title that you purchased but had to delete for some reason, or just as a simple way to keep track of all the games and Channels you've purchased so far. Use the arrows to scroll and change pages, or click on a game or Channel name to go to the information page for that title. Click Back to return to the Shopping menu.

✔ **Settings:** Adjust the following settings specific to the Wii Shop Channel:

• **My Nintendo Membership Settings:** If you've signed up for a My Nintendo account on Nintendo.com, you can use this option to link your Wii Shop Channel account and your My Nintendo account together. Linking the accounts adds your Wii Shop Channel purchases automatically to the list of Wii games stored on your My Nintendo account. If you don't have a My Nintendo account, you can sign up for one for free by visiting http://my.nintendo. com/cpp/mynintendo/myNintendo.do.

To link the accounts, click the username and password fields on this submenu and use the on-screen keyboard to enter your personal data. Remember that your password is case-sensitive, so use those Shift and Caps Lock keys if necessary. Then click the Link button to confirm. You can unlink the accounts later by choosing the My Nintendo Membership Settings option again and then clicking Unlink. You can link and unlink your account as many times as you want.

- **Gift Settings:** If, for some reason, you don't like receiving downloadable games and Channels as gifts from your Wii Friends, you can turn off your system's ability to receive gifts by using this menu option. Doing so automatically refuses any and all such gifts your Wii Friends try to send you. (You can turn on the gift-receipt feature later by using the same menu option. Before you do, though, could you possibly tell your friends to send all those gifts to me instead?)

- **Remove Wii Shop Channel:** Be careful! This menu option removes your Wii Shop Channel account and *deletes all the software you've already downloaded* from your system. The only reason you might want to do this is if you're selling your Wii and you don't want your personal data to be accessible to the system's new owner. Short of that, just stay far, far away from this option.

✔ **Wii Menu:** Return to the Wii Menu, shockingly enough!

✔ **Wii Points:** This area displays your current balance of Wii Points. Click this number to add Wii Points to your account.

✔ **Shopping Guide:** This option opens up an interactive guide that tells you how to use the Wii Shop Channel. (You won't be needing it, though, because you have this book, right? Right?! Right.)

Turning Dollars into Wii Shop Points

In a real store, you can exchange crisp bills and shiny coins or plastic for goods and services. Because the Wii doesn't have slots for bills, coins, or credit cards, you need another way to purchase games and Channels from the Wii Shop Channel. This means converting your hard-earned legal tender into the Wii Shop Channel's exclusive currency, Wii Shop Points.

Do not put bills, coins, or credit cards into the Wii's disc slot. This advice may seem obvious, but you'd be surprised what some people will try.

Wii Shop Channel game pricing

Before purchasing your Wii Shop Points (sometimes referred to as Wii Points), it would probably be good to know how many you need for the specific game or Channel you want. This information is displayed prominently next to each game and Channel name as you browse the selection on the Wii Shop Channel (see "Browsing, Purchasing, and Downloading" later in this chapter).

In general, original WiiWare games can vary in price anywhere from 500 to 1,500 Wii Shop Points (that is, $5 to $15). The downloadable Channels available as of this writing are generally free, with one exception: The Internet Channel, which costs 500 points ($5). Interestingly enough, even the Internet Channel was free until June 30, 2007, when Nintendo took the Channel out of beta testing and upped the price. (Sorry, late adopters; you have to shell out a Lincoln for Web browsing on your TV.)

For classic games available on the Wii Virtual Console, pricing is largely dependent on the system the game was originally released for. This pricing system is detailed in Table 6-1. Some rare and/or foreign games might be priced slightly higher than the prevailing rates listed in Table 6-1, but the prices apply to the vast majority of the Virtual Console games available on the Wii Shop Channel. (Whether each game is worth the price is a matter of personal discretion, of course.) See Chapter 15 for a list of some games that are definitely worth the money, in my humble opinion.

Table 6-1	Virtual Console Game Prices	
System	*Price in Wii Points*	*Price in U.S. Dollars*
NES	500	$5
Sega Master System	600	$6
NEC TurboGrafx-16	600	$6
Super NES	800	$8
Sega Genesis	800	$8
SNK Neo-Geo	900	$9
Nintendo 64	1,000	$10

Purchasing Wii Shop Points

When you know what game or Channel you want to buy and how much it costs, you need to actually convert your money into the Wii Shop Points necessary to get it. To do this, simply click the Wii Points button that appears at the bottom of nearly every screen of the Wii Shop Channel. (Refer to Figure 6-2.) Doing this brings up the Add Wii Points menu, shown in Figure 6-4.

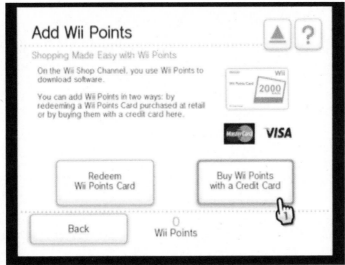

Figure 6-4:
The Add
Wii Points
menu.

Adding Wii Points by Wii Points Card

As you can see, there are two main ways to add Wii Points to your Wii Shop Channel account. The first is by redeeming a Wii Points Card, a prepaid plastic card sold at most electronics and gaming retailers (and shown in Figure 6-5).

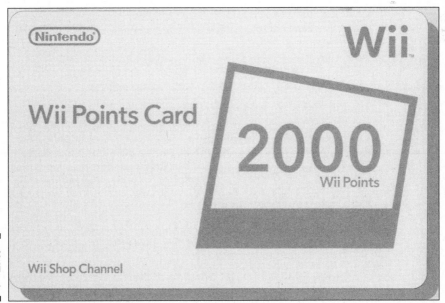

Figure 6-5:
The Wii
Points Card.

Wii Points Cards currently come only in denominations of 2,000 points; these sell for roughly $20 in the U.S. (You can occasionally find slightly better deals as part of store promotions or bundles.) While purchasing a prepaid card from a brick-and-mortar store largely ruins the convenience of shopping from the comfort of your couch, these cards are the only way for people who don't have major credit cards to get Wii Points into their account. Wii Points Cards also make good gifts for your Wii-owning friends, although savvy Wii owners can use the Shop Channel's gift-giving function to subvert even this need to leave the couch. (See the later section, "Gift-giving.")

After you get home with your Wii Points Card, here's the drill:

1. **Scratch off the silver foil on the back using a coin or a key to reveal the Wii Point Card Activation Number.**

2. **Click Redeem Wii Points Card on the Add Wii Points menu shown in Figure 6-4, and enter this number using the on-screen keypad.**

   Make sure you enter all 16 digits correctly or the Wii won't recognize the card.

3. **Click OK, and your Wii account is credited with the requisite number of Wii Points.**

   You can now discard the card, or keep it as a stylish reminder of your Wii Points purchase.

Adding Wii Points by credit card

By far the more convenient and flexible way to add Wii Points to your account is to use a major credit card. To do this, click the Buy Wii Points with a Credit Card button on the Add Wii Points menu (refer to Figure 6-4). Then follow these steps:

1. **Choose the number of Wii Points you want.**

   Wii Points are available in increments of 1,000, 2,000, 3,000, or 5,000 (if you really just want 4,000 Points, you can buy two 2,000-Point increments). Refer to the "Wii Shop Channel game pricing" section to figure out how many points you actually need. Don't worry if it looks like you're going to end up with leftover points — they're saved in your account for your next purchase (see "The surplus Points problem" sidebar).

2. **Choose your credit card type.**

   Only Visa and MasterCard are currently accepted. Wii owners with other credit cards need to go out and purchase a Wii Points Card. Sorry, Diner's Club members.

3. **Enter your credit card number, expiration date, and security code.**

   Use the on-screen keypads and arrows to enter your personal data. Your security code is a numeric code found on the back of your card, usually in the signature area. You only need to enter the last three digits of this code.

The surplus Points problem

By now, you may have noticed that the pricing of some Virtual Console and WiiWare games doesn't line up very nicely with the sales increments for Wii Points themselves. Buying 1,000 Wii Shop Points and then purchasing a 900-point Neo-Geo game (for instance) leaves your account with 100 leftover Points. With the cheapest downloadable games coming in at 500 Wii Points, the questions quickly become: What am I supposed to do with these leftover points? And why can't I buy just the Wii Points I need?

Unfortunately, there's no wholly satisfying answer to either of these perfectly fine questions. The best defense I've heard for Nintendo's 1,000-Point-at-a-time sales practice has to do with the credit card fees associated with purchasing Wii Points online. Selling points in smaller increments, the argument goes, would bury Nintendo in credit card fees that it can't really afford. (Note that this defense did not come from Nintendo itself, but from a business-savvy friend of mine.)

While this explanation is plausible, conspiracy-minded readers have probably come up with an equally plausible explanation for the practice: Nintendo is trying to bilk Wii owners out of their hard-earned dough. After all, if those leftover points don't get spent, they represent, in essence, extra, unearned money in Nintendo's pockets. And if you do want to use these leftover Points, you have to buy at least 1,000 *more* Wii Points, which puts more money in Nintendo's coffers. Even after the extra purchase, you often *still* have more leftover Points, which leaves more unearned money in Nintendo's pockets. And the cycle continues.

This problem really isn't as bad as some people might make it out to be. You can usually get your Wii Points balance down to that magic level of zero through some creative game-purchasing combinations. And frankly, if you can't find enough games to justify spending $10 more on Wii Shop Channel content, then you aren't looking hard enough. (Check out Chapter 15 if you're really having trouble.) Still, it is really annoying being forced to purchase Wii Shop Points that you may never actually use. You may just have to suck it up and eat the remainder, just as you do when buying incompatible packages of hot dogs and hot dog buns. Of course, the extra buns *do* tend to taste better than the extra Wii Shop Points.

Don't worry too much about the security of your personal credit card data when you're using the Wii Shop Channel. The Wii automatically encrypts all the sensitive data it sends to Nintendo, so unscrupulous characters listening in won't be able to make sense of your information even if they somehow intercept it. While no security system is perfect, this is relatively safe as these things go. If you really want some extra protection, look into a wireless router with WEP or WPA security.

4. **Enter your billing address information.**

Use the on-screen keyboard to enter the required information.

Note that the last field is County, not *Country* (this little wrinkle messed up quite a few transactions for me).

5. Click Yes to confirm your purchase.

After a short confirmation process, your credit card is billed and the Wii Points are added to your account. You can now continue shopping with your virtual wallet filled.

Browsing, Purchasing, and Downloading

After your virtual wallet has been virtually stuffed with virtual currency in the form of Wii Points, it's time to spend those Points on Virtual Console games and Channels for your, er, non-virtual Wii.

Browsing

To browse the Shop Channel's selections, go to the Shopping menu (refer to Figure 6-2) and choose either the Virtual Console, WiiWare, or Wii Channels option. The difference between the content available behind each of these options is described in the earlier section, "Browsing the Virtual Aisles."

While choosing the Wii Channels option brings you directly to a scrollable menu of downloadable Channels (much like the one shown in Figure 6-7), choosing either WiiWare or Virtual Console brings up a submenu like the one shown in Figure 6-6, which shows the browsing submenu for WiiWare titles; the menu for Virtual Console titles is very similar.

Figure 6-6: WiiWare browsing options.

The WiiWare and Virtual Console browsing options menus both include the following options:

- ✔ **Popular Titles:** Choose this option to browse a list of the games downloaded most often by other Wii owners. This option is useful if you have no idea what you're looking for — after all, millions of other Wii owners can't be wrong (about games, anyway).

- ✔ **Newest Additions:** Choose this option to browse a list of all available games in reverse chronological order, based on the date they were added to the Wii Shop Channel. This option is particularly useful for seeing what's been added since your last visit to the Channel.

- ✔ **Search by Publisher/Genre:** Choosing these options brings up yet another submenu where you can choose to restrict your browsing to a particular publisher or genre. (See Chapter 11 for advice on genres and how to choose games you might enjoy.)

  In the case of the Virtual Console menu, these options are hidden behind the Search by Category option. They are also joined by a third filtering option — Search by System — which lets you restrict your browsing to games originally released on a specific classic system.

- ✔ **Search by Game Title:** Enter a full or partial game title using the on-screen keyboard, and then click OK to browse a list of games that have that phrase as part of their title. Remember that spelling *does* count here, so only enter part of the game title if you're unsure of how to spell the whole thing.

After choosing your browsing options (as described in the preceding list), you're presented with a list of games much like the one shown in Figure 6-7.

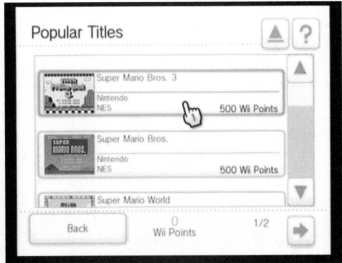

Figure 6-7:
The Wii Shop Channels game-browsing menu.

Click the arrows and slider on the right side to scroll through this list, or use the up and down arrows on the Wii Remote's control pad. Browsing is limited to only ten games per page, so use the blue arrows in the lower-right corner to scroll through multiple pages of results (the current page and total number of pages can also be seen in the lower right). Click the Back button to go back to the previous menu. You can also click the question mark for help with navigating, or you can keep reading and I'll prove to you that I can help you out just as well as any silly on-screen help files.

If you see a game that you're potentially interested in, click its name on the browsing list to bring up an information page, as shown in Figure 6-8. As you can see, this page presents a wide variety of data about the game, including the original release date, publisher, genre, number of players, and ESRB rating. (See Chapter 11 for more on game ratings.) Click the More Details button to view some sample screenshots from the game and read a short synopsis of the gameplay.

Although the Wii doesn't offer demos of WiiWare and Virtual Console games, you can view sample videos of generic gameplay by visiting www.nintendo. com/wii/virtualconsole. You can also view videos of many WiiWare and Virtual Console games directly on your TV using the downloadable Nintendo Channel. (See Chapter 10 for more on this Channel.) Incidentally, you should definitely feel comfortable buying *Super Mario 64*, the game shown in Figure 6-8, without consulting any videos, because it's the greatest game of all time. And I'm totally objective about that. Honest.

Figure 6-8: A Wii Shop Channel game information page.

Purchasing and downloading

After you've read all the information about a game and/or Channel and are sure you want to actually purchase it, click the Download button at the bottom of the screen (as shown in Figure 6-8). Make sure you already have enough Wii Points attached to your account to make the purchase — if you don't, the Wii greets you with a rather rude error message.

If you do have enough Wii Points, you're taken to a list of the controllers that the game or Channel is compatible with. Pay close attention to this information before moving on, as it would be a shame to go to all the trouble of downloading a game or Channel just to find that you didn't have the right controller to use it. For more information about which controllers work with which games, see the "Which controller do I need?" section later in this chapter, or refer to Chapter 3.

After you confirm that you have one of the compatible controllers, you're presented with a download-confirmation page (shown in Figure 6-9), which outlines the effects the download will have on your Wii Points balance and on your Wii's internal-memory situation. (See Chapter 5 for more on managing the Wii's internal memory.)

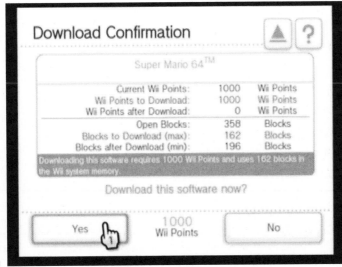

Figure 6-9:
The Wii Shop download confirmation page.

If this all looks acceptable, click Yes to begin the download. An old-school, two-dimensional Mario runs down the screen collecting coins and bashing blocks (as shown in Figure 6-10). This may just seem like a cute animation, but those blocks and coins actually represent the progress of the download.

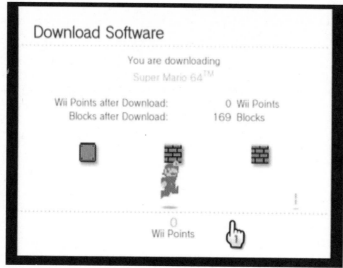

Figure 6-10: The download progress screen.

For some downloads, you may notice the Mario on the download progress screen is taller and wears white overalls. When this happens, you can press the A button on the Wii Remote during the download to make Mario shoot fireballs. Neat!

After Mario finishes bashing the rightmost block, the Wii tells you that the download is complete, and updates you on the number of blocks left on the Wii's internal memory. Click OK and read a quick parental-control warning, and then press A to return to the Wii Shop channel.

When you return to the Wii Menu, your newly downloaded game or Channel is ready to go, with no need for any manual installation.

You may have to scroll past the first page of the Wii Menu to find your new download.

Gift-giving

In addition to downloading games and Channels for your own personal use, the Wii Shop Channel also lets you purchase titles as gifts for your registered Wii Friends. The process for purchasing these gifts is very similar to the process for downloading your own titles — just click the Gift button on the game information page instead of the Purchase button (refer to Figure 6-8). After reading the controller information page, you're asked to pick the recipient of your gift from a list of your registered Wii friends (see Chapter 4 for more on registering Wii Friends).

After choosing your friend, you're allowed to write a personal message and attach a Mii to your gift, as shown in Figure 6-11. The process for writing this note is similar to the process for writing a Wii Message Board message (described in Chapter 4).

Figure 6-11:
The Wii
Shop
Channel's
Gift Giving
Message
screen.

After you confirm your message and the gift purchase, the Wii Points are deducted from your account and your gift are sent across the Internet. Your friend receives the gift in the form of a Message on his or her Wii Message Board that includes a button. Your friend clicks this button to download the gift from the Wii Shop Channel for free. Be sure to alert any such lucky friends to your philanthropy; have them check their systems.

Playing Downloaded Games

Playing WiiWare and Virtual Console games downloaded from the Wii Shop Channel is a lot like playing Wii games that come on a disc, only there's no disc! Simply click the appropriate icon on the Wii Menu and click Start to load the game right up. (See Chapter 5 for more in the Wii Menu.)

The following sections discuss the few other wrinkles with playing downloaded games that don't apply to normal, disc-based games.

Which controller do I need?

Classic games downloaded for the Wii Virtual Console are identical to the original versions in nearly every respect. But there is one important way in which they differ: the controllers. Unfortunately, the Wii doesn't let you plug in the original controllers used with the classic systems that the Virtual Console games were originally designed for.

Fortunately, many Virtual Console games are playable with the Wii Remote that's included with each system. Some downloaded games, though, require you to use a Wii Classic Controller or GameCube controller. Which games work with which controllers can be a bit confusing for Virtual Console games. Consult Table 6-2 to determine what controller is needed for which game, based on the system the game was originally released for.

Table 6-2	Picking a Controller with Virtual Console Games		
System	*Wii Remote*	*Classic Controller*	*GameCube*
NES	Yes	Yes	Yes
SNES	No	Yes	Yes
Nintendo 64	No	Yes	Yes
Sega Genesis	Some	Yes	Yes
Sega Master System	Yes	Yes	Yes
SNK Neo-Geo	Some	Yes	Yes
NEC TurboGrafx-16	Yes	Yes	Some

As you can see from Table 6-2, you can control every game in the Virtual Console Library with the Wii Classic Controller. If you don't have one, though, a GameCube controller can act as a decent substitute, working with all games save some designed for the TurboGrafx-16, according to Nintendo's Web site. (As this book was written, though, all 49 TurboGrafx-16 games offered on the Wii Shop Channel actually *do* work with the GameCube controller. Frankly, I can't see any reason why future games would break this trend.)

If you just have a Wii Remote, you won't be able to play a large chunk of the Wii's Virtual Console library. This is due to the distinct lack of buttons and joysticks on the Wii Remote, which makes controlling Super NES and Nintendo 64 games with the motion-sensitive controller impossible. Note that some Genesis and Neo-Geo games work with the Wii Remote, although this compatibility varies from game to game.

If you only have a Wii Remote, pay close attention to the controller-compatibility confirmation screen when you're downloading games originally designed for these systems; make sure you're actually able to play your purchase.

Suspending play

With most games, if you haven't saved your progress before you turn the system off, you've lost all your hard work (or hard play, as the case may be). With many Virtual Console games, though, this isn't true. The Virtual Console has a game suspension feature that lets you automatically save your progress at any point in many games.

Suspending a game couldn't be simpler. When you're done with a play session, simply press the Home button on the Wii Remote and choose to return to the Wii Menu. The Wii automatically creates and saves a *suspend state* for the game that captures the in-game situation exactly as it was when you pressed the Home button. When you come back to the game, the game resumes from this exact point as if you had never stopped playing.

Note that this suspension feature doesn't work for games that were originally designed for the Nintendo 64 or the Neo-Geo, owing to technical issues. Also note that you have to actively return to the Wii Menu to create a suspend state — simply turning the system off in the middle of a Virtual Console game erases your progress, forcing you to start over from the beginning the next time you play. Suspending play doesn't work at all for downloaded WiiWare titles.

Also note that resuming play from a suspend state destroys that suspend state. This means that you have to create *another* suspend state before you end your next play session to continue your game again.

Aside from the suspend function, many Virtual Console games include a built-in save function to chronicle progress in the game. If the original version of a game originally supported saving game data, then the Virtual Console version does too. Saving a Virtual Console game using an in-game menu creates a save file in the Wii's internal memory, just as it would for a disc-based game.

Operations Guide

All downloadable Virtual Console and WiiWare games also come with an in-game Operations Guide that tells you the rules and controls behind the game. To access the guide, press the Home button on the Wii Remote at any point during play, and then click the Operations Guide button on the Home menu.

Click the section names to open them up for reading on-screen. You can scroll through the various sections using the up and down buttons on the Wii Remote's directional pad. The + button returns to the table of contents. Press the Home button again to return to the game.

The Operations Guide is especially useful for determining how the buttons on the various Wii controllers relate to the original buttons used in downloaded Virtual Console games. Each Operations Guide has a handy diagram for this, as well as a detailed explanation of what each button does. Read it, use it, live it — but most of all, play it.

Chapter 7

Those Marvelous Miis

For years, playing video games primarily meant taking control of someone else (someone virtual, anyway), and escaping your normal, boring life to become a super-powered alter-ego. As games have become more complex and game systems have become more powerful, more game makers are letting players create controllable, "realistic" digital versions of themselves, their friends, or anyone at all. The Wii is no different, allowing players to create customized Miis to represent themselves in games and Channels and the Wii Message Board.

No one is going to mistake these cartoon-like, large-eyed, round-headed Mii characters for digital photographs, but Miis still do a good job of capturing the essence of a wide variety of facial characteristics. This chapter discusses how to create and download Miis using the Mii Channel and share those Miis with the world, using the Check Mii Out Channel.

The Mii Channel and You

The Mii Channel is your main gateway for creating new Miis to use in games and Channels. It's also the place where your created Miis hang out in the Mii Plaza when they're not being used, and the home of the Mii Parade, where your friends' Miis might wander over to you through your Internet connection.

Creating a Mii

The first time you start up the Mii Channel (see Chapter 5 for more on using Channels from the Wii Menu), you're immediately asked to create a Mii. After that, you can create additional Miis by clicking the Create Mii button on the Wii Plaza menu (see the later section, "Mii Plaza").

First you have to select the gender of your Mii by clicking the appropriate on-screen option (don't worry, you can change it later). If this is your first Mii, you have to start with an extremely generic Mii model. If this is not your first Mii, you can choose to start from scratch or use the Choose a Look-Alike screen to pick a Mii that's already close to the Mii you envision in your head. If you choose to use a look-alike, you're first asked to choose a starting face from a variety of randomly generated faces. You can then tweak that face toward the one you envision, using the look-alike menu shown in Figure 7-1. Simply click the face closest to your desired Mii to see a new selection of Miis that tweak that Mii just slightly. Click Use This Face to start editing that face to your precise specifications, as described in the following section.

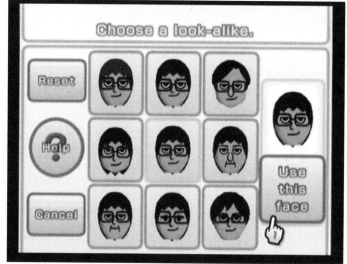

Figure 7-1:
The Mii
Channel's
look-alike
menu.

Editing your Mii's facial features

After you've set up your Mii's basics, it's time to shape your Wii's face like a virtual plastic surgeon. This is done primarily through the facial editing menu, as shown in Figure 7-2. There are a lot of options available here, and even more are available by clicking the tabs on the top.

Click the Mii shown on the left side of the editor to make it spin around quickly. Click the Mii again while spinning to stop the spin and hold position. This is the only way to see the back of a Mii's hairstyle, as well as a side view of certain facial features.

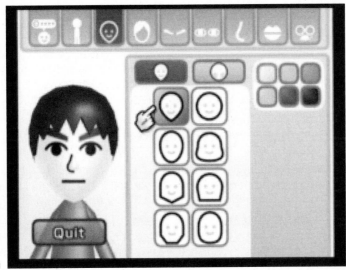

Figure 7-2:
The Mii
Editor main
menu.

The following list describes the Mii editing options you can access by clicking the tabs at the top of the Mii editing menu; the tabs are described from left to right:

  ✔ **Edit Mii Profile:** Click this tab to configure the vital statistics for your Mii, as shown in Figure 7-3:

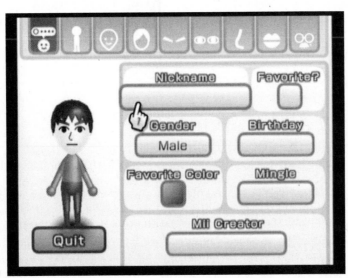

Figure 7-3:
The Edit
Mii Profile
Screen.

- **Nickname:** Click this area to bring up an on-screen keyboard which you can use to enter a nickname for your Mii. (See Chapter 5 for more on using the on-screen keyboard.) Note that nicknames can have a maximum of ten characters. This is the only personal information that is absolutely required for every Mii — everything else on the Edit Mii Profile menu screen is optional.

- **Favorite?:** Check this option to designate this Mii as one of your favorites. These Miis tend to show up more often in the crowd scenes of Mii-compatible games. If you created the favored Mii, its pants change from blue to red in the Mii Plaza as well.

- **Gender:** Toggle your Mii's gender between male and female. The only real difference between the two is that female Miis wear a slightly longer, tapered blouse rather than a plain shirt.

- **Birthday:** Designate a birthday for this Mii, first by choosing the month and then the day. You can choose today's date or whatever you want. Choose the question mark to leave the birthday as unknown.

- **Favorite Color:** Despite the name, all this option really does is change the color of the Mii's shirt. Click whichever colored square you'd like to choose that color.

- **Mingle:** Toggle whether or not this Mii can travel to your friends' Wiis as part of the Mii Parade feature (see "The Mii Parade" section, later in this chapter). By default, your Miis are not shared with others. Click this box to allow a copy of the Mii to travel to your Registered Wii Friends (see Chapter 4 for more on registering Wii Friends). Note that for this feature to work, both you and your friends must allow for sharing through the Mii Parade.

- **Mii Creator:** Like an artist signing a canvas, you can put your name (or a pseudonym) to your Mii creations. Click this button and then click Reenter to bring up an on-screen keyboard to enter a name with up to ten characters. You can also choose from a list of creator names that have already been entered without going through the keyboard.

✔ **Body Type:** Choose this tab on the top of the Mii editing menu to bring up the body type sliders shown in Figure 7-4. Click and drag the sliders with the Wii Remote pointer to adjust the height and weight of your Mii. As you move the sliders, the Mii shown on the left side of the screen changes in real time. Remember, you can get a full body view of your Mii by clicking the figure to the left with the Wii Remote pointer.

✔ **Facial Features Menus:** Click any of the remaining seven tabs at the top of the Mii editing screen to bring up a variety of facial feature options. Click any of these facial feature options to assign it to the Mii shown on the left. Don't like how it looks? Just click another feature in the center area to change it again. Other options for editing the look of particular facial feature are shown in Figure 7-5 and discussed in the list that follows:

Body Type

Edit Mii Profile

Facial Features menus

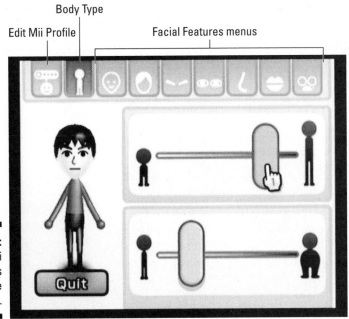

Figure 7-4:
The Mii
Channel's
body type
menu.

Flip page

Colors

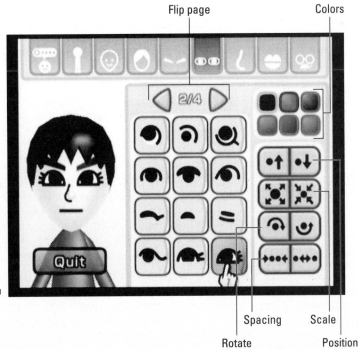

Figure 7-5:
The Mii
Channel's
eye style
editing
menu.

Spacing

Scale

Rotate

Position

- **Flip page:** Use these buttons to scroll through multiple pages of facial feature options. The current page number and total number of pages are shown in the center. Note that some facial features only have one page of options to choose from.

- **Colors:** Click a color box to change the color of the currently selected facial feature. Refer to Figure 7-5.

- **Position:** Use these buttons to change the vertical position of the current facial feature. This effect can be quite extreme if you click multiple times. Try moving your Mii's mouth above its eyes for a really freaky effect. (See the "Making mysterious Miis" sidebar.)

- **Scale:** Use these buttons to change the size of the current facial feature.

- **Rotate:** Use these buttons to rotate the current facial feature clockwise or counterclockwise. The Rotate buttons are only available in the Eyes and Eyebrows menus.

- **Spacing:** Click these buttons to tighten or broaden the space between the eyes or eyebrows on your Mii. (Like the Rotate buttons, the Spacing buttons are only available on the Eyes and Eyebrow menus.)

- **Flip Part:** On the hairstyle menu, use this button to reverse the direction of certain nonsymmetrical parts.

Note that some of the facial feature submenus have further submenus of their own. On the Facial Shape menu, click the circle above the facial shape options to add subtle features like freckles, rosy cheeks, eye shadow, and more. In the Miscellaneous submenu, you can find further menus for beards, mustaches, and even a beauty mark. Don't be afraid to click around and explore — remember, you can always undo whatever you've done.

✔ **Quit:** When you're done creating your Mii, click Quit to return to the Mii Plaza. Don't worry; you're asked to save your Mii before quitting out of the menu (you can also quit without saving if you aren't happy with how your Mii turned out).

If you haven't given a nickname to your Mii yet, you have to enter one using the on-screen keyboard before saving your Mii. Don't worry if there's still something you don't like about the Mii — you can come back and edit it later.

Mii Plaza

The Mii Plaza is where the Miis you've created or downloaded from the Internet hang out when they're not being used in games or Channels. It also serves at the main menu of sorts for the Mii Channel, letting you create, delete, manage, and share your Miis with others. This section provides a complete guide to doing all these things.

Making mysterious Miis

The wide variety of facial feature options in the Mii Channel's Mii maker means you can mimic practically any human face. But why stop there? Using some creative positioning, coloring, and sizing you can create much more than just human faces. Here are some basic tips:

🖊 The right combination of mustache, beard, and hairstyle can make an animalistic Mii.

🖊 Try arching the eyebrows and positioning them inside the hair to make a faux crown!

🖊 Why go with the regular facial order? Turn a Mii's face upside down by moving the mouth above the eyes.

🖊 Try hiding facial features in other facial features for noseless, mouthless or even eyeless creations.

🖊 Use the Check Mii Out Channel for inspiration!

You can store only 100 Miis in your Mii Plaza at any one time. If the plaza is full, you won't be able to create new Miis or download Miis from the Mii Parade or the Check Mii Out Channel. Delete some of your least favorite Miis, or store them in the Mii Parade (see the later section, "The Mii Parade").

Navigating the Mii Plaza

The Mii Plaza is like an aquarium for your Miis — a featureless void where they wander around, chat, fall asleep, and even occasionally wave at the camera. Your initial view of the Mii Plaza is only a small section of that aquarium, though. Use the following controls to view and interact with the rest of the Mii Plaza:

🖊 **Zoom:** If there are a lot of Miis in your Plaza, it can be hard to see them all on the screen at once. To fix this problem, use the + and – buttons on the Wii Remote to zoom the camera in and out, respectively. There are four levels of zoom.

🖊 **Identify:** Point and click a Mii with the A button to see the Mii's name appear in a word balloon above his or her head. If the Mii was created by one of your registered Wii Friends, the creator's name is also shown. You'll also notice a gray circle in the identifying word balloon. Click this circle to designate the Mii as one of your favorites. Your favorite Miis tend to show up more often in Mii-compatible games. Click anywhere else on the screen to make the name bubble disappear.

🖊 **Scroll:** Point the Wii Remote at the Mii Plaza screen and hold the B button to bring up a scrolling interface with four arrows on the edges of the screen. While still holding the B button, move the pointer in any direction to scroll your viewpoint in that direction. Let go of the B button to stop scrolling. You can also use the directional pad on the Wii Remote to scroll.

✔ **Picking up:** Hover the pointer over a Mii and press the A and B buttons simultaneously to pick the Mii up, as shown in Figure 7-6. You can move the Mii around by moving the Wii Remote pointer. Hold the Mii near the edge of the screen to scroll in the direction of that edge. Let go of either button on the Wii Remote to drop the Mii in its current location.

While carrying a Mii, you can also drag it to the Edit Mii, Erase Mii, or Send to Mii Parade buttons. The functions are discussed in the next section.

Figure 7-6:
Carrying a
Mii with the
Wii Remote
pointer.

Mii Plaza menu

While you're in the Mii Plaza, point the Wii Remote at the screen to bring up the menu shown in Figure 7-7. The options on this menu let you create, edit, and share your Miis, as well as download new Miis from the Mii Parade. These menu options are described in further detail in the following list, starting from the upper-left corner:

✔ **Wii Menu:** Click this button to return to the Wii Menu. Remember, you can also return to the Wii Menu at any time by pressing the Home button on the Wii Remote.

✔ **Edit Mii:** Not happy with how one of your Miis looks? Drag it over to this circle to rejigger it in the Mii Editing menu, as described in the earlier section, "Editing your Mii's facial features."

Note that you can only edit Miis that were created on your personal Wii. Miis downloaded from the Mii Parade or the Check Mii Out Channel are locked and can't be edited.

✔ **New Mii:** Click this button to create a new Mii. When you're done, the freshly created Mii drops into your Mii Plaza.

✔ **Erase Mii:** Is your Mii Plaza getting too cluttered? Pick up and drag a Mii over to this circle to remove it from your system permanently.

Be careful! There's no way to undo this Mii erasure, so think long and hard before you confirm the deletion.

Edit Mii

Wii Menu

Transfer Mii

Mii Parade

Help

Arrange

Figure 7-7
The Mii
Plaza menu.

Erase Mii

Wii Friend

New Mii

Note that you can also clear space in the Mii Plaza by sending a Mii to the Mii Parade for long-term storage. (See the Mii Parade bullet.)

When you erase a Mii from the Mii Plaza, you also erase its data from any Wii games that might use that Mii as a character. This can cause you to lose important progress data. Be careful erasing Miis you use in games.

✔ **Help:** Bring up on-screen directions for navigating the Mii Plaza. These are all covered in the "Navigating the Mii Plaza" section, though, so you can just pretend this button doesn't exist. Just look away whenever your eyes happen to hover over it. Maybe put a little piece of paper on the screen to block it from your sight permanently.

✔ **Mii Parade:** Click this button to bring up the Mii Parade, which is discussed in further detail in the following section. You can also pick up a Mii from the Mii Plaza floor and drag it over to this icon to transfer it from the Mii Plaza to the Mii Parade. This frees up space in the Mii Plaza while still allowing you to recover the Mii from the Mii Parade at a later date, if you so desire. Note that Miis in the Mii Parade can't be used in games and other Channels without first being brought back to the Mii Plaza.

✔ **Transfer Mii:** That Wii Remote in your hands isn't just good for navigating games and menus. You can also use it to store up to ten Miis, which you can then use on a friend's Wii. Follow these steps to transfer Miis on and off your Remote:

1. **Click the Transfer Mii button.**

   A list of the Remotes currently connected to the Wii is displayed.

2. **Click the icon for the Remote which you want to use to transfer Miis.**

   If the Remote you want to use is not connected to the Wii, first press the 1 and 2 buttons on that Remote simultaneously, then choose its icon on the screen.

3. **Drag the desired Mii to one of the empty white circles.**

   After you've chosen a Remote, the contents of that Remote are shown at the top of the Mii Plaza menu, as shown in Figure 7-8. Pick up and drag a Mii to one of the empty white circles to transfer a copy on to the Remote. Alternatively, you can drag a Mii from one of those circles on to the Mii Plaza floor. This takes the Mii off the Remote and adds it to the Mii Plaza. Note that if there's a copy of the Mii already in the Plaza, it's replaced with the version from the Remote.

   You can also Erase Miis from the Wii Remote or the Mii Plaza by dragging them to the Erase Mii button on the left side of the screen.

4. **Click Save & Quit when you're done transferring Miis.**

   The Wii spends a few seconds transferring the Miis in the white circles on to your Wii Remote. You can now take this Remote over to a friend's Wii and use your personal Miis over there.

✔ **Wii Friend:** Use this button to send a Mii to one of your registered Wii Friends over the Internet (see Chapter 4 for more on connecting your Wii to your broadband Internet connection). First, click the envelope button to display the mail icon at the top of the screen, as shown in Figure 7-9. From here, pick up and drag the Mii you want to send to the white circle in the envelope.

Figure 7-8: The Transfer Mii menu.

Figure 7-9: The Mii mailing submenu.

After dropping the Mii in the envelope, a menu pops up with a list of your registered Wii Friends (see Chapter 5 for more on registering Wii Friends). Click the friend you want to send the Mii to and confirm by clicking Yes. The Mii appears in your friend's Mii Plaza the next time he or she starts up the Mii Channel. Click the Quit button when you're done sending Miis.

✔ **Arrange:** Tired of seeing your Miis meandering around the Plaza like a bunch of lazy layabouts? Click the Arrange button (it looks like a whistle) to call the Miis to attention in nice, orderly rows and columns. Clicking the Arrange button also brings up a new row of options on the bottom row of the Mii Plaza menu:

- **Number:** Clicking this icon doesn't do anything, but the number tells you exactly how many Miis are in your plaza. (Remember, you can only have 100 Miis in your Plaza at any one time.)

- **Whistle:** Click the whistle again to disband the Wiis and let them wander and mingle as they please.

- **Alphabetical:** Arrange your Miis in alphabetical order by their nicknames, starting in the bottom-left corner and proceeding to the right and upward.

- **Favorites:** The Miis you've designated as your favorites line up in the front, while the rest of the riff-raff are arranged in the back. To designate a Mii as a favorite, click the Mii and then click the gray circle that appears in the word balloon above the Mii's head. You can also click the Favorite box on the Edit Mii Profile tab when you're editing or creating the Mii.

- **Color:** Arrange your Miis in rows by the color of their shirts. The lines look almost like the bars of a rainbow, don't they?

- **Gender:** Click the Gender button to separate the males and females. Boys to the left, girls to the right, everybody's gonna party tonight!

The Mii Parade

If your Wii is connected to the Internet, Miis from your registered Wii Friends can wander over and gather in the Mii Parade area. The Miis in the Mii Parade can't be used in games or other Channels until you transfer them to the Mii Plaza.

Setting up the Mii Parade

To get Miis in your parade, first make sure your Wii is connected to the Internet and that WiiConnect24 is turned on. You also have to register some Wii Friends to share Miis with (see Chapter 4) and both you and your friends have to turn on the travel settings for your Mii Parades (see the next section).

After this is done, any Miis that have been set to mingle start to meander over through the Internet ether (see the "Editing your Mii's facial features" section for more on mingling Miis). Be patient — it may take a few days after setting everything up for the first Miis to wander over to your parade.

Using the Mii Parade menu

Click the Mii Parade button to bring up the Mii Parade screen, as shown in Figure 7-10. Click a marching Mii to stop him or her marching and see his or her name, or click one of the options on the Mii Parade menu, also shown in Figure 7-10 and described in the following list:

✔ **Send to Mii Plaza:** Pick up a marching Mii and drag him to this circle to add him to your Mii Plaza (see the "Navigating the Mii Plaza" section for more on picking up and moving Miis). This Mii drops into your Mii Plaza, ready to be used in games, other Channels, and the Wii Message Board. Note that you can't edit the features of Miis created by other people. Also note that you can only hold 100 Miis in your Plaza at any one time.

✔ **Erase Mii:** If your parade is getting too crowded, pick up and drag any of the marching Miis to this circle to remove them from the Parade permanently. Note that the Mii Parade can hold up to 10,000 Miis at once, so the only real reason to remove Miis is if you don't like the way they look.

Send to Mii Plaza   Return to Mii Plaza

Figure 7-10:
The Mii
Parade and
menu.

Erase Mii   Speed

Travel Settings

✔ **Mii Plaza:** Return to the Mii Plaza.

✔ **Travel Settings:** Before any Miis can join your parade, you and your registered Wii Friends first have to turn on the Travel Settings through this menu. Click the Travel Setting icon, and then the Travel button to turn the feature on. Choose Don't Travel to stop the automatic inflow and outflow of Miis through the Internet.

See the "Setting up the Mii Parade" section for more requirements for filling up your Mii Parade. Remember, only Miis set to mingle travel to your friends' systems. The more registered Wii Friends turn on this feature, the more Miis wander into your parade.

✔ **Speed:** Click the running-man icon to toggle the Miis' marching speed between a slow walk and a fast trot.

Checking Out the Check Mii Out Channel

We human beings have things like fashion magazines, reality shows, and beauty pageants to tell us who to deify for physical attractiveness. Miis have the Check Mii Out Channel, an online clearinghouse for Wii owners to put their creations up to be evaluated by the harsh criticism of the public. The following sections tell you everything you need to know to become one of the nervous Mii artisans, one of the public evaluators, or both!

Checking Mii Out for the first time

To use the Check Mii Out Channel, you first have to get your Wii hooked up to a high-speed Internet connection (see Chapter 4 for more on this). When you're online, head over to the Wii Shop Channel and download the Check Mii Out Channel from the Channels section. (See Chapter 6 for more on using the Wii Shop Channel.) The Check Mii Out Channel is absolutely free and takes up 91 blocks of space on your Wii's internal memory (see Chapter 5 for more on memory management). After the Channel is downloaded, you start it just as you would any other Channel from the Wii Menu.

The first time you load up the Check Mii Out Channel, you're presented with some on-screen information about how to use it. You can skip through these screens by pressing the A button. (You won't need them . . . that's what you have this book for!) You then are asked to choose a Mii to represent you as an "artisan." This serves as your public face for people evaluating the Miis you upload to the Channel. Use the on-screen arrows to scroll through the list of Miis in your Mii Plaza then click your desired Mii to select it.

If you pick a Mii with an inappropriate nickname as your artisan, Nintendo might block your access to the Channel.

After picking your artisan, the Channel asks if you want to sign up for the Check Mii Out Channel messaging service. This service sends you Wii Message Board messages whenever a new contest is available for evaluation on the Check Mii Out Channel (see Chapter 5 for more on the Wii Message Board). If you turn this service on now, you can always turn it off later from the Settings menu.

After this brief setup process, you see the Check Mii Out Channel's main menu, as shown in Figure 7-11. The Posting Plaza and Contests options are detailed in the following sections. The other menu options are discussed in the following list:

✔ **Wii Menu:** Return to the Wii Menu. Remember, you can also return to the Wii Menu at any time by pressing the Home button on the Wii Remote.

✔ **Mii Artisan Info:** Click the face of your currently selected Mii artisan to access data about your Mii posting history. This information includes your average star ranking, your most popular posted Mii, and the quality of your contest judging (see the "Contests" section). Click the on-screen arrows to scroll through the information screens. You can also click the Change button in the upper-left corner to choose a new Mii artisan, just as you did the first time you used the Channel. Click the Back button to return to the Check Mii Out Channel's main menu.

✔ **Settings:** Use the on-screen buttons to change your status on the Check Mii Out Channel's messaging service. You can also change the language the messages are delivered in from English to French or Spanish, if you're into that sort of thing.

Figure 7-11:
The Check Mii Out Channel Main menu.

Return to Wii Menu   Mii Artisan Info   Settings

Navigating the Check Mii Out Channel

You can use your Wii Remote to navigate around both the Posting Plaza and Contest evaluation screens. Use the following Wii Remote commands to get around:

- ✔ **Viewing a Mii:** Click a Mii to bring up a larger view of it, along with a menu with more options for viewing and evaluating the Mii and its ilk. See the "Viewing Mii details" section for more on viewing posted Miis.

- ✔ **Scrolling:** There are two ways to scroll through the Posting Plaza. The first (and simpler) is to use the up and down arrows on the Wii Remote's directional pad. The second is to point the Wii Remote at the screen, hold down the B button, and move the Remote pointer up and down. Let go of the B button when you're done scrolling.

- ✔ **Zoom:** Use the + and – buttons on the Wii Remote to change the number of Miis you can see at once, from a minimum of three to a maximum of 50.

- ✔ **Grabbing and moving a Mii:** If you don't like where a particular Mii is standing, you can changes its location by pointing at the Mii and grabbing it by pressing and holding the A and B buttons on the Wii Remote simultaneously. While still holding the buttons, move the Mii to your new desired location with the Wii Remote pointer, and then let go of the buttons to set the Mii down in its new position.

Posting Plaza

The Check Mii Out Channel Posting Plaza, as shown in Figure 7-12, is like an Internet-enabled version of the Mii Plaza. In the Posting Plaza, Miis submitted from Wii owners worldwide hang out, waiting for people like you to gawk at them and evaluate them like a piece of meat! Best of all, you can add your own Miis to this feeding frenzy.

The Posting Plaza menu

Use the Wii Remote Commands described in the "Navigating the Check Mii Out Channel" section to browse the Miis. You can click the menu buttons surrounding the edge of the screen for more options. These buttons are shown in Figure 7-12 and described in the following list:

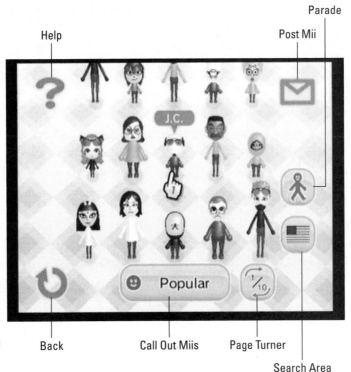

Help

Parade

Post Mii

J.C.

Figure 7-12:
The Posting
Plaza Main
menu.

Back

Call Out Miis

Page Turner

Search Area

✔ **Help:** Click the question mark to get on-screen information about the general navigation. (You can use the "Navigating the Check Mii Out Channel" section just as easily.)

✔ **Back:** Return to the Check Mii Out Channel main menu.

✔ **Call Out Miis:** Click the button initially labeled "Popular" to bring up a submenu outlining all the different ways you can filter the Miis in the posting plaza, as shown in Figure 7-13:

- **Popular:** Calls out Miis that have recently been popular with other users of the Check Mii Out Channel.

- **Top 50:** The top 50 highest-ranked Miis submitted to the Check Mii Out Channel, as determined by Star rating (see the section, "Viewing Mii details").

- **Grab Bag:** Call out a random selection of Miis submitted to the Check Mii Out Channel.

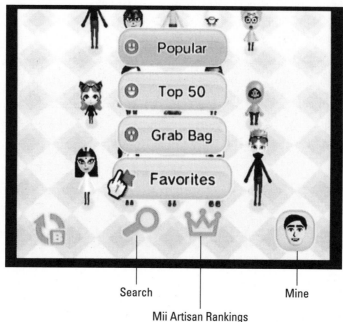

Figure 7-13:
The Call Out
Miis
submenu.

Search

Mine

Mii Artisan Rankings

- **Favorites:** Call out Miis that you've designated as your favorites using the I Like It option on the Mii Details screen (see the section, "Viewing Mii details").

- **Search:** Click the magnifying glass to filter the Check Mii Out Channel Miis according to specific criteria, as shown in Figure 7-14. Click the Change buttons to toggle the Gender or Skill you want in your results, and then click Search to bring up the resulting Miis.

  You can also click the Rotate button in the upper-right corner to bring up a search by specific entry number. These entry numbers are unique to each Mii in the Channel and can be found in the Profile screen when viewing a Mii's details. Click Enter # and then use the on-screen keypad to enter the entry number for the Check Mii Out entry you want to see, and then click Search to bring that Mii up on the screen.

- **Mii Artisan Rankings:** Click the crown to display a list of the top 100 Mii artisans for the current month, as ranked by their Miis' average Star Rankings. The arrows next to each artisan name show their change in position since the previous month. Click the on-screen arrows or press the up and down arrows on your Wii Remote's directional pad to scroll through the list. Click an artisan name to see a lineup of popular Miis submitted by that artisan. From this lineup, click the Leave button in the lower left to go back to the artisan rankings.

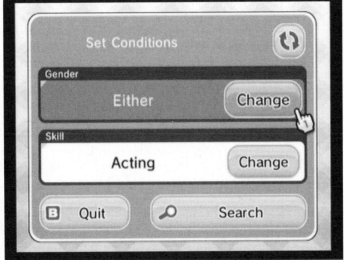

Figure 7-14:
The Check Mii Out Channel search menu.

- **Mine:** Click the picture of your Mii artisan to view the Miis that you've posted to the Check Mii Out Channel. This is a handy way to keep track of how popular your postings are, and for getting the posting numbers to share with friends.

✔ **Page turner:** Cycle through multiple pages of Miis that meet the current Call Out criteria.

✔ **Post Mii:** Click the envelope to add your own Mii creations to the Posting Plaza, using the following instructions:

1. **Click the Post Mii button (the envelope) in the Posting Plaza menu.**

   This brings up a selection of ten Miis from your Mii Plaza.

2. **Choose which Mii you want to post.**

   Click the on-screen arrows or use the left and right buttons on the Wii Remote's directional pad to scroll through the pages of Miis. When you find the Mii you want to post, click it, and then click Yes to confirm. Note that you can only post Miis that were created on your system, not Miis that you downloaded from friend or from the Mii Parade.

3. **Enter initials for the Mii.**

   The Check Mii Out Channel uses two-letter initials, rather than nicknames, to identify Miis. Use the on-screen keyboard to choose the initials you want to identify the Mii.

4. **Choose a skill for the Mii.**

This skill is used to further identify the Mii to other users of the Check Mii Out Channel. Click the up and down arrows on the screen or press the up and down buttons on the Wii Remote's directional pad to scroll through the list, and then click your choice. If the Mii is a caricature of a famous celebrity, choose a skill that reflects what the celeb is known for. Otherwise, just pick a skill that reflects his or her face, or just be random.

5. **Confirm your posting.**

Look over your Mii and confirm that you actually want to post it and that the data you entered is correct. When you click Yes, the Mii is shared with the world, with no way to take it back.

After posting your Mii, the Wii displays an entry number for your submission. This number is a unique identifier for your posting that can be used by others to find it easily using the Search function in the Call Out menu (discussed earlier). You can write this number down for safekeeping, or get it later by viewing your submissions through the Call Out menu.

✔ **Parade:** Click the button with the picture of a stick figure to have the current selection of Miis present themselves in a parade format. The Miis walk from the top of the screen in groups of three, posing in a large spotlight before moving on. Click any Mii during this parade to pause the marching and see that Mii's details. Click the Parade button again to go back to the arranged, grid view of the Miis.

✔ **Search Area:** Click the American-flag icon to bring up a menu allowing you to toggle between a regional and a worldwide search. Click the Change button to toggle and then click Exit to go back.

Viewing Mii details

While browsing the Posting Plaza, you can click any Mii to view its face up close. You can also view more details about the Mii and access further menu options, as shown in Figure 7-15. These menu options are discussed in the following list:

✔ **Profile:** Click the book icon in the upper-right corner to bring up more information about the current Mii, including its popularity (out of five stars), its Mii artisan, the region it comes from, and its unique entry number, as shown in Figure 7-16. Click the book again to go back to the menu view as shown in Figure 7-15. Pushing the + or – buttons on the Wii Remote also toggles the view.

✔ **Import Mii:** Save a copy of the current Mii to your local Mii Plaza. Before making the copy, use the on-screen keyboard to enter a personal nickname for the Mii. (Mii nicknames can have up to ten characters.) Click OK to copy the Mii to your Mii Plaza.

Profile

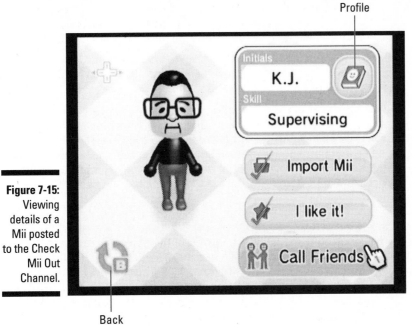

Figure 7-15:
Viewing
details of a
Mii posted
to the Check
Mii Out
Channel.

Back

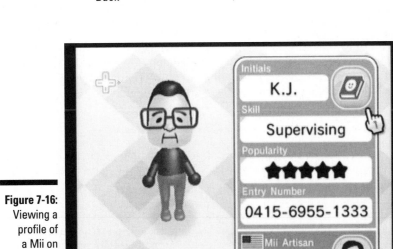

Figure 7-16:
Viewing a
profile of
a Mii on
the Check
Mii Out
Channel.

Note that the Mii Plaza can only hold 100 Miis. If you have too many you won't be able to import Miis from the Check Mii Out Channel. Erase some Miis or move them to the Mii Parade to clear out some space.

✔ **I Like It:** Click this button to add the Mii to your personal favorites. This helps increase the Mii's star ranking and makes it easy to find later using the Favorites option on the Call Out menu.

✔ **Call Friends:** One of the most interesting features on the Check Mii Out Channel, click this button to see a collection of Miis that are similar to the current Mii in some way. This could mean they have a similar face, the same initials, or the same artisan. It's interesting to see how slight changes can have a large effect. When you're done browsing the friends, click the Leave button in the corner to go back to the Posting Plaza menu.

When viewing Mii details, you can press the B button on the Wii Remote or click the Back button in the lower-left corner of the screen to return to the wider Posting Plaza view. You can also use the directional pad on the Wii Remote to scroll through the details of other Miis without first backing out into the Posting Plaza menu.

Contests

Posting random Miis for public approval is all well and good, but sometimes having a specific goal can help focus your thinking. The Check Mii Out Channel's contests are designed to bring out your creativity by asking you to design a Mii to match a specific goal, as shown in Figure 7-17.

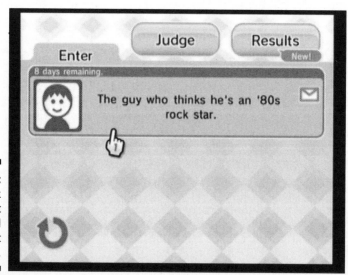

Figure 7-17: The Check Mii Out Channel contest menu.

Entering contests

The list of currently running contests is displayed as soon as you click the Contests button on the Check Mii Out Channel main menu (refer to Figure 7-11). Click a contest to expand the menu with the options to enter the contest or click the Make a Mii button. Clicking Make a Mii returns you to the Wii Menu to create a Mii using the Mii Channel.

When you have a Mii you'd like to enter in a contest, click Enter Contest and then click Next to read through the few pages of disclaimers. Then choose from the Miis available in your Mii plaza, using the on-screen arrows or the arrows on the Wii Remote's directional pad to scroll through the pages. You can submit only one entry per contest, but you can change the entry by entering the contest again.

Judging contests

If you'd rather judge than be judged, you can judge a contest as follows:

1. **Click the Judge button on the Contest menu (refer to Figure 7-17).**

2. **Click the contest you'd like to judge.**

   This brings up the judging menu, as shown in Figure 7-18.

Figure 7-18: The Check Mii Out Channel contest-judging menu.

Swap Out

3. **Choose some candidates by clicking a Mii and then clicking Select This Mii?**

   Pick which Miis you think best embody the theme of the contest. The selected Mii is highlighted. To deselect a candidate, click it and then click Deselect.

   Alternatively, you can hover over the Mii with the Wii Remote pointer and press the + or – buttons to select and deselect more quickly.

4. **Click the Swap Out button to get more choices.**

   If you can't find three candidates you want to vote for among the first ten, click the Swap Out button in the bottom right to get more Miis to select from. Any Miis you've selected in Step 3 stay on the screen, while new candidates run in to replace those you ignored.

5. **Repeat Steps 3 and 4 until you're happy with the three candidates you've chosen.**

6. **Click Cast a Vote, and then click Yes to confirm.**

   Your vote is cast. You can change your vote at any time up to the end of the contest judging period by going back to Step 1 and repeating these steps.

Viewing contest results

Click the Results button (refer to Figure 7-17) and then choose the completed contest you'd like to view the results for. The relative popularity of your selections for the contest is shown in a cute animation set against a mountaintop. After this, the Mii that garnered the most votes overall walks out and waves. Click the Congratulations button, or click the Skip button in the lower-right corner to get to the top 50.

Browse the top 50 the same way you'd browse Miis in the Posting Plaza. Use the Parade button to switch between an arrangement and a parade. Click a Mii to see the artisan and get the option to import the Mii to your local Mii Plaza.

Chapter 8

The Photo Channel

*T*here's a lot to love about digital cameras: the capability to review your shots instantly; the option to touch up blemishes on the computer; freedom from expensive film and development costs. But when it comes time to view those digital pictures, things aren't always so convenient. Squinting at a tiny camera or cell phone screen is hardly the ideal way to view those party shots, and gathering a large group around the office PC to see your vacation photos is just as cumbersome.

Luckily, your Wii makes it easy to view digital photos and videos on your TV. Just pop in a SmartDigital card full of pictures and fire up the Wii's Photo Channel to browse through your shots with ease from the comfort of your couch. You can even create musical slide shows and play around with your photos directly on the screen. Sound complicated? Don't worry. This chapter gives you everything you need to become a Photo Channel pro.

Viewing Photos and Videos

When you first select the Photo Channel from the Wii's Home menu (see Chapter 5 for more on this), you're greeted with a screen asking, "Which photos do you want to view?" as shown in Figure 8-1. I cover viewing Wii Message Board photos later in this chapter — for now, I focus on viewing photos by choosing Digital Camera/Cell Phone.

Figure 8-1:
The Photo
Channel
introduction
screen.

Getting photos and videos onto an SD card

The first step to getting your photos onto your TV through the Wii is getting them onto an SD card. (You can see a picture of an SD card on the Photo Channel introduction screen, shown in Figure 8-1.) Many digital and cell phone cameras can store images directly to an SD card as you take them. If you have such a camera, congratulations — you have a lot less work to do.

If you're one of those unfortunate souls who has digital photos stored on a different medium (such as a CD-ROM, a computer hard drive, a CompactFlash card, and such), you need to transfer your photos to an SD card before viewing them with the Wii. Some newer computers come with a built-in SD card slot for copying photos and files to an SD card. For older computers, an external SD card reader that hooks up to your computer's USB port can provide the same functionality. If neither of these is an option, your local photo processor can probably help you transfer your photos over to an SD card.

The Wii's SD card slot only accepts pictures on full-size SD cards — not the microSD or miniSD cards used by most cell phone cameras (and some smaller digital cameras). You can find adapters to make these smaller cards fit into the Wii's standard-size SD slot at most electronics retailers — they should set you back only a couple of bucks.

After you have your photos on an SD card, simply slide the card into the slot on the front of the system. Figure 8-2 shows how to open the SD slot's protective cover and correctly insert the SD card. The card slides in with a slight click. To remove the card later, simply push in slightly and the card pops right out.

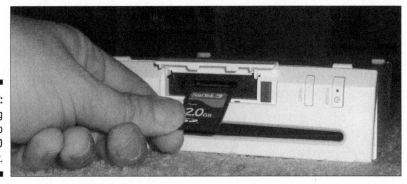

Figure 8-2:
Inserting
a card into
the Wii's SD
card slot.

After the SD card is in the system, turn it on and choose the Photo Channel from the Wii's Channel menu (described in Chapter 5). Click the Digital Camera/Cell Phone button and the system automatically scans the SD card for photos and videos (it doesn't matter what folder they're in — the Wii finds them all). This process may take a few seconds. When it's done, click the View button to see these photos and movies arranged chronologically as a grid of thumbnails on the screen, as shown in Figure 8-3.

The Wii Photo Channel starts to break down if it tries to display more than 1,000 photos at a time. If your SD card has more than 1,000 photos on it, consider backing them up or deleting them. (Also consider being a little more discriminating with your future shot selections.)

Figure 8-3:
The Photo
Channel
thumbnail
menu.

Navigating the thumbnail menu

Getting around the thumbnail menu is as simple as clicking the on-screen buttons, as shown in Figure 8-3 and explained in the following list. Note that many on-screen buttons have analogues on the Wii Remote that perform the same function. Using the Wii Remote buttons makes navigation much quicker and simpler.

- ✔ **Zoom –:** Reduce the size of the thumbnails so you can show more on screen at once. Pressing the – button on the Wii remote has the same effect.

- ✔ **Up Arrow:** Scroll upward through the list of thumbnails. Pressing up on the Wii Remote's directional pad has the same effect.

- ✔ **Zoom +:** Increase the size of the thumbnails so you end up showing fewer on-screen at the same time. Pressing the + button on the Wii remote has the same effect.

- ✔ **Back:** Return to the Photo Channel's main menu.

- ✔ **Down Arrow:** Scroll downward through the list of thumbnails. Pressing down on the Wii Remote's directional pad has the same effect.

- ✔ **Slide Show:** Start a slide show of all the photos and movies on the menu. See the "Watching photo slide shows" section for more on this.

You can also scroll through the thumbnail menu by holding down the B button on the Wii Remote and pointing toward the top and bottom of the screen. The on-screen pointer icon changes to a picture of a B button when you do this. This is especially useful for scrolling through massive sets of zoomed thumbnails quickly.

Viewing photos

Now that you can find your way around the thumbnail menu, simply click a thumbnail to blow it up to full screen size. The photo may appear slightly blurry for a few seconds, but it becomes sharper when the Wii finishes loading it.

The Photo Channel won't work with photos with resolution greater than 8192 x 8192 pixels, according to the manual. It would take a 67.1-megapixel camera to generate an image that big, so it's not going to be an issue for most shutterbugs. I just thought I'd warn you in case you're planning to view a hyper-detailed map of the Interstate highway system or something.

Pointing the Wii Remote at the screen displays the time and date the picture was taken. It also brings up a translucent menu with a variety of navigation options, as shown in Figure 8-4 and described in the following list:

08/08/2007 09:25

Figure 8-4:
The photo-
navigation
menu.

✔ **Zoom –:** Zoom out from the photo. Pressing the – button on the Wii Remote has the same effect.

✔ **Previous:** View the previous photo in the thumbnail list. Pressing left on the Wii Remote's directional pad has the same effect.

✔ **Rotation Arrows:** Change the orientation of the picture by rotating it 90 degrees clockwise. These arrows are useful for correcting photos taken with a rotated camera.

✔ **Next:** View the next photo in the thumbnail list. Pressing right on the Wii Remote's directional pad has the same effect.

✔ **Zoom +:** Zoom in to the photo. Pressing the + button on the Wii Remote has the same effect.

When zoomed in, you can use the arrow buttons on the bottom-right quadrant of the picture to pan around the photo. Alternatively, you can hold the B button and point the Wii Remote toward the edges of the screen to scroll around.

✔ **Back:** Takes you back to the thumbnail menu. Pressing the A button on the Wii Remote while pointing at the photo itself has the same effect.

✔ **Post:** Saves the picture to the Wii's internal Message Board. See the "Posting and Sharing Photos: The Wii Message Board" section, later in this chapter, for more.

✔ **Fun!:** Applies a selection of fun effects to the photo. See the "Playing with Your Photos: The Fun! Menu" section, later in this chapter for more.

✔ **Slide Show:** Presents a slide show of all the pictures in the list. See the following section, "Watching photo slide shows," for details.

A blur in your saddle

One of the odder features of the Wii's Photo Channel is the capability to pixelate a small section of the photo while viewing it. To do this, simply point the Wii Remote at the photo and push up or down on the Wii Remote's directional pad. This also works during slide shows. As an added bit of weirdness, pressing down during a video also distorts the soundtrack, making it higher pitched.

Why was this feature added? Perhaps Nintendo wanted parents to be able to edit lascivious photos on the fly? Maybe it was required to meet the FCC's decency standards? No . . . more likely, the developers were simply bored while working on the Channel and added the hidden feature as a sort of Easter egg for intrepid users to find. Intrepid users like you!

Watching photo slide shows

Tired of manually clicking through each and every photo in your collection? Choose the Slide Show option from the thumbnail or picture menus and the Wii shows each of your photos in sequence, automatically. While you don't have *that* much control over these slide shows, you can alter the experience a bit by pressing the A button at any time during the show and choosing the Change Settings option. Doing so brings up the menu shown in Figure 8-5, explained in the following list:

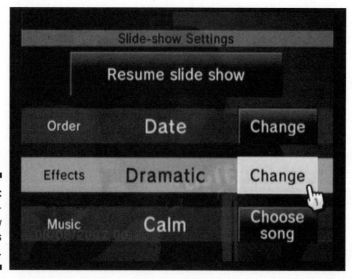

Figure 8-5:
The Slide-show Settings menu.

- **Order:** Click Change to toggle between a chronological viewing order and a random one.

- **Effects:** Click Change to toggle among the following options:

  - *Dramatic:* The default "slow pan" over the images — kind of like a Ken Burns documentary.

  - *Simple:* No effects — just a simple, full screen view of each picture.

  - *Nostalgic:* Pictures are shown in sepia tone, like an old-timey photo, complete with the dramatic slow pan.

- **Music:** Click Choose Song to pick from six built-in background songs: Calm, Fun, Bright, Nostalgic, Beautiful, or Scenic, or turn off the music entirely. If there are any MP3 files on the SD card, you can use them as the background music as well. You can also turn off the music entirely.

Want to control the pace of your photo slide show? Use the left and right buttons on the Wii Remote's directional pad to advance the slide show backward and forward. You can also use the + and – buttons on the Wii Remote to control the volume of the background music that plays over the slide show. (Or, you know, you *could* use your TV remote to control the volume. But really, where's the fun in that?)

Watching videos

Watching digital videos stored on an SD card works much like viewing pictures: Simply click the thumbnail and the video starts playing in full-screen mode. Videos can be identified on the thumbnail menu by the filmstrip icon on the lower-right corner of the thumbnail. You can zoom and rotate a video just like a still picture, but picture-editing effects and message-board posting work a little differently for videos. (I give you more details about posting and editing in the following section.)

The Wii Photo Channel only plays videos recorded in the Motion JPEG (PCM) format, which is supported by most digital cameras and camera phones. If you have videos in another format, you can convert them to the Wii format using software such as Red Kawa's free Wii Video 9. Find it online at www.redkawa. com/videoconverters/wiivideo9/.

There are no on-screen controls for fast-forwarding and rewinding a movie while it's playing. However, you can jump back approximately three seconds by pressing the 1 button on your Wii Remote, or jump ahead three seconds by pushing the 2 button. You can hold either button for quicker scanning. There's no way to pause a video, however, so don't go thinking your Wii's going to replace your DVD player.

Posting and Sharing Photos: The Wii Message Board

Storing photos on an SD card is all well and good, but sometimes you want a backup of your precious memories with a version that's always available on the Wii itself. Posting photos to the Wii's internal Message Board does just that. Posting to the Message Board also lets you send photos to your friends' Wiis over the Internet.

Posting and viewing Message Board photos

Getting photos onto the Wii Message Board couldn't be simpler. While viewing a photo, simply point the Wii Remote at the screen and click the Post button on the bottom line of the on-screen menu. Another menu appears, asking if you want to post a copy of the picture to the Wii Message Board. Choose Post to the Wii Message Board and the picture is posted. Wasn't that easy? Choose OK to move on.

What happens if you try to post an image that's already on the Wii Message Board? No, the Wii won't explode in a logic error — it just posts a second copy of the photo to the Message Board, complete with any doodles and mood effects you may have applied and permanently saved. Thank goodness for the Wii's anti-paradox circuitry!

While you can't post entire videos from an SD card to the Wii Message Board, you can post individual frames from a video. To do this, simply watch the video as you normally would, and click the Post button as soon as you see the frame you want to capture. If you mess up and choose the wrong moment, don't panic — simply choose Don't Post and try again.

You can use the 1 and 2 buttons on the Wii Remote to quickly rewind and fast forward, respectively, while watching videos.

The Wii has a limited amount of space to store Message Board photos — 512 megabytes, to be exact. These photos have to share space with things like games and applications downloaded from the Wii Shop Channel (see Chapter 6 for more about the Wii Shop Channel). This only really becomes an issue if you plan on storing hundreds of photos on the system, but it is something to keep in the back of your mind as you post.

After a photo has been posted to the Wii Message Board, you can always view it by choosing the View Wii Message Board Photos from the initial Photo Channel menu. Note that photos on the Message Board are arranged chronologically by the date they were posted to the Wii, *not* by the date they were taken.

Sending Message Board photos over the Internet

In addition to permanent, SD-card-free viewing, posting a photo to the Wii Message Board lets you e-mail the images to your friends' Wiis. Follow these steps to e-mail a photo to a friend's Wii:

1. **Make sure your Wii is connected to the Internet and that you and your friend have exchanged and registered each other's Wii Friend Codes.**

   See Chapter 4 for more information on how to make those preparations.

2. **Post your image to the Wii Message Board as described in the previous section.**

   If you've already posted the photo to the Message Board, you can skip this step — you don't need to do it again.

3. **Push the Home button on the Wii Remote and choose Wii Menu.**

4. **Click the Envelope icon in the bottom-right corner of the Wii Menu.**

   Doing so brings up the Wii Message Board, as shown in Figure 8-6.

Figure 8-6:
The Wii
Message
Board.

5. **Find the picture on the Message Board.**

If you posted the picture to the Wii Message Board today, it should immediately appear as an envelope on the screen. If you posted the photo earlier, you need to find it by navigating to the appropriate day. (See Chapter 4 for more on navigating the Message Board.)

6. **Click the Envelope icon with your image in it.**

A message pops up with a thumbnail of your picture and the words "From the Photo Channel" prominently displayed.

At this point, you can delete the photo from the Message Board by clicking the Trash Can icon in the upper-left corner of the screen and then choosing OK. This is useful for keeping your Message Board organized and for freeing up space for newer photos if your Message Board is getting too crowded.

7. **Click the picture thumbnail.**

This brings up a full-screen view of the photo.

8. **Choose Send.**

A list of the friends you've registered on your Wii appears.

9. **Choose the friend you want to send the picture to and click his or her name.**

You may need to scroll through the list using the arrows on the sides of the screen.

10. **Complete your message and click Send.**

You can add text and attach a Mii to your photo before sending it off. Or choose Quit to abort the process.

Playing With Your Photos: The Fun! Menu

Because the Wii is, at its heart, a video-game system, it shouldn't be too surprising that the Photo Channel lets you *play* with your photos in addition to just viewing them. The Photo Channel's Fun! menu lets you play around with the mood of a photo or video, doodle on it with the Wii Remote, and even play a simple sliding puzzle game created from your photo.

To play with all these options, simply view any photo and choose Fun! to bring up the menu shown in Figure 8-7. I discuss each of the Fun! menu options individually in the following sections.

Figure 8-7:
The Fun!
menu.

That darn cat

If you're hanging around on the Fun! menu long enough (about five seconds or so), you'll notice a small black cat walking around the yellow title bar at the top of the screen. (You can see him at the top of Figure 8-7.) If you leave little Blackie (I like to call him Blackie) alone for a minute or so, the cutie pie sits down and start meowing through your speakers. When he's sitting, Blackie also follows your pointer around with his head as you wave it around the screen. Be careful not to move the pointer too close, though — Blackie scares quite easily.

What initially seems an adorable throwaway feature is actually much more. If your Remote hand is quick and steady enough, you can actually catch Blackie and click him as he's running away from your pointer. Your reward is an on-screen tip about getting the most out of the Photo Channel — navigation shortcuts, hidden features, and the like. (Hey . . . wait a minute . . . that's what I'm doing in this chapter! Blackie's trying to horn in on my business! Doesn't he know I'm the hot-shot author around here?)

Mood

The Mood menu lets you apply four different visual effects to your photos and videos, as shown in Figure 8-8 and described in the following list:

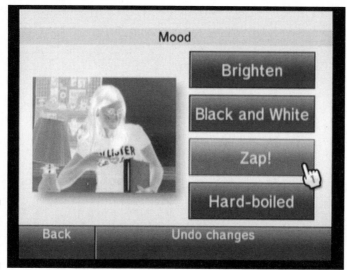

✔ **Brighten:** Click this button to add some more light to your shots — perfect for photos taken at dark parties. Clicking the Brighten button multiple times cycles through eight different levels of brightness.

✔ **Black and White:** Distills the picture into a colorless grayscale image. This is what the entire world looked like before the invention of color photographs. It's true!

✔ **Zap!:** Transform your photo in a crazy, alternate-universe version of itself. This is what the film negative of the image would look like on a traditional camera.

✔ **Hard-Boiled:** By far the oddest mood-changing option, this button creates a rough black outline of the objects in the picture — kind of like a coloring book. It may not look quite right when you first click the button, but clicking again cycles through different levels of, er, hard-boiling.

Each mood change comes with an accompanying change in the background music for the Photo Channel. When viewing videos, the actual soundtrack from the video is altered as well.

When you're happy with the mood you've chosen, choose Back to go back to the Fun! menu. To view your mood-altered picture, choose Back again. If you want to save a copy of the altered picture, choose Post to copy it to the Wii Message Board. (See the previous section for more on this.) If you don't like the edits, don't panic! Just go back to the Mood menu and choose Undo Changes.

Posting to the Message Board is also the only way to layer the mood options on top of one another. Simply choose a mood, save the picture to the Message Board, and then open up the new copy and choose a new mood to put on top of it. You can repeat this process as many times as you want, but remember to delete the earlier versions of the photo when you're finished; otherwise your Message Board could get pretty crowded.

It's important to note here that any changes made to your photos *cannot* be saved to an SD card. On the one hand, this means your moods and doodles are trapped on the Wii, and impossible to get to a computer with a professional editing program. On the other hand, it means the original version of the photo on the SD card remains unchanged, so you don't have to worry about ruining your raw shots. So go nuts!

Doodle

Some of the most fun you can have with the Photo Channel can be found by clicking the Doodle button on the Fun! menu. This mode offers a variety of tools to draw on top of your photo, as shown in Figure 8-9 and explained in the following list:

Figure 8-9:
The Doodle menu.

✔ **– button:** Zooms out of the picture. Pressing the – button on the Wii Remote has the same effect.

✔ **Color Dropper icon:** Lets you extract a color from the photo. Click the dropper once to select it; then click anywhere on the photo to absorb the color at that point on the photo. You can now draw on top of the photo using that color. This is a great way to get more complex colors than the simple color selections offered by the pencil icons.

✔ **Pencil icons:** Lets you sketch all over the photo in a variety of colors. Click a pencil to choose a color, and then click and drag on the photo to draw over the photo in that color.

✔ **Eraser:** Lets you erase all or part of the doodles you've already made. Click to select the icon, and then click and drag over the doodles to erase. Note that the eraser only erases the doodles you've added to the picture — it can't erase the original picture itself.

✔ **+ button:** Zooms in to the picture. Pressing the + button on the Wii Remote has the same effect.

✔ **Back:** Goes back to the Fun! menu. Choose Back again to go back to the picture viewer. Don't worry — your doodles are still there.

✔ **Stamps:** Make your mark on a photo with these fun-filled stamps. Click the stamp once to select it, and then click the image to stamp it down. Note that the sunglasses stamp cycles randomly through three different styles as you stamp it down repeatedly.

✔ **Scissors:** Lets you replicate part of an image elsewhere. Click the scissors to choose them, and then click anywhere on the image to choose a starting point for the area you want to replicate. Move the pointer to create an oval, or press the 1 button on the Wii Remote to select a rectangular area instead. Either way, click the A button once more to pick up a copy of that area. Now click anywhere on the photo to stamp down replicas of your selection. Pressing the 1 button on the Wii Remote after you've made your selection flips the stamp horizontally — great for creating a mirror image of yourself.

Did you know you can copy a section from one photo and apply it to another? It's true. Simply make your selection with the scissors as normal, and then click Back three times to get back to the thumbnail menu. Choose another photo, choose Fun!, and then choose Doodle, and the selection from the previous photo is available to stamp on to the new photo. Neat!

✔ **Undo All:** As you might expect, this button undoes all your doodles and reverts the photo to its original state. The erasure comes complete with a cute little rocketship animation flying over the photo. (Aww.)

You can change the size of the Pencil, Eraser, and Stamp tools by pushing the Wii Remote closer (to make them bigger) or by pulling the Wii Remote farther away (to make them smaller) from the Wii Sensor Bar. In addition, you can change the orientation of the Stamps and Scissor tool selections by twisting the Wii Remote in your hand like a key. Note that the relative size of these tools also changes as you zoom in and out of the picture using the + and – buttons on the Wii Remote. Experiment with the rotation and size until you're happy with the effect.

Remember to save your doodles by posting the edited photos to the Wii Message Board, as described in the earlier section, "Posting and Sharing Photos: The Wii Message Board." If you try to start a second doodle before saving the changes to the first, the edits you've made to the original photo will be lost. Also note that after you save the doodles to the Wii Message Board, you won't be able to undo the doodles using the Eraser tool or the Undo All command.

Yes, you can doodle on movies, too — the doodles just float statically on top of the moving images below them. These doodles show up if you post a frame of the movie to the Wii Message Board, but they will not be saved on top of the original movie when you turn off the system. Also note that the Scissors tool captures a portion of the current frame when you finish your selection, so time your cuts wisely.

Puzzle

Even though the Wii is a video-game system, this is the only portion of the Photo Channel that actually plays like a traditional game. Choose your photo, choose Fun!, and then click Puzzle to get your image chopped up into a two-row-by-three-column grid, as shown in Figure 8-10.

To set things right, simply point at a section of the picture and move it by clicking and dragging it where you think it should go. Don't worry about pieces overlapping each other — the old section moves to accommodate the one you're placing.

The direction buttons at the bottom of the puzzle shift the entire puzzle in that direction, with one side looping around to the opposite end. The Cheat button lets you study the original picture; choose Back to the Puzzle! to return to solving.

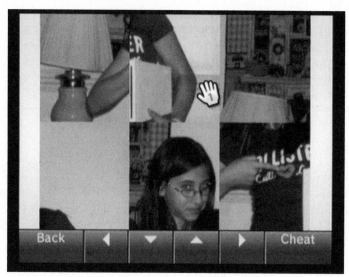

Figure 8-10:
A basic,
six-piece
puzzle.

When the puzzle is finished, the Wii plays a jaunty melody and gives you a round of applause for a job well done. It also tells you your solve time, which is saved to the View Records menu if it's the fastest. After you complete a six-piece puzzle, buttons appear, giving you the option to try harder puzzles with 12, 24, or 48 pieces.

The puzzle sizes don't actually top out at 48 pieces. If you hold down the 1 button on the Wii Remote while on the difficulty selection menu, the 48-piece puzzle option transforms into a ridiculous 192-piece puzzle option! This one is definitely not for the faint of heart.

For a really neat experience, try playing a puzzle based on a video. The video continues to play and loop as you solve the puzzle, creating a moving, movable mosaic that's really something to behold (and also much more difficult to solve than puzzles made from a static photo).

You can also create your own puzzle, in effect, by doodling on a picture, saving it to the Wii Message Board, and then starting a puzzle based on it.

Chapter 9

The Internet Channel

In This Chapter

▶ Surfing the World Wide Web on your TV using the Wii's Internet Channel

▶ Using Favorites and Remote shortcuts to navigate the Channel more easily

▶ Visiting some useful and entertaining Web sites specifically designed for the Wii

T he World Wide Web has truly been a communications revolution, allowing people the world over to find information and publish their thoughts quickly and conveniently. For too long, though, this revolution was limited to personal computers that were, quite frankly, way too powerful and expensive for mere Web browsing. As technology has continued to get cheaper, though, full-scale Web browsers have begun to drift away from the PC and toward devices such as cell phones, MP3 players, and yes, even game consoles.

Other boxes have tried to bring the Web to the living room TV — most notably Microsoft's now-defunct WebTV — but none have done it nearly so well as the Wii's Internet Channel. It's hard to overstate how freeing it is to surf the Web while sprawled on the couch rather than hunched over the computer desk. It's the difference between seeing the Web as part of your entertainment center and seeing it as part of your workstation.

This chapter outlines how to use the Wii's Internet Channel to navigate the Web, using shortcuts to help speed up your surfing. It also introduces you to some sites specifically designed for couch-bound surfing.

Web Surfing from Your Couch

The first step to enjoying the Internet Channel is actually downloading the Internet Channel. To do this, you need to have your Wii hooked up to your TV (as described in Chapter 2) and to a high-speed Internet connection (Chapter 4). After this is done, you can purchase and download the Internet Channel from Wii Shop Channel (see Chapter 6 for more on using the Wii Shop Channel).

Note that you have to spend a one-time fee of 500 Wii Points ($5) before downloading the Internet Channel. This might seem a little ridiculous when computer-based browsers such as Firefox and Internet Explorer can be downloaded for free, but it's really a small price to pay to unlock the world of the World Wide Web on your TV.

If you downloaded the Internet Channel before April 11, 2007, you are using the "beta" version of the Channel. The rest of this chapter discusses the "full" version of the Channel, which features many improvements over the beta release. You can upgrade to the full release by downloading a free update available on the Wii Shop Channel.

The Internet Channel Start Page

After you've downloaded the Internet Channel, start it up by clicking the icon on your Wii Menu and then clicking the Start button. A Wii: Opera Powered logo shows up on a white background for a few seconds, followed by the Internet Channel Start Page (as shown in Figure 9-1). This page may look intimidating, but it really has only a few key options, as described in the following list:

Figure 9-1: The Internet Channel Start Page.

✔ **Search:** Type in a search term using the on-screen keyboard to search the Web for pages on a specific topic (see Chapter 4 for more on using the on-screen keyboard). The results appear as a Web page that can be navigated like any other (see the later section, "Web page navigation"). You can change your preferred search engine using the Settings menu, as discussed in the Settings bullet.

✔ **Favorites:** Also known as bookmarks, the Favorites list is a collection of frequently visited sites that you can access quickly without having to type in their full Web address. As you can see in Figure 9-2, the Wii's Internet Channel comes pre-configured with a few Favorites right off the bat. Just click any of the large icons and the applicable page loads in the browser. If and when the list of Favorites extends past one page, you can scroll through it just as you would a normal Web page.

You can edit, amend, and share your Favorites list using the navigation buttons at the bottom of the Favorites screen, as follows:

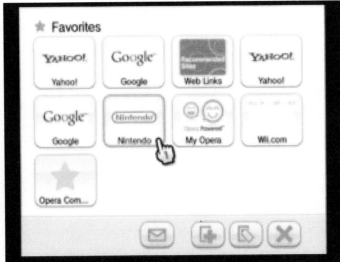

Figure 9-2:
The Internet Channel Favorites screen.

- **Send Favorite:** Send the address of a saved Favorite to any of your Wii Friends (for more on registering Wii Friends, see Chapter 4). After you click the envelope icon, click the icon for the site you want to send, and then choose a registered friend from the list that pops up. You can enter an optional message to accompany the site using the on-screen keyboard, and then click Send. Your link appears as a message on your friend's Wii Message Board, along with the option to open the site directly in the Internet Channel.

  When you're done sending, click the Star icon to go back to your Favorites list, or click the X icon to go back to the browser itself.

- **Add Favorite:** Click this button to add the last Web page you viewed to your Favorites list. Use the Edit Favorites option if you want to move or delete this new Favorite.

- **Edit Favorites:** Click this icon and then the Favorite you want to edit to bring up the menu seen in Figure 9-3. Choose Delete to permanently remove the Favorite from the list. Choose Rename to change the title of the Favorite using the on-screen keyboard. Choose Move to change the position of the Favorite icon to another location on your list (simply click your new preferred position for that favorite). Click Close to close the menu. When you're done editing Favorites, click the Star icon to get back to the Favorites menu or the X icon to go back to the browser.

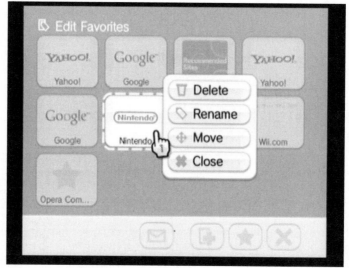

Figure 9-3: The Edit Favorites menu.

- **Close:** Click the X icon to exit the favorites menu and return to the Web browser itself.

✔ **Web Address:** Click the big "www" balloon to bring up an on-screen keyboard where you can enter a Web address (also known as a URL) for any site you'd like to view. Note that the Internet Channel usually doesn't usually require you type in the `http://www.` prefix that goes before many Web addresses, so you can just type **wiley.com** to view the site for the publisher of this fine book. However, sites that start with `https` (note the `s` at the end) or a prefix other than `www` may require you to type the full address.

✔ **Operations Guide:** This menu item tells you all about how to use the Wii's Internet Channel. (Of course, this chapter does the same thing, with a lot more wit and vivacity than some sterile on-screen guide.)

✔ **Settings:** Click this button to bring up a page of general Web browsing settings, as shown in Figure 9-4. Click and drag the scrollbar on the right side of the screen or use the up and down buttons on your Wii Remote to scroll through the list. The options in the Settings menu are as follows:

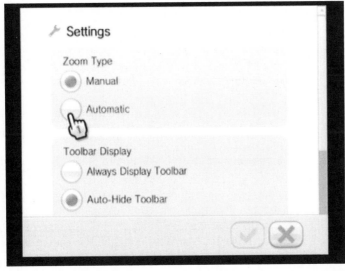

Figure 9-4:
The Internet
Channel
Settings
menu.

- **Zoom Type:** Web pages designed for a computer monitor can
  sometime look blurry when displayed on a TV screen. The Internet
  Channel offers a zoom feature to enlarge these blurry pages to
  make them more readable. This option lets you toggle between two
  options for how this feature will work. (See the later section, "Web
  page navigation," for more on zooming in and out when viewing
  Web pages.)

  Choose Manual for a zoom function that moves in and out in small
  increments with each press of the Zoom button. Choose Automatic
  to have the Web browser guess automatically at an optimized
  zoom level when you press the Zoom button.

  The Automatic option might seem a good way to save some button
  presses, but it takes away the ability to have precise control over
  your zoom level. Use your discretion.

- **Toolbar display:** Use this option to toggle the appearance of the
  small toolbar at the bottom of the Web browser (refer to Figure 9-1
  to see the toolbar; it's discussed in the later section, "The toolbar").
  The Always Display Toolbar option is pretty self-explanatory — the
  toolbar is always there, waiting for you to click its shapely buttons.
  Choose the Auto-Hide Toolbar option to have the toolbar disappear
  when you move the pointer away to other parts of the page — move
  the pointer off the bottom of the screen to reveal the toolbar once
  more. Choosing Button Toggle lets you show and hide the toolbar
  by pressing the 1 button on the Wii Remote.

- **Search Engine:** This setting determines what search engine is used by the Internet Channel's built-in search function. The only options as of this writing are Google and Yahoo!, but you can access other search engines directly by typing in their URL using the Web Address option. Or, better yet, you can save your preferred alternative search engine as a Favorite for easy access.

- **Delete cookies:** Cookies are little digital breadcrumbs left by some Web sites to help identify you automatically the next time you visit. These cookies aren't dangerous per se, but they can be a security risk if you visit some unscrupulous Web sites that try to search your cookies for personal data. It's a good idea to delete your cookies periodically, just in case.

- **Adjust Display:** On some TVs, the Internet Channel won't extend all the way to the edge of the screen. Use the Adjust Display option to fix. Simply click the on-screen arrows to widen or narrow the display until the blue borders reach all the way to the edge of your screen.

- **Proxy Settings:** Advanced users can use this option to set up a proxy server for their Web browsing. Most users (including all those who don't know what a proxy server is) shouldn't worry about these settings.

✔ **Wii Menu:** This returns you to the Wii Menu, oddly enough. Remember you can always return to the Wii Menu by pressing the Home button on the Wii Remote.

✔ **Controls:** Click the controller on the Start Page to get a basic overview of the Internet Channel's Web page navigation controls. These controls are discussed in much, much greater detail in the "Web page navigation" section, later in this chapter.

The toolbar

At the bottom of Figure 9-1, you can see a few buttons that are not discussed in the list in the previous section. That's because these buttons are not strictly part of the Start Page — they're part of the toolbar that lets you access many of the Internet Channel's functions quickly as you surf the Web. (See the preceding section for more on hiding the toolbar to get a better view of the Web page.) The toolbar buttons are shown and discussed in more detail in the following list:

✔ **Back and Forward:** Use these buttons to return to the last page visited or advance to the next page in your visitation history, respectively. These buttons become grayed out if there is no previous or next page in your history list.

✔ **Reload:** Click this button to download the latest version of the Web page you're currently viewing. This is useful for getting the latest data from a page that's frequently updated, or to retry a page that may have encountered an error on the first attempt. Note that when a page is actively loading, this button changes to a Stop sign. Click that stop sign to stop the browser from loading the current page.

✔ **Search:** Type in a search term using the on-screen keyboard to search the Internet for pages on a specific topic. You can toggle your preferred search engine using the Settings menu, as discussed in the previous section.

✔ **Favorites:** Opens up the Favorites menu, as discussed in the previous section.

✔ **Enter Address:** Brings up an on-screen keyboard where you can enter a Web address (also known as a URL) for any site you'd like to view. See the Web Address entry in the "Internet Channel Start Page" section for more on entering URLs on the Internet Channel.

✔ **Start Page:** Returns you to the Start Page, as discussed in the previous section.

✔ **Page Information:** Click this button to view general information about the page you're currently viewing, as shown in Figure 9-5. The icon changes to a lock if the currently viewed page is encrypted.

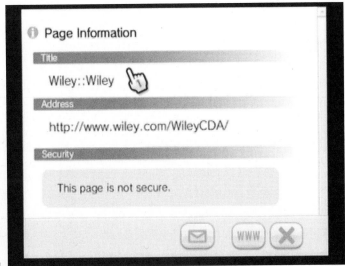

Figure 9-5: The Web Page Information screen.

Web page navigation

Even if you already know how to surf the Web with a mouse and keyboard, navigating Web pages on the Internet Channel may take a bit of a learning process. The following list discusses the variety of Remote-based shortcuts used to navigate around a page once it's been loaded:

- ✔ **Following links:** Just as you find on the computer, following a link on the Internet Channel is a matter of pointing and clicking. When you move the on-screen pointer over a Web page, certain words and pictures are highlighted in a light blue box when you hover over them. Simply push the A button when hovering over such a link to be redirected to the linked Web page.

   The Remote might rumble slightly and emit a clicking noise from the speaker when you hover over a link. You can turn these features off using the Wii Remote Settings menu. (See Chapter 3 for more on how to find and use this menu.)

- ✔ **Scrolling:** On Web pages that don't fit on one screen, you can use the directional pad on the Wii Remote to scroll the entire contents of the page in the desired direction. Note that some pages scroll left to right as well as up and down.

   For a quicker scroll, you can use the free scrolling option, which scrolls based on the direction you move the on-screen pointer. To activate free scrolling, point the Remote anywhere on the Web page and press and hold the B button. The on-screen pointer changes to a giant B button, as shown in Figure 9-6. While still holding B, move the pointer in any direction to scroll the Web page in that direction. The farther you move the pointer, the faster the page scrolls. To stop the quick scrolling, simply let go of the B button.

Figure 9-6:
Quick
Scrolling
with the Wii
Remote.

✔ **Zoom:** Because TVs weren't designed to display Web pages, some sites can look incredibly small and blurry when viewed on your home-entertainment setup. Luckily, you can enlarge the text, graphics, and anything else on the Web page using the + button on the Wii Remote. Use the − button to zoom out again if you get too close — a small 100% icon briefly appears in the upper-right corner of the screen when you're back to the default zoom level. Note that some graphics and video may look pixelated or have jagged edges if you zoom in too close.

See the earlier section, "The Internet Channel Start Page," for more on the two different styles of zooming supported by the Internet Channel.

✔ **Single Column Mode:** Tired of constantly zooming and scrolling from side to side just to see all the content on your favorite Web page? The Internet Channel's single-column viewing mode can help simplify the display of larger, more complex Web pages. Just press the 2 button on the Wii Remote to show the contents of the page condensed into a single vertical column with blown-up text, as shown in Figure 9-7. Scrolling and following links work normally in this mode, but the zoom function is disabled. Press 2 again to go back to the default viewing mode.

Figure 9-7:
A Web page displayed in the Internet Channel's single-column mode.

On the plus side, single-column viewing mode makes it much easier to quickly skim a complicated Web page. On the downside, the page's content is pushed out of position, ruining the intended design and layout. Some pages won't display correctly at all in single-column mode. Use your discretion.

✔ **B button shortcuts:** The B button isn't just good for quickly scrolling through Web pages — you can also use it to quickly access some common Web browsing commands. Use the following button combinations on the Wii Remote to bring up the noted Web-browser functions without the need to point and click anything on the toolbar. (Note that the directions listed apply to directions of the Wii Remote's directional pad.)

- **B+– (minus):** Go to the last visited page.

- **B++ (plus):** Advance to the next page.

- **B+↑ (up on the directional pad):** Reload the current page.

- **B+↓ (down on the directional pad):** Open the Favorites menu.

- **B+← (left on the directional pad):** Open the on-screen keyboard to enter a Web search term.

- **B+→ (right on the directional pad):** Open the on-screen keyboard to enter a Website address.

✔ **Search by selection:** The Internet Channel's search function is great and all, but it can be annoying typing in long, complex search terms using the on-screen keyboard. Luckily, you can use the Wii Remote to quickly search using any text that appears on a Web page. Just point at the starting point of the text you want to use as your search term, and then press and hold the A button. While still holding the A button, move the pointer to the end of your desired text — your selection is highlighted in blue, as shown in Figure 9-8. From here, open up a Web search using the button on the on-screen toolbar (or the B+← [left] shortcut discussed earlier). Your selected text is placed in the search box automatically! Click OK to perform your search.

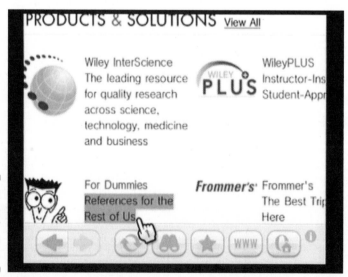

Figure 9-8:
Selecting
text for
a Web
search.

Limitations of surfing on the Internet Channel

Although the Wii's Internet Channel is a full-featured Web browser, it does have some limitations when compared to popular computer Web browsers such as Internet Explorer and Firefox:

- Some sites designed specifically to work with the Firefox or Internet Explorer browsers may not display properly on the Wii Internet Channel.
- The Internet Channel can't display Adobe PDF files.
- The Internet Channel can't run applets written in the Java programming language.
- The Internet Channel can't display content written for Flash Player Version 8 or above. This unfortunately includes many popular Flash-based sites, such as YouTube. Fortunately, there are some sites that get around this problem (see the "Must-Wii Web Sites" section).
- The Internet Channel can't play movies in Windows Media (WMV), QuickTime (AVI), or RealPlayer formats.
- The Internet Channel can't play audio in MP3 format.
- You can't upload or download files using the Internet Channel.
- You can't search through the contents of a specific Web page for a specific word or phrase using the Internet Channel.
- You can't copy and paste content from a Web page into an e-mail or Web address using the Internet Channel.

Must-Wii Web Sites

While you can visit practically any Web page on the Internet using the Wii's Internet Channel, some Web pages have been specifically designed with television browsing in mind. These sites can turn your Wii into a free arcade, a radio, a video player, and more!

Games: WiiCade

URL: www.wiicade.com

Most anyone who's been bored while a Web-enabled computer is nearby will tell you that the Internet is a great place to kill some time playing free Web games. Put that same Internet on a system *designed* to play games, and the possibilities for time wasting grow exponentially. Amateur game developers have taken to the Wii's Internet Channel in a big way, creating games specifically designed to take advantage of the Wii Remote.

WiiCade, shown in Figure 9-9, is the oldest and most popular hub for such games on the Internet. You can enjoy hundreds of free games, in genres ranging from action to puzzle to old-school run-and-jump-platform games, all specifically designed to be playable using the Wii Remote. Not all these free games are winners, of course, but you can harness the power of independent user rankings to separate the good from the bad. It's hard to be upset with even the clunkers, though, considering the cost. (Did I mention they were all free?)

Figure 9-9:
WiiCade, as seen on the Internet Channel.

Similar sites: www.wiiplayable.com, www.wiiwant2play.com, http://wii.knibble.com

Video: MiiTube

URL: http://miitube.co.uk

While YouTube is great for watching short videos of dogs on skateboards and such, hunching over your computer desk isn't really the ideal way to watch these videos. Unfortunately, sites such as YouTube aren't really designed with the Wii's Internet Channel in mind, meaning watching those amusing videos on your living room couch isn't as easy as it should be. Enter MiiTube, a site that converts the video content on YouTube into a form that works well with the Wii's Internet Channel.

The MiiTube site , shown in figure 9-10, features large, TV-friendly buttons, tabs for browsing featured and popular videos, and a search function to find videos on specific subjects. With all these free Web videos available, you may never watch network TV again!

Figure 9-10: MiiTube, as seen on the Internet Channel.

Similar site: http://wiitube.com

Music: Finetune

URL: `www.finetune.com/wii`

Ever since Napster started a revolution in downloadable music, billions of Internet users have downloaded countless MP3s to their personal collections, both legally and illegally. Unfortunately, you can't use the Wii's Internet Channel to permanently download such songs for later listening. Fortunately, there are a few sites that let you turn the Wii into an ad-free radio station for the latest hits.

Finetune, shown in Figure 9-11, is by far the best-designed of these sites, featuring big buttons and text that's perfect for viewing on your TV. You can listen to preselected mixes of everything from rock and pop to rap and country, or create a personalized station centered on a specific artist or keyword. Best of all, unlike the car radio, this player lets you skip ahead past songs you don't like. Next time you have a party, forget the CDs and fire up the Wii!

Figure 9-11:
Finetune,
as seen on
the Internet
Channel.

Similar sites: `www.wiihear.com`, `www.imeem.com/wii`

Search: Clusty

URL: www.clusty.com

While the Internet Channel's built-in Web searching capabilities are great, the results returned by both Google and Yahoo! were designed for viewing on a computer screen, not a TV. This means search results on the Wii Internet Channel are often too small to read and onerous to scroll through.

Web search upstart Clusty.com, shown in Figure 9-12, has attempted to solve this problem with a Web searching interface designed specifically for the Wii. Results are displayed in large, friendly letters that are easy to view on a normal TV screen. The site also accompanies each search with a convenient sidebar of links to follow-up searches on potentially related terms.

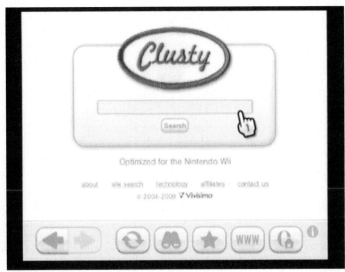

Figure 9-12: Clusty, as seen on the Internet Channel.

Similar Site: http://search.onlywii.com

Community: MapWii

URL: www.mapwii.com

The Wii makes it relatively easy to connect with your real-life friends that happen to own a Wii (see Chapter 4). But what if you don't know anyone who owns the system? For all its connectivity, the Wii doesn't exactly make it easy to find and connect with new people to chat and play with. MapWii, shown in Figure 9-13, helps fix this problem. It offers a public clearinghouse for Wii owners to share their Friend Codes using a simple map-based interface.

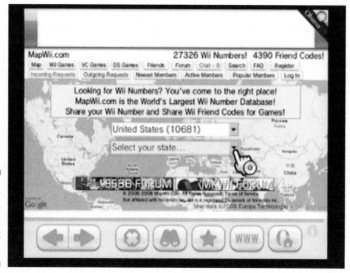

Figure 9-13:
MapWii,
as seen on
the Internet
Channel.

After you register with the site, you can search for potential friends by geographic location or common game interests, and then easily share your Friend Codes for chatting and playing together. The site's tens of thousands of users also maintain a vibrant discussion forum and chat room for all things Wii-related and not. The site does encounter some display problems on the Internet Channel, but it's by far the best place to search out new Wii owners to engage with.

Similar Sites: http://miiplaza.net, www.nintendo-play.com

Chapter 10

News, Weather, and More

· ·

· ·

So many Channels are available for the Wii, I just can't devote an entire chapter to each one. The Channels discussed in this chapter aren't necessarily the most popular or useful Channels, but they're no less important for being squeezed together here.

Reading the News Channel

Sure, you could get the latest headlines by using the Internet Channel to head to your favorite news Web site (see Chapter 9). But the Wii's News Channel is designed to display those headlines in a format specifically tailored for the Wii and your TV screen. Scanning the headlines with the News Channel is so simple, you may find yourself turning on the Wii instead of unfolding the paper with your morning coffee.

Starting up the News Channel

To access the News Channel, first you have to connect your Wii to the Internet through a broadband connection. You should also make sure you have WiiConnect24 turned on so you can download headlines automatically when the system is off (see Chapter 4 for more on connecting the Wii to the

Internet and WiiConnect24). The News Channel is available on the Channel menu when you first start your Wii, so there's no need to download anything from the Wii Shop Channel.

When you first start the News Channel, it may take a few minutes to download and display the latest headlines. This process takes longer the less often you use the Channel, so be sure to check in on current events often. When the loading is done, you see the News Channel topic menu, as shown in Figure 10-1.

Clicking on the cat while the headlines are downloading brings up a random tip on using the News Channel. It also changes the loading animation to a group of cats. This won't speed up the sometimes painfully long download process, but it is very cute.

If you accessed the News Channel recently and have WiiConnect24 turned on, you can view recent headlines scrolling on the News Channel icon from the Wii Menu. These headlines also available on the Channel preview screen, before you even fully start the Channel. (See Chapter 5 for more about the Wii Menu and Channel preview screens.)

Figure 10-1:
The News Channel topic menu.

Scanning the headlines

Click the on-screen arrows or press the up and down buttons on the Wii Remote's directional pad to scroll through the topics list. You can also hold down the B button and move the Wii Remote pointer up and down to scroll through the list. Click a topic to bring up a set of recent headlines for that topic, as shown in Figure 10-2.

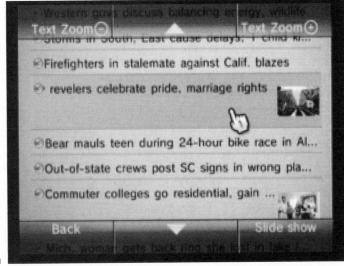

Figure 10-2:
The News
Channel
headline
menu.

You can scroll through this list in the same manner as you scrolled through the topics list. You can also enlarge or shrink the text by clicking the buttons in the upper corners of the menu, or by pressing the + and – buttons on the Wii Remote.

A blue dot next to a headline means the story hasn't been read yet. If that blue dot is blinking, the story was posted within the last hour or two. A gray dot means you've already read that story.

Clicking a headline displays the full story, as shown in Figure 10-3. Scroll through the text of the article by clicking the on-screen arrows or pressing the up and down arrows on the Wii Remote's directional pad. You can increase or decrease the size of the text by clicking the buttons on the top of the menu, or by pressing the + and – buttons on the Wii Remote, respectively. You can also hold down the B button and move the Wii Remote pointer up and down to scroll through the story. Click the Back button to return to the headline menu, or press the left or right button on the Wii Remote's directional pad to jump directly to another story.

Global news

When viewing a news story, click the Globe button at the lower right of the menu to bring up a decidedly global view of the day's news, as shown in Figure 10-4. This global view gives you a visual indication of where the news is happening and how much of it is happening where. Controls for this view are described in the following list:

Figure 10-3:
The News
Channels
news story
view.

Figure 10-4:
The News
Channel's
Global news
view.

✔ **View Stories:** The pieces of paper on the global view each represent
a distinct news story with a dateline from the named location on the
globe. Click a single piece of paper to bring up the applicable story in
the news story view described earlier. Click a stack of papers (with a
number next to the name of the region) to bring up a list of the recent
stories from that area in the headline view.

✔ **Spin the Globe:** Click and hold the A button with the Wii Remote pointer over an empty patch of land or water to grab the globe at that point. Move the Remote pointer while still holding the A button to spin the globe in that direction. If you let go of the A button quickly, the globe continues spinning in that direction, just like a real globe!

✔ **Zoom:** Click the buttons in the upper corners of the menu or press the + and – buttons on the Wii Remote to zoom the camera in and out from the globe. Note that as you zoom out, stories may rearrange themselves by region rather than specific city. For instance, a story that shows up as coming from Boston when zoomed in may show up as part of the "Washington Area" when zoomed farther out. The closer you zoom the view, the more tightly targeted the sets of headlines are.

✔ **Tilt:** Click the curved arrow buttons on the bottom of the menu or press the up and down buttons on the Wii Remote's directional pad to tilt the camera's view of the globe higher or lower. A lower angle makes the stacks of papers look like soaring towers of news, while a higher view makes them look flatter. Click the Restore button at the lower right when tilted to get back to a straight overhead view.

When zooming and tilting around the global view, take a moment to glance at the starry background on the screen: This starry night view is based on real astronomical data culled from NASA. (I bet you didn't know you were getting a basic planetarium with your News Channel, but the Wii is nothing if not full of surprises.)

News slides

Tired of the simple headline view? Bored with spinning the globe? Click the Slide button in the lower-right corner of the headline menu to view a dynamic slide-show view of the headlines, as shown in Figure 10-5.

Each headline is automatically replaced by a new one every few seconds, or you can press the left and right buttons on the Wii Remote's directional pad to scroll at your own pace. You can also use + and – buttons on the Wii Remote to increase and decrease, respectively, the size of the headlines.

If a headline looks interesting, press A at any time to see the entire story in a full screen view. When you're done reading a story, click the Continue button at the lower right to go back to the slide show. When you're done watching the news slide on by, click the End button in the lower left to go back to the basic headline view.

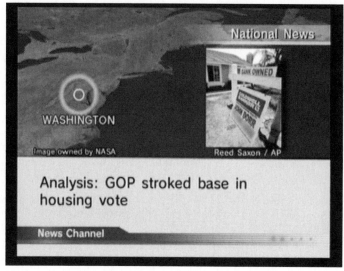

Weathering the Forecast Channel

Bob Dylan famously said you don't need a weatherman to know which way the wind blows. For those who want more detailed weather information and predictions, though, consulting some form of meteorologist is probably a good idea. Read on for more information on how to use the Wii's Forecast Channel to get the current temperature, forecasts, and global weather conditions on-demand on your TV.

Setting up the Forecast Channel

To use the Forecast Channel, you first have to make sure the Wii is hooked up to a broadband Internet connection. The Forecast Channel is built into the system right out of the box, so there's no need to download anything from the Wii Shop Channel.

The first time you turn the Channel on, you're asked to confirm the current time and date. If either is incorrect, you're sent back to the Wii System menu to correct them (see Chapter 2). You're then asked to choose your default location, first by choosing your state or territory and then choosing your city. Only major cities are listed, so if you live in a small town, pick a larger city that's close by. After you've chosen your state and city, confirm your selections by clicking Yes.

The Forecast Channel menu

After you've gone through the initial setup, you come to the Forecast Channel main menu, as shown in Figure 10-6. This is the screen that appears initially every subsequent time you start up the Channel.

Figure 10-6:
The Wii
Forecast
main menu.

This initial weather data screen shows current conditions for your area, but there's more data hidden just above and below. Click the up and down buttons on the edges of the screen or press the up and down buttons on the Wii Remote's directional pad to bring up the additional information, described from top to bottom in the following list:

- ✔ **UV Index:** The amount of ultraviolet radiation in the air today, measured on a scale from 1 (low) to 11+ (extremely high). A UV Index of 6 to 8 or above is considered dangerous; you should take special precautions if you decide to go out in such conditions.

- ✔ **Current:** The most recent temperature, weather, and wind conditions for your area. Weather data is updated multiple times per day; check the message in the lower-right corner of the screen for the time of the last update. This is the default view, as shown in Figure 10-6.

Forecast Channel data won't update when you're actively using the Channel. To get new data, first quit out of the Channel and then start it up again from the Wii Menu.

- ✔ **Today:** The predicted high temperature and weather conditions for later in the day (or later in the night, depending on the time of day).

- ✔ **Tomorrow:** The predicted weather conditions and high temperature for tomorrow.

- ✔ **Five-day Forecast:** Shows predicted weather conditions and temperatures for the next five days. The top number is the predicted high temperature and the bottom one is the predicted low.

Weather data displayed on the Forecast Channel does not include severe weather warnings and watches. Consult TV or radio for updates on severe weather in your area.

Settings

Click the Settings button in the upper-right corner of the Forecast menu to bring up the Change Settings menu. Click the appropriate Change buttons to toggle to the following options:

- ✔ **Closest Location:** Choose a new default location for the default Weather data view, as described in the "Setting up the Forecast Channel" section.

- ✔ **Temperature display:** Toggle between Fahrenheit and Celsius display for temperature data.

- ✔ **Wind Display:** Toggle between miles per hour (mph) or kilometers per hour (km/h) for the wind speed display.

Global view

Click Globe in the lower-right corner of the Forecast menu to bring up a worldwide view of the weather, as shown in Figure 10-7. Details about the controls for this view are described in the following list:

- ✔ **View detailed forecast:** To view more detailed weather information for a city, simply click the city's name on the globe. This brings up the current weather information for that city, as discussed in "The Forecast Channel menu" section. From here you can scroll up and down to get forecasts and more weather information, just as you would for your default location. When you're done taking in this info, simply click the A button in the middle of the screen to return to the Global view.

- ✔ **Zoom:** Click the zoom buttons in the top corners of the menu or press the + and – buttons on the Wii Remote to zoom in and out of the globe. Note that some smaller cities are only visible when zoomed in close to the globe — they are subsumed by larger cities when the view is zoomed out. Your default location is always visible, no matter the zoom level.

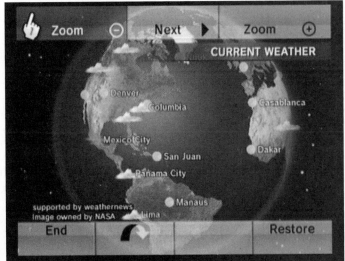

Figure 10-7:
The
Forecast
Channel's
Global view.

✔ **More Information:** By default, the global view shows a small icon representing the current weather conditions next to each city name. You can change this display by clicking the Next button at the top of the screen or by pressing the left and right buttons on the Wii Remote's directional pad. This cycles the displayed data through the following list:

- Current weather conditions
- Current temperature
- Today's predicted weather conditions
- Today's predicted high temperature
- Tomorrow's weather conditions
- Tomorrow's predicted high temperature

✔ **Spin the Globe:** To see other parts of the globe, click and hold the A button while the Wii Remote pointer is hovering over an empty spot of land or water. While still holding A, move the Wii Remote pointer in any direction to move the globe in that direction. If you let go of A quickly while moving the pointer, the globe continues to spin in the indicated direction, just like a real globe.

✔ **Tilt:** Tired of looking at the world from above? Click the curved arrow button at the bottom of the menu or press the up and down buttons on the Wii Remote's directional pad to look at the world from a different vantage point. When in a tilted view, click the Restore button to go back to the view from directly above.

Canvassing the Everybody Votes Channel

Have you ever seen that show *Family Feud,* where 100 Americans are surveyed, and the contestants have to guess the most popular answers? Ever wish you could give your opinion in a survey like that? Well, with the Everybody Votes Channel, you can! You can even take part in a game-show style game to predict what answer will be most popular. It's not quite *Family Feud* — you don't win any cash or prizes for participating — but this hidden gem of the Wii's Channel selection is still a surprising amount of fun. Read on for more on how to vote in polls, predict the results, and view your personal voting and predicting statistics.

Starting up the Everybody Votes Channel

First things first: To use the Everybody Votes Channel, your Wii has to be hooked up to the Internet through a broadband connection. You also have to download the Everybody Votes Channel from the Channels area of the Wii Shop Channel (see Chapter 6). The Everybody Votes Channel doesn't cost any money and doesn't take up much space on your Wii's internal memory, so there's really no reason not to try it out. Remember, if you don't like it, you can always delete it later.

The first time you start the Everybody Votes Channel, you need to confirm the general region you live in. This is the region you set up when going through the Wii System menu. If the region is correct, click OK. Otherwise, choose No to be taken back to the Wii System menu to choose a new region (described in Chapter 2). You're also asked to confirm your selected language from an on-screen list.

After your region and language settings are confirmed, you need to choose at least one Mii to represent you in the online voting. The Miis available in your Mii Plaza are displayed on-screen, ten at a time. Click the on-screen arrows to scroll through the selection of Miis, and then click your preferred Mii to choose him or her. Click Yes and then OK to confirm.

If more than one person uses the Channel, you can register more Miis at this time — just click Yes when asked and then repeat the steps in the previous paragraph. You can register up to six total Miis as voters on the Everybody

Votes Channel at any one time. You can always add more voters later, so don't worry if you're not sure if the rest of your family will want to join in on the fun (they probably will, if my experience is any indication).

Voting

After the initial setup, you're taken to the Everybody Votes Channel main menu, as shown in Figure 10-8. This is also the first screen that's shown on subsequent uses of the Channel.

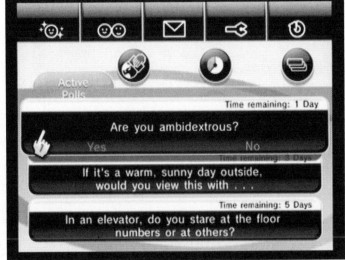

Figure 10-8: The Everybody Votes Channel main menu.

For now, just ignore the top row of options and focus on the tabs/circles just below it. Specifically, the first two on the left — Active Polls and Worldwide Polls — are the ones that let you express your opinion on the hot-button issues of the day (like how many times a day you brush your teeth, to take one recent example). These tabs are labeled as "New!" if there are new questions to respond to. Click either of these tabs to see a list of the three most recent active-poll questions available, and then click the poll question itself to bring up the Voting menu, as shown in Figure 10-9.

The Everybody Votes Channel only shows three Active Polls and one Worldwide Poll at a time. If you don't vote before a poll closes, you won't be able to go back and add your thoughts — it's gone for good. New polls come up regularly every other day, so be sure to visit the Everybody Votes Channel frequently. As Al Capone used to say: Vote early, vote often!

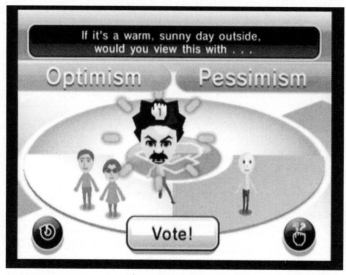

If it's a warm, sunny day outside,
would you view this with . . .

Optimism   Pessimism

Vote!

Figure 10-9:
The
Everybody
Votes
Channel vot-
ing screen.

On the Voting menu, any of your registered Miis that haven't yet voted are shown in the center of the teal voting circle. To place a vote for that Mii, first pick that Mii up by pointing the Wii Remote pointer at it and pressing and holding the A and B buttons on the Wii Remote simultaneously. While still holding A and B, drag the Mii over to the semicircle for your preferred choice. Let go of the buttons on the Remote to place the Mii in that voting area.

After you've placed any number of registered Miis in this manner, click the Vote! button at the bottom of the screen and then click Yes to officially confirm your vote (or votes). The voting Miis' shirts change to the color of the option they picked, indicating that their vote is locked and can't be changed. You can leave some Miis undecided for now, but remember: When a poll is done, it's done for good.

Predictions

After you make your personal vote comes the fun part — predicting which option will get the most votes overall. Click the Yes button when the on-screen prompt asks you if you want to "predict the response that will get the most votes." You don't have to do this if you're in a hurry, of course, but you're missing out on the best part of the Channel if you click No. I'm just saying . . .

The Miis that just voted run back to the center of the blue voting platform under the question "Which will be more popular?" Make your prediction by picking up your Mii with the A and B buttons and placing him or her in the appropriate semicircle (as described in the "Voting" section). After placing all voting Miis, click the Predict! button and then click Yes to register your predictions. Each Mii raises up a small, colored sign to indicate which option he or she predicted would be more popular. You're then taken back to the Everybody Votes Channel main menu.

Results

If you've already cast a vote or two, you're ready to move on to the rightmost two circles on the main menu: the Recent Results and Poll History tabs. The former allows access to the most recently concluded regional and international polls, while the latter contains archives of up to 12 more recently concluded polls (click the on-screen arrows to scroll through the list). These tabs are labeled with New! if there are any unviewed results to peruse.

Click the name of a poll question under either of these tabs to bring up the Results screen, as shown in Figure 10-10. First your Miis' picks and predictions will be recapped via the same colored shirts and signs discussed in the previous sections. After this, a drumroll and spotlight accompany a bunch of tiny Miis running in to fill in a pie chart, which shows the percentage results for the poll. Click the Skip button at the lower right to get past this rigamarole quickly.

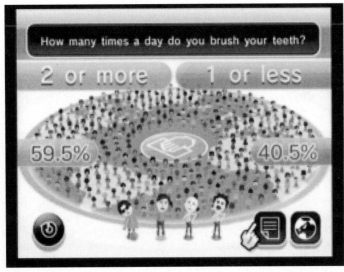

Figure 10-10:
The Everybody Votes Channel results screen.

After the results are up on the screen, you can click the icons at the lower right to get more information about voting patterns. Click the icon that looks like a piece of paper to view results split by gender and to see how accurate respondents were in their predictions. Click the scroll icon to see how the poll results broke down by state: The darker a state's color, the stronger that state's results broke in favor of that colored option.

For worldwide polls, click the globe icon to view a bar graph ranking of how each country responded to the poll. Click the on-screen arrows or press the up and down buttons on the Wii Remote's directional pad to scroll through this list of countries. Click Rearrange to order the countries by a different method, including their prediction accuracy.

Options and user data

This section discusses that top row of tabs on the Everybody Votes Channel's main menu screen (refer to Figure 10-8). From left to right, they are:

- ✔ **Register New Voter:** Add more Miis to that central blue voting circle. The process for registering new Miis is exactly the same as the one discussed in the "Starting up the Everybody Votes Channel" section.

- ✔ **Voter Data:** What good is all this voting and predicting if you can't keep track of who's actually winning? The Voter Data option lets you track your progress in the Everybody Votes Channel.

  First, click a registered Mii to bring up a screen tallying his or her vote count and prediction win/loss record. Click the right arrow on-screen to bring up the How Tuned In Are You? screen, a highly unscientific measure of your character traits based on how your votes gibe with those of others. Click the right arrow again to view the equally unscientific Distance from Popular Opinion screen, which measures how often you agree with the majority. The more pedestrian your personal picks, the shorter the distance.

  Click Close to go back to the Mii selection menu, or simply click a Mii on the left side of the screen to bring up his or her data without backing out. When you're done viewing voter data, click the Back button to get back to the main menu.

  Incidentally, the Voter Data screen is also where you go to *un*register a voter who's been signed up for the Channel. Click the Mii as normal, and then click the Erase button in the upper-left corner of the screen. Confirm your selection, but be careful — when you unregister a voter, all that Mii's accumulated voting and prediction data is lost forever.

✔ **Suggest a question:** Got a burning desire to know whether Wii owners prefer peas to carrots? Maybe you want to know if more Wii owners use a car or ride a bike to work or school? Suggest one of these or your own (doubtless better) questions to Nintendo and maybe it will get asked on the Everybody Votes Channel.

To suggest a question, click the question and answer area of this submenu to bring up an on-screen keyboard where you can enter your question and two responses.

Your question can have only two responses, so don't ask anything too open-ended. Keep it family-friendly and be sure to check your spelling before clicking the Send button to submit your question.

✔ **Options:** Brings up a submenu with the following options:

- **Confirm Polling Region:** Confirms your polling region. Click Change Your Polling Region to be taken to the Wii System menu, where you can change your Wii's region.

- **Erase All Data:** Be careful! This option unregisters _all currently registered voters_ and _erases their voting and prediction history for good._ Think long and hard before clicking the Yes button to confirm this drastic step. Think of the children!

- **Change Question Language:** Get questions in English, French, or Spanish.

✔ **Wii Menu:** Return to the Wii Menu to await further questioning. Remember, you can return to the Wii Menu at any time by pressing the Home button on the Wii Remote.

Getting Informed with the Nintendo Channel

There are plenty of ways to keep informed about new games for your Wii (see Chapter 11 for but a few) but there's only one way to stream videos and information about the latest games directly from Nintendo to your Wii. The Nintendo Channel is basically a giant Nintendo marketing zone on your Wii, providing video trailers and advertisements along with basic information about Wii games right on your TV screen. There are some interesting features to the Channel, though, such as interviews with game developers and downloadable demos for your Nintendo DS. Read on for more information on navigating this treasure-trove of marketing information.

Starting up the Nintendo Channel

Before getting into the Nintendo Channel, you need to connect your Wii to the Internet via a broadband connection. Then you have to download the Channel itself from the Channels area of the Wii Shop Channel (see Chapter 6). The Nintendo Channel is free, and worth a look even if you're not particularly interested in watching Nintendo advertisements.

When you first start the Nintendo Channel from the Wii Menu, the Channel downloads and plays the latest Digest Video summarizing the latest products and videos on the Nintendo Channel service. You can watch this video using the control discussed in the following section, "Viewing videos," or click the To The Video List button to jump right to the video list, as shown in Figure 10-11. Scroll through the pages of the list by clicking the on-screen arrows or pressing the left and right buttons on the Wii Remote's directional pad. Click a video name to view that video.

Figure 10-11:
The
Nintendo
Channel
Video List.

Viewing videos

Click the name of a video from the Video List menu to play that video on your TV, as shown in Figure 10-12. These videos are streamed directly from Nintendo's servers, so there may be a slight downloading delay before the video starts.

Figure 10-12:
Watching a
video on the
Nintendo
Channel.

After the video starts playing, click the video image itself to expand the video further to a full-screen view, or click the Back button in the lower-left corner to reduce the video to thumbnail size and return to the Video List menu. Click the Pause button to stop playback temporarily; click the Play button that appears in its place to resume the playback.

 While watching a Nintendo Channel video, hold down the B button to bring up a slider showing your current position in the video playback. While still holding B, move the Wii Remote pointer to move the slider and let go of B to jump to that position in the video.

 If videos are taking too long to download and start playing, there may be a problem with your Wii's Internet connection. Try restarting the Channel and/ or the system to see if the problem improves. If not, you might be better off just using your computer to view the similar information available on www. nintendo.com.

Viewing game information

When you're viewing a video, click the More Information button to bring up a page containing more information about the featured game, oddly enough. The top part of such an information page is shown Figure 10-13. Scroll down the page by clicking the on-screen arrows, by pressing the up and down buttons on the Wii Remote's directional pad, or by clicking the menu buttons at the right side of the screen, as shown in the figure.

Super Mario Galaxy

Wii

Mild Cartoon Violence

Experience a gravity-defying adventure!

Purchase

Figure 10-13:
A Nintendo Channel game information page for Super Mario Galaxy.

Each game information page can have some or all of the sections described in the following list:

- **Basic information:** Review the basics about the game in question, including the supported controllers, ESRB Rating, genre, number of players, and more. Click the Purchase button to go to the Internet Channel (for disc-based games) or the Wii Shop Channel (for downloadable games) where you can buy that game directly. After making your purchase (or just browsing), you have to leave the new Channel and restart the Nintendo Channel to get back to where you were.

- **Videos:** A list of all available Nintendo Channel videos about the current game. Click a video name to view the video, as described in the "Viewing videos" section. Click the Back button to return to the game information page.

- **Recommended Games:** For some games, the Nintendo Channel recommends other games you may like, basing their guess on the usage patterns and recommendations of other Nintendo Channel users. Click the name of a recommended game to go to the information page for that game.

- **What people are saying . . .:** This section graphs the recommendations of other Nintendo Channel users for this game (see the section, "Find titles for you"). This includes whether the game is better for hardcore or casual gamers and whether the game is more fun with friends or played alone. Hover over a graph with the Wii Remote pointer to see the answers and percentages for a specific question. Click the Filter Results button to narrow down the results to a specific age group or gender.

✔ **Time Spent Playing/Times Played:** Shows how popular the game is among people who decide to share gameplay data with Nintendo (see the "Settings" section, later in this chapter). Hours measures total number of hours data-sharing players have put into the game. Times measures how many distinct times data-sharing players have turned on the game (limit one per system per day). The Per Person numbers for each statistic average out the results over all the people sharing data. Remember this is a self-selected sample, so this data might not be indicative of how popular the game is among Wii owners as a whole.

✔ **Related Titles:** A selection of games that are related to the currently viewed game by series, character, or genre. Click a game name to bring up the information page for that game.

✔ **Web Page:** A list of some Web pages associated with the game. Click any of the listed Web page names to open up that page in the Internet Channel.

Find titles for you

Instead of just browsing around the videos on the Video List menu, you can look for videos of specific games by clicking the Find Titles For You button. This brings up a submenu with the following options:

✔ **View New Titles:** Click this option to bring up a list of titles that have been released recently or that will be released in the near future. This list initially includes titles for all Nintendo systems, including the Nintendo DS. Click the All Platforms button in the upper-right corner; then click the Wii button that pops up to restrict the results to Wii games. You can also choose to view only WiiWare or Virtual Console games.

✔ **Search by Category:** Click this option to bring up another submenu letting you choose a variety of filters for your game listings, including publisher, genre, recommendation status (see the Make a Recommendation bullet), or more. Click a filtering option, and then choose the desired criteria from the list that pops up. When all your options are set, click Search to bring up a list of games matching your search criteria. Click a game name on this list to get more information about the game (see the earlier section, "Viewing game information").

✔ **Search by Name:** Click this option to bring up the on-screen keyboard, where you can type in all or part of the name of the game you want more information on. (Remember: Spelling counts, so only type in the part of the title you're sure you know how to spell.)

✔ **Make a Recommendation:** Click this option to bring up a list of Wii games and Channels you've played for at least an hour. Click a game or Channel name to go through a series of questions about your experience with the game, including your gender and age, how much you generally enjoyed the game, and whom you think the game is best suited for. Use the Wii Remote pointer to answer all the questions, and then click Register to add your opinion to the Nintendo Channel's recommendations.

✔ **DS Download Service:** If you have a Nintendo DS, you can click this option to download trial versions of Nintendo DS software through your Wii. Note that you have to sign up for the Nintendo Channel's data sharing service before you can use the DS Download service (see the "Settings" section later in this chapter).

Here's how the DS Download Service works:

1. **Choose DS Download Service from the Find Titles for You menu.**

2. **Choose the game demo you want to download from the list.**

   This brings up a screen that says Preparing. When this message changes to Transmitting (as shown in Figure 10-14), proceed to the next step. This process can take a few minutes, so be patient.

3. **Turn on your Nintendo DS.**

4. **On the Nintendo DS, tap DS Download Play.**

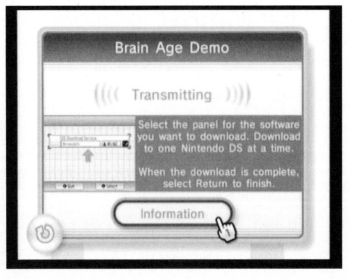

Figure 10-14: The DS Download Service game download preparation screen.

5. **On the Nintendo DS, tap the name of the demo, and then tap Yes to confirm the download.**

   A message on the DS says that the demo is downloading. After a few seconds, the game demo should appear on the DS screen.

6. **Play the demo.**

   After the demo has started, you can click the Back button on the Wii to go back to the demo list, or click Information to get more information about the game.

   When you're done with the demo, just turn off the Nintendo DS. Note that the demo is not permanently saved to your Nintendo DS, so you have to download it again from the Wii if you want to try it another time.

Settings

Click the wrench icon in the upper-left corner of the Video List menu to access the following options through a submenu:

✔ **Video Volume:** Change the volume at which Nintendo Channel videos are played. Click the on-screen arrows to move the volume setting up and down. Of course, you can just use your television remote to change the volume as well.

✔ **Commercial Message Settings:** The Nintendo Channel can occasionally send information about new games or products to your Wii Message Board. If you want this kind of information sent to your system periodically, click the Opt In to Commercial Messages From This Channel button. Otherwise click the Opt Out button.

✔ **Data Sharing Settings:** The Nintendo Channel has the ability to collect information on what games you play and how often you play them. This data is used to compile region-wide gameplay statistics for many games. Don't worry — this data is anonymous and can't be tied back to you in any way. Click I Agree (to share the data) or I Disagree (to stop sharing).

You need to agree to data sharing in order to access DS Game Downloads.

✔ **About Nintendo Channel:** Read more about the Nintendo Channel.

✔ **How Your Information Is Used:** Read more about how Nintendo uses the data you agree to share in the Data Sharing Settings. To summarize all the legalese and technical stuff here, Nintendo basically collects data on what games you play and how long you play them, as well as how you've set your Wii's System Settings. This data is all anonymous; it's not identifiable with you personally, but Nintendo may use it in the aggregate — whether for internal market research purposes or publicly to make game recommendations.

Getting Specific with Game-Specific Channels

While the games portion and the Channels portion of the Wii tend to keep a respectable distance from each other, a couple of Channels are specifically designed to work with certain disc-based games. These game-specific Channels can be run even when the associated game disc isn't in the system, providing some basic, gamelike functionality even if the game is buried at the bottom of your toy chest.

The following sections give you some basic information about these Channels, which can be installed onto your Wii Menu directly from the game disc. Consult the instruction manual for the games for more detailed information on using these Channels.

Mario Kart Channel

To install the Mario Kart Channel from the *Mario Kart Wii* disc, follow these steps:

1. **Start up *Mario Kart Wii* using the Disc Channel.**

2. **Press A to advance to the License menu.**

3. **Click the Settings icon.**

   This icon can be found in the upper-right corner of the screen.

4. **Click Install Channel.**

5. **Click OK, and then click Install.**

   The system quits to the Wii Menu and displays a somewhat cryptic "Save to Wii System Memory" message. Click OK once more to start the installation. The progress bar should fill up in a matter of seconds.

The Mario Kart Channel is now installed. You're returned to the game for now, but the next time you go to the Wii Menu, the Mario Kart Channel will be ready to go.

This Channel takes up 79 blocks on your Wii's internal memory (see Chapter 5 for more on memory management).

The Mario Kart Channel lets you monitor the online happenings in the *Mario Kart Wii* universe without having the game disc in the system. If your Wii is hooked up to the Internet, you can use the Channel to register new *Mario Kart Wii* friends, see if currently registered friends are online, or view how your time trial results measure up in the worldwide rankings. Of course, to actually race against your friends or their downloaded ghost data, you need to put the game disc in the system.

Wii Fit Channel

To install the Wii Fit Channel from the *Wii Fit* disc, follow these steps:

1. **Start up *Wii Fit* using the Disc Channel.**

2. **Click the Settings icon.**

   This icon can be found in the upper-right corner of the screen.

3. **Click Install Channel.**

4. **Click OK, and then click Install.**

   The system quits to the Wii Menu and display a somewhat cryptic "Save to Wii System Memory" message. Click OK once more to start the installation. The progress bar should fill up in a matter of seconds.

The Wii Fit Channel is now installed. You're returned to the game for now, but the next time you go to the Wii Menu the Channel will be ready to go.

Note that the Wii Fit Channel takes up 109 blocks on your Wii's internal memory (see Chapter 5 for more on memory management).

The Wii Fit Channel menu looks a lot like the Wii Fit Plaza (as discussed in Chapter 13), so it's not too surprising that most every function of the Wii Fit Plaza is available on the Wii Fit Channel. This includes viewing a graph of your daily exercise progress, performing a basic Body Test, and receiving your daily BMI and Wii Fit Age rankings. You can even jump into your daily training exercises, if the *Wii Fit* disc is in the system. Even if the disc is far, far away, the Wii Fit Channel is a great way to do your daily weigh-in and Body Test without a lot of hassle.

Part III
The Games

"Oh, that's disgusting! Using the Wii Fit as a tray table for your pizza!"

In this part . . .

After reading about all those Channels in Part II, you'd be forgiven if you momentarily forgot that the Wii was primarily designed to play video games. Well, this part will help remind you. First you discover how to pick out games that are right for you and your family. Then you figure out the ins and outs of two of the most popular games on the system, Wii Sports and Wii Fit. This part finishes up with a quick description of 15 great games designed for all sorts of situations.

Chapter 11

Picking Out Games

*W*alking into a video-game store for the first time can be a scary and baffling prospect. Rows and rows of largely identical-looking games, packaging that stresses flashy graphics over gameplay, and retail employees trained to cater to hardcore gamers can make choosing a game at the store a risky move. A $50 video game that you'll be playing for dozens of hours shouldn't be an impulse buy. You have to do your research to make sure you're not getting a lemon.

Of course, you could skip all that research and just head over to Chapter 14 for a list of recommended games for a variety of situations. As time goes on, though, and that list gets out of date, you'll eventually want to know how to pick out appropriate games for yourself. That's where this chapter comes in. Read on to find out more about the major genres of video games, the industry-standard content-rating system, good sites to consult for independent reviews, and tips for getting more games for less money.

Checking the Genre

Anyone who's watched a movie knows there's a huge difference between a summer blockbuster and an independent art-house flick. Similarly, games range from fast-action thrill-fests to more contemplative puzzle games. The first step to deciding whether or not to buy a game is determining whether its genre is a good fit for your tastes.

In the following list, I provide some of the most common video-game genres, along with a brief description of the games that fall into each genre. When you come across a genre you like, look for games that fit that genre on the Nintendo Web site (www.nintendo.com) or in your perusal of reviews (see the following section). Or you can simply ask about that specific genre at your local game retailer.

- ✔ **Action/Adventure:** Probably the most overcrowded genre in all of gaming, action/adventure games are those that focus on fast-paced thrills (the "action") and/or exploration (the "adventure"). Action games tend to require quick reflexes and have a lot of on-screen action, so new players may find these games difficult to play.

  That said, some action games are specifically designed to be easy for anyone to pick up and play (such as *Lego Star Wars: The Complete Saga*). Remember to check the box for an ESRB Rating, because many action games have excessive violence and other content that might not be appropriate for young children. (See the section on family-friendly adventure games in Chapter 14 for some recommended games in this genre.)

- ✔ **Fighting:** Games in this genre focus on individual or group combat between fighters, to the exclusion of pretty much all else. As of press time, the Wii library is notably lacking in fighting games, save for one major exception: *Super Smash Bros. Brawl.* This game features familiar characters from across Nintendo's history battling in frenetic, accessible battles that support up to four players at once. Outside of that, fighting game fans might want to look for classic fighting games such as *Street Fighter II* or *Eternal Champions* on the Wii Shop Channel (see Chapter 6).

- ✔ **Life Training:** A relatively new genre, Life Training games combine entertainment with personal betterment. This includes games such as *Wii Fit* (see Chapter 13), which exercises your body or *Big Brain Academy: Wii Degree* (see Chapter 14), which exercises your mind. The selection of Wii games in this genre is somewhat limited as of this writing, but look for it to take off in the near future.

- ✔ **Party:** As the name implies, party games are designed to be played in a group setting. While most party games have a single-player mode, the focus of the design is on multi-player carousing. Many party games are simply collections of mini-games that can be played in bite-size chunks of a few minutes apiece — ideal for the short attention span of a group setting. The quality of party games can vary wildly, with many companies trying to cash in with shoddy, quickly developed products. Even a bad game can be fun with the right friends, though. (See Chapter 14 for some party games that deliver on their promise of group fun.)

- ✔ **Puzzle:** This wide-ranging genre name is applied to games that generally require contemplative thought to solve in-game puzzles. These can range from destruction-fests such as *Boom Blox* to reflex tests such as *Mercury Meltdown Revolution* to point-and-click adventure games such as *Zack and Wiki: The Quest for Barbaros' Treasure.* Any game can fit in this genre, as long as it taxes your brain.

Beware the box

While the front of the box is what usually gets your attention in a store, flipping that box over can give you a better idea of what a game is actually like. As opposed to the front of the box, which usually includes highly stylized art designed to catch your eye, the back of the box usually includes descriptive text and representative screenshots of what a game will actually look like on your TV.

Of course, this text and these screenshots are created by the publisher to make the game look as good as possible, so it's still a good idea to consult some reviews for independent confirmation before you go to the store (see the "Reading Reviews" section). That said, the back of the box can provide an extra bit of confirmation that a specific game is actually what you're looking for.

While you're perusing the back of the box, remember to check the icon in the upper-right corner that indicates which controllers the game supports (see Chapter 3). Also be sure to check the lower-left corner for the game's ESRB rating (refer to Figure 11-1).

- ✔ **Racing:** Not surprisingly, this genre includes games that require driving around a course faster than the other players (human or computer). Racing games can range from relatively realistic simulations such as *MX vs. ATV Untamed* to totally off-the-wall games that involve fantastical characters and elaborate weaponry such as *Mario Kart Wii*. Many racing games on the Wii let you use the Wii Remote as a makeshift steering wheel, turning the entire controller in your hands as you would a real steering wheel.

- ✔ **Role-playing:** Technically this category includes any game that asks you to play a role. Role-playing games (or RPGs) tend to focus on elaborate, epic storylines told over many hours of gameplay. They typically involve turn-based battles with elaborate enemies and require you to manage a wide array of personal statistics and equipment to make your characters the best they can be. Generally, these games aren't great for quick, pick-up-and-play gaming sessions; they should be reserved for when you have a long period of time to devote to becoming engulfed in an entire world.

- ✔ **Rhythm/Music:** This genre includes games that turn on the player's musical and/or rhythmic ability. These can range from games that use the Wii Remote to tap out a quick beat, such as *Battle of the Bands,* to games that come packaged with their own musical controllers to measure the player's musical abilities, such as *Rock Band.*

- ✔ **Sports:** Games that simulate real world sports on your TV. As with racing games, these can range from accurate, lifelike depictions of popular sports (*Tiger Woods PGA Tour 08, Top Spin 3*) to games that stretch the definition of the sport with outlandish characters and superhuman abilities (*Super Swing Golf, Sega Superstars Tennis*). Usually one look at the box art is enough to tell one group from the other.

✔ **Strategy & Simulation:** A wide-ranging genre covering everything from realistic war simulations to wacky courtroom dramas, from tense medical dramas to relaxing scuba-diving trips under the sea.

If you're running low on new Wii games that fall into your preferred genre, remember that the Wii can also play games designed for the Nintendo GameCube. There also might be games in your preferred genre listed for download from the Wii Shop Channel (see Chapter 6).

Checking the Ratings

Games aren't just kid stuff anymore. Since the arcade heyday of *Pac-Man* and *Donkey Kong,* video gaming has grown into a multibillion-dollar industry, with content catering to everyone from preschoolers to adults. Just as you wouldn't let a young child go to an R-rated movie, you shouldn't let him or her play an M-rated game.

Fortunately, a large majority of the games available for the Wii are appropriate for even relatively young children (see sidebar, "Are game ratings effective?"). That said, you still have to be vigilant to make sure your children aren't playing anything meant for those outside their age range. That means checking the packaging for a rating before you buy the game. It also means reviewing the ESRB warning displayed on-screen before downloading a game from the Wii Shop Channel (see Chapter 6). The following sections give you all the information you need to review these ratings effectively.

The Wii has built-in parental controls to make sure your children can't play inappropriate games on your system. (See Chapter 2 for more on setting up parental controls.)

How games are rated

Console video games are rated in the United States by the Entertainment Software Rating Board, a group created by the Entertainment Software Association trade group. Ratings are assigned by a panel of at least three specially trained adults (mostly parents) whose identities are kept strictly secret. These panelists watch a video of "all pertinent content" in a game before its release to determine what ages that content is appropriate for. Raters may also sit in on a play session led by an experienced gamer and review the responses to a questionnaire on the contents of the game before making their ratings determination.

Other regions have their own game rating systems, including the British
Board of Film Classification (England), the Pan-European Game Information
system (Europe), and the Office of Film and Literature Classification
(Australia).

Games ratings explained

The Entertainment Software Rating Board groups all games released for the
Wii in the United States into one of the following six categories:

- ✔ **EC — Early Childhood:** Assigned to games suitable for children aged
  three or older, according to the ESRB. EC-rated games are the friendliest
  of the friendly, with absolutely no potentially controversial material.
  These are usually educational games, targeted at small children or
  toddlers. As of this writing, there are no EC-rated games available for
  the Wii.

- ✔ **E — Everyone:** Assigned to games with content suitable for ages six and
  older. E-rated titles are roughly equivalent to G-rated movies; they may
  contain minimal cartoon, fantasy, or mild violence and/or infrequent use
  of mild language, according to the ESRB. Generally this kind of content
  won't be anything worse than you would see in a Looney Tunes cartoon.
  Still, it might be too much for extremely young children.

- ✔ **E10+ — Everyone 10+:** As the name suggests, the E10+ rating is
  assigned to games containing content that's suitable for children
  ten years of age and older, according to the ESRB. E10+-rated games
  are roughly equivalent to PG-rated movies; they may contain mild
  language or cartoon/fantasy violence. The difference between E and
  E10+ is usually a question of degree — the more violence and/or
  rough language contained in a game, the more likely it will get the
  E10+ rating. Be sure to check the content descriptors for more on
  why exactly the rating was assigned.

- ✔ **T — Teen:** Assigned to games suitable for ages 13 and older. T-rated
  titles are roughly equivalent to PG-13-rated movies; they may contain
  violence, suggestive themes, crude humor, minimal blood, simulated
  gambling, and/or infrequent use of strong language, according to the
  ESRB. In general, violence in a T-rated game is slightly more realistic and
  gory than similar violence in an E or E10+-rated game.

- ✔ **M — Mature:** Assigned to games with content suitable for people 17
  and older. M-rated titles are roughly equivalent to R-rated movies; they
  may contain intense violence, blood and gore, sexual content, and/or
  strong language, according to the ESRB. This includes games with
  extremely realistic depictions and violence and gore that might be
  disturbing to children. Most retailers voluntarily refuse to sell M-rated
  games to unaccompanied minors, and some stores don't carry
  M-rated games at all (see the sidebar, "Are game ratings effective?").

✔ **AO — Adults Only:** Assigned to games with content that is unsuitable for children under 18. AO-rated games are roughly equivalent to NC-17-rated movies; they usually include strong sexual content or *very* extreme graphic violence. The rating is given out very rarely and only for the most extreme cases of sex and/or violence in games. Nintendo has pledged to block the release of any game that receives an AO rating on the Wii. As such, there are no AO games for the Wii as of this writing.

Content descriptors

ESRB ratings aren't just limited to the ratings described in the previous section. Each rating also comes with a more detailed description of the specific types of potentially objectionable content in the title. These content *descriptors* are displayed prominently along with the letter rating on the back of the box, as shown in Figure 11-1, and can include everything from "mild comic mischief" to "strong sexual content."

Don't just disregard this important information. A T-rated game with "crude humor" or "strong language" can be very different from another T-rated game with "minimal blood" or "violence" descriptors. The content descriptors can help you distinguish a title that might be inappropriate for your child from one that should be just fine.

For a full explanation of all these descriptors, as well as a searchable database of all ESRB ratings, visit www.esrb.org.

Are game ratings effective?

It's important to remember that even though the game industry has widely adopted the ESRB's rating system, the ratings don't have the force of law. No state or local government currently has any restrictions on what types of games can be bought or sold to minors, and attempts at such legislation have routinely been overturned on constitutional grounds.

That said, most major retailers voluntarily enforce ESRB ratings by refusing to sell M-rated games to children under 17 years of age. Other retailers go even further by agreeing not to carry M-rated games in their stores at all. Of course, enforcement isn't perfect. A 2008 "secret shopper" study conducted by the FTC found that children aged 13 to 16 could purchase M-rated games nearly 20 percent of the time. And even if your child can't buy a game, he or she might be able to play it at a friend's house.

As of this writing, there are there are no AO-rated games and only 13 M-rated titles mixed in among the Wii's 200+ game library. In contrast, nearly half of the current Wii game library is rated E10+ or younger, meaning the large majority of games for the system will be appropriate for a large majority of the gaming audience. So there are really only a handful of Wii games a watchful parent has to keep an eye on.

Figure 11-1:
An ESRB
rating, as
displayed on
the back of
a Wii game
box.

EVERYONE ENFANTS ET ADULTES

™ E

Mild Cartoon Violence

Légère violence en animation

ESRB CONTENT RATING   www.esrb.org

The ESRB doesn't rate the online portions of video games, instead issuing a blanket warning that "online interactions are not rated by the ESRB." This means that even if a game is rated E, your children could be subjected to adult language or inappropriate content by other players when playing online. Most Wii games have extremely limited chat functions, but children could still be exposed to the occasional crude username or other inappropriate content that can slip through during online play. (See Chapter 2 for more on turning on the Wii's parental controls to limit your children's access to this potentially harmful content.)

Other rating sources

While the ESRB rating is a great source of information for appropriate game content, some parents may want a second opinion before going into the store. The following Web sites can provide more information on a game's content:

- ✓ **What They Play (www.whattheyplay.com):** A site that takes a parent's-eye look at the gaming industry as a whole. In addition to parent-centric game reviews and features targeted at gaming neophytes, What They Play uses reader polls to determine age ratings that might be more accurate and precise than those given by the ESRB. In general, the site is a great resource for parents looking to learn more about the favorite hobby for a large segment of today's youth.

- ✓ **Common Sense Media (www.commonsensemedia.org):** An independent, not-for-profit group, Common Sense Media offers detailed game reviews with a focus on age-appropriateness. They also give their own ESRB-style ratings that slice the gaming landscape into content appropriate for each year of a child's age, from 2 through 17. The site also reviews TV, movies, and music, making it a one-stop shop for parents concerned about youth media.

- ✓ **Gaming with Children (www.gamingwithchildren.com):** Run by well-respected game journalist Andrew "GamerDad" Bub, this site covers myriad issues surrounding parenting and gaming, providing general information on the sometimes confusing game industry and answering reader questions in a useful column. While the site doesn't contain a comprehensive reviews section, it's still an invaluable resource for parents who might just be wading into the strange world of "interactive entertainment."

Reading Reviews

While the ESRB and other content rating organizations detailed previously in this chapter tells you if a game is age-appropriate, they don't give you much information as to whether or not a game is actually any good. Although personal taste is highly subjective and everyone's definition of a good game is different, there are some generally agreed-upon standards for what makes a quality title, including these:

- ✔ **Controls:** Probably the most important element of a game, the controls determine how easily your personal twiddling with the Remote and Nunchuk (or other controller) relate to the on-screen action. If the controls aren't intuitive and responsive, the game is going to be hard to salvage, no matter how good the other aspects are. Some controls may start out difficult but get easier with time. Others may seem all right at first, but fall short of offering fine enough control for complex maneuvers later in the game. Any review worth its salt will detail how the controls hold up, so read carefully.

- ✔ **Graphics:** Does the game have a pleasing aesthetic and generally consistent art direction? Note that a game's graphics don't necessarily have to be lifelike or realistic to be "good" — some of the best graphics can be the least realistic. You can read about graphics in reviews, but you can also judge them for yourself using online screenshot and movie galleries that accompany those reviews.

- ✔ **Length:** Games are expensive, so they generally need to be able to sustain themselves for at least a few hours to justify a purchase. A story-heavy game that reaches its conclusion after only five or six hours might feel like a rip-off, no matter how good it is. That said, just because a game is long doesn't mean it's worth the money. Even if a review notes that a game has "hundreds of hours of unique content," it doesn't matter if all that content sounds boring and derivative.

  On a related note, some games are good for picking up and playing in small bursts; others are better suited for hours-long play sessions. The former group of games might not be good for gamers who like to get lost in an experience, but the latter group might be hard to fit into a busy schedule.

- ✔ **Multiplayer:** Even the worst games tend to be redeemed somewhat if you can play them with a good group of friends. In fact, sometimes bad games are fun precisely *because* you can play them with friends! Use review sites to determine how many players a game supports, and whether they can all play at once or have to hand off the controller for alternating play. If your Wii is hooked up to the Internet, look for a discussion of any online options the game might have. (See Chapter 14 for more on picking great games for a party.)

When you know what you're looking for in a new game, you need to know where to find reliable reviews. The following list provides you with a few good sources for game reviews:

- **GameRankings (www.gamerankings.com):** Sometimes you're just too busy to read 1,000 or so words that give a comprehensive explanation of a game. Sometimes you just want the quality of a game distilled into a single number. GameRankings is perfect for those times. The site compiles dozens of independent reviews for a game and compiles them into a single aggregated percentage that gives a good general idea of the game's critical reception. Games that come in at over 90 percent are considered universally praised by critics. Games above 80 percent are pretty good for fans of the genre. Games that score between 70 and 80 percent are generally for diehard fans only. You should probably avoid anything with a game ranking under 70 percent. If you like GameRankings' scoring style, you may also want to check out similar review aggregator MetaCritic.com.

- **GameSpot (www.gamespot.com):** One of the oldest video game sites on the Web, GameSpot is also one of the most comprehensive. Practically every Wii game released gets a review here, along with a ranking on a 10-point scale. GameSpot reviews tend to be some of the harshest in the industry, meaning it's pretty hard to get a perfect 10 out of 10. Though the reviews are generally written for a hardcore audience of experienced gamers, even relative newcomers can get a feel for the gameplay through GameSpot's detailed prose.

- **GameCritics (www.gamecritics.com):** While not as comprehensive as a site such as GameSpot, GameCritics is a great site for a different take on the biggest releases. GameCritics reviews generally take a more artistic, more holistic look at a game, examining not only its technical merits but also the societal impact of the content (if any). The site also offers handy consumer guides that detail potential objectionable content for parents and possible difficulties that might be encountered by handicapped gamers. I might be a little biased in its favor (since I got my start reviewing games there roughly six years ago), but trust me, GameCritics reviews are great for getting a unique perspective on a potential purchase.

Getting a Deal

With new video games consistently retailing for up to $60 (or sometimes more if the games come with peripheral controllers), gaming can quickly become a rather expensive hobby.

Here are some tips for maximizing the number of games you get to play while minimizing the amount of money you have to spend:

✔ **Buy it used:** If you don't care much about the physical appearance of the game disc or box, buying used is a great way to save a substantial sum. You can find used games at a number of retailers, though Gamestop is probably the leader in the used game, er, game — with over 5,000 stores worldwide, roughly 4,000 of which are in North America. Many online retailers, such as Amazon (`www.amazon.com`), also offer a wide selection of used games. Used games aren't available the same day as brand-new games, of course, but you can usually pick up used versions of the biggest releases just a few days after the initial release. Used game prices go down quickly over time, so if a game is too much to shell out for today, just wait a few months and it might come into your price range.

✔ **Trade it in:** The flipside of buying used games is selling your own used games for money toward new purchases. While most stores no longer offer cash for your old games, Gamestop and many other retailers offer store credit for your gently used games. You get more for your trade-in if you still have the box and instruction manual, so keep them handy if you plan on cashing in later. You also get more for a game the closer it is to release — beat that brand new game in a week and you can sometimes trade it in for up to half the $50 purchase price. Stores occasionally offer trade-in specials for games exchanged toward the purchase of a specific new title, so watch your local store for promotions.

✔ **Rent it:** Why spend $50 on a game you'll only play for a week when you can rent that same game for only a few bucks? Your local movie-rental store probably has a video game section where you can try before you buy (or, if the game's a clunker, try *instead of* buy). For serial renters, Blockbuster Video offers a Games Pass program that lets you rent a set number of games at a time with no late fees, starting at $21.99 a month. Another way to rent games is through online rental programs that mail you a game along with a prepaid envelope to exchange it for a new one when you're done. GameFly (`www.gamefly.com`) is probably the best of these services, starting at $8.95 a month.

✔ **Download it:** Don't forget that Wii games aren't limited to those you see in the stores. If your Wii is hooked up to the Internet, you can download a wide range of Virtual Console and WiiWare titles without even leaving the house. These games tend to be a lot cheaper than those found at retail stores, generally falling in the $5 to $15 range. (See Chapter 6 for more on downloading games from the Wii Shop Channel and Chapter 15 for some recommended downloadable games.)

Chapter 12

Wii Sports

. . . .

In This Chapter

▶ Using the Wii Remote to control the five different sports available on the *Wii Sports* disc

▶ Strategies and tips to become a master at each sport

▶ Unlocking hidden secrets and Easter eggs to get the most out of the game

▶ Using the training games to perfect your technique

. . . .

*T*o a large extent, no two Wii owners will have exactly the same experience with their Wii systems. Given the hundreds of games currently available for the system, it's possible for two Wii owners to have massive libraries that don't overlap in the slightest. That said, there is one game that every Wii owner is guaranteed to have access to: *Wii Sports,* the game that comes packaged with every Wii system sold in the United States.

Because every Wii owner has this game, it's a great reference point for getting used to using the Wii Remote as a game controller. This chapter discusses how to use the Wii Remote to control each of the five games on the *Wii Sports* disc, including the training games that can refine your technique. This chapter also discusses basic strategy for each sport and unlockable secrets that you might not know about.

Getting Started

Before you head into this chapter, I assume that you already connected your Wii to your TV (as discussed in Chapter 2), connected your Wii Remote(s) to the system (Chapter 3), and you know how to start Wii games using the Disc Channel (Chapter 5). I also assume you've used the Mii Channel (Chapter 7) to make some personal avatars. (This last bit isn't strictly necessary, but I find *Wii Sports* is much more fun when the on-screen players actually look like you and your friends.)

If you've brushed up on your Wii basics, here's the drill:

1. Put the game in the Wii and start it up from the Wii Menu.

2. **On the title screen, press the A and B buttons on the Remote simultaneously to advance to the main menu.**

   This menu is shown in Figure 12-1. At this point, you have some options:

   - You can select single- or multi-player versions of each sport by clicking the appropriate buttons on the left side.

   - Clicking the barbell starts the Training mode, a set of fifteen mini-games designed to improve your technique in each sport.

   - Clicking the graph starts the Wii Fitness mode, which ranks your performance in three randomly selected training games.

     Training and Fitness options are discussed further in the "Training Mode" section at the end of this chapter.

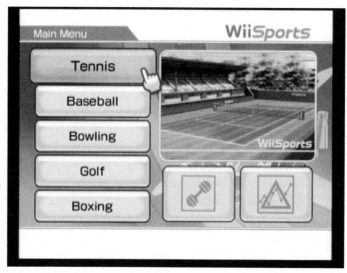

Figure 12-1:
The Wii
Sports main
menu.

Choosing the number of players

After selecting your sport, you're asked how many players are playing on a menu like the one shown in Figure 12-2. If there aren't enough Remotes connected, some player selection options may be grayed out. In this case, click More to connect more Wii Remotes to the system (see Chapter 3 for details).

Note that baseball and boxing can only be played by a maximum of two players. Also note that you don't need multiple Remotes to play the multiplayer versions of bowling and golf — players can simply hand off the controller in between rounds for these sports.

Figure 12-2:
The player-
selection
screen.

Choosing Miis

After choosing how many people are playing, you have to choose which Mii
will represent each player, using the menu shown in Figure 12-3. Only Miis in
your Mii Plaza are available here — Miis from the Mii Parade or the Check Mii
Out Channel won't be selectable (see Chapter 7 for more on Miis).

Figure 12-3:
The Mii
selection
screen.

If you have a lot of Miis in your plaza, you can scroll through the list by clicking the arrows on the right and left sides of the screen. If you have no Miis, click Guest to choose from a small selection of pre-made avatars. If you or one of your friends has saved any Miis to a Remote, they can be selected by clicking the Wii Remote tab (see Chapter 7).

In multiplayer games, each player has to use his or her own Remote to select his or her Mii.

After each player chooses a Mii, each player is asked to confirm which hand he or she uses for each sport, as shown in Figure 12-4. This selection affects how the Remote interprets that player's movements into in-game actions, and also which hand the player's on-screen Mii uses when playing each sports. Click the L (for left-handed play) or the R (for right-handed play) in each row; click OK when you're done.

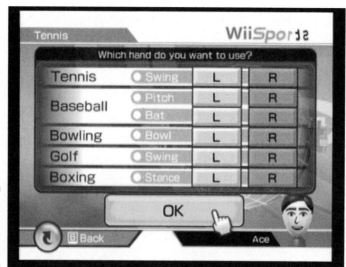

Figure 12-4:
The hand-
selection
screen.

Skill levels

You may notice that some of the Miis in these figures have individual "skill level" numbers next to their names. These skill levels keep track of your progress when playing single-player sports — they go up when you do well and go down when you do badly. Your computer opponents get better as your skill level gets higher in the competitive sports (tennis, baseball, and boxing). In games without computer opponents, the skill level has no effect on the gameplay.

Each sport has its own distinct skill level, so performance in one game won't affect your skill level in another. If you reach a skill level of 1,000 in a sport, the word "Pro" appear next to your skill level to indicate your achievement. Pro status also unlocks some hidden features in certain sports, as discussed in the "Secrets and Easter eggs" sections. The game also sends a message to your Wii Message Board when you achieve Pro status in a sport (see Chapter 4).

Skill level statistics are linked to a specific Mii, so be sure to use the same Mii every time you play a single-player match if you want to keep track of your progress. If you delete this Mii from the Mii Channel, your progress will be lost, so be careful.

Pressing the + button on the Wii Remote at any time during play pauses the game and brings up a menu that allows you to quit, start over, or return to the main menu.

Tennis: The Racquet Racket

The exact origins of the game of tennis are up for debate, but the game (as we know it) has been around since at least the mid-nineteenth century. *Wii Sports Tennis* has been around since at least the 2006 Electronic Entertainment Expo, where it was first demonstrated to a crowd of industry insiders at the Kodak Theater in Hollywood, CA. Tennis is probably the most easily accessible of the *Wii Sports* games, and a great way for beginners to learn about using the Wii Remote.

Getting started with tennis

After selecting Tennis from the main menu, you're presented with the player positioning screen as shown in Figure 12-5. You can use this screen to arrange which player will play on which team — the pair on one side of the net works together against the pair on the other side (singles matches are not available). The gray, question-mark player icons represent computer-controlled players; these can be opponents or teammates. Click one of these gray icons to put your Mii into that position, and click again to toggle back to a computer-controlled player. In games with multiple players, note that all players have to click the positions they want with *their* Wii Remotes — another player can't do it for them.

A single player can control more than one position at a time, as shown in Figure 12-5. Each swing of the Wii Remote swings the racquet for all the Miis controlled by that Remote. You can even set it up so one player controls all four players at once, which is a great way to practice your ball-watching and timing skills.

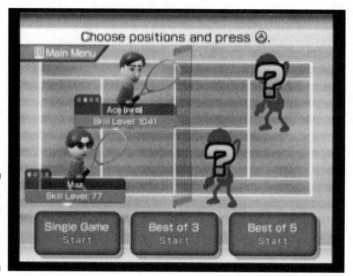

Choose positions and press Ⓐ.

Main Menu

Ace [hiro]
Skill Level: 1041

Yax
Skill Level: 77

| Single Game | Best of 3 | Best of 5 |
| Start | Start | Start |

Figure 12-5:
The tennis
position-
selection
screen.

After you're done setting up the positions, choose your desired number of games from the choices at the bottom. A Best of 3 match ends as soon as one team wins two games, while a Best of 5 match ends as soon as one team wins three games.

Gameplay basics for tennis

In a nutshell, tennis involves hitting a ball back and forth over a net and into the large white box drawn on the ground on the other side. A team loses a point if a player on that team hits the ball outside that box or into the net, or if a player fails to hit the ball before it bounces twice on that team's side. Because this is doubles tennis, the boundaries are determined by the outer lines, as shown in Figure 12-6.

Scoring in tennis may seem a little odd for newcomers to the sport. Instead of counting up points normally (0-1-2-3-4), scoring in *Wii Sports Tennis* runs 0-15-30-40-Game, the final one indicating a side has won that game. When both teams are tied at 40 each, the game enters a different mode of scoring called a *deuce*. The winner of a deuce point is said to have the advantage, and that pair wins the game if they win the next point. If the pair with advantage loses, the score goes back to deuce.

The players in *Wii Sports Tennis* are initially arranged as shown in Figure 12-6. The player with Server over his or her head has to put the ball in play, as described in the "Controls for tennis" section. The player across the court from the server diagonally is the one to return the serve back across the net. After that, either player can hit the ball at any point.

Figure 12-6:
The initial
setup of the
tennis court
and players,
including
the server.

At the end of a game, the serve alternates to the other team. There are no "sets" or "matches" in *Wii Sports Tennis*: The first team that wins the set number of games wins immediately.

This gives the team serving first a distinct advantage, so you might want to put the weaker players on the left side of the net when you're arranging players.

If there are two human players on different sides of the court, the screen is split into two halves with two different camera angles. In general, you should focus on the side with your Mii at the bottom of the screen, because this makes it easier to plan your shots. You might also want to position yourself around the TV so that you're closer to your player's side of the screen.

Controls for tennis

First off, each player should be holding the Wii Remote in the standard, vertical position.

Grip firmly but not too tight, and be sure you have your wrist strap and Wii Remote jacket attached before starting. Stand up with your knees slightly bent and make sure there's lots of room to maneuver without hitting other players or any objects in the room. I can't stress this last point enough — you need a *lot* of space to make sure you don't cause physical damage to anyone or anything around you.

Serving

To start a game of tennis, the ball is put into play by the server, as indicated by the yellow Server over that player's head on-screen (refer to Figure 12-6). The server first throws the ball up by either swinging the Wii Remote upward or by pressing the A button. Either way, when the ball is in the air, it can be served by swinging the Remote forward quickly, just as if it were a real tennis racquet.

Don't worry about the speed or angle of your serving motion — all that matters is the height of the ball when you hit it; the higher the better. If you serve the ball when it's at the very top of the throwing arc, it zooms quickly to the other side of the net with a white trail of smoke behind it. Such serves are very hard to return effectively, so work on your timing.

Hitting the ball

You don't have to worry about moving your Miis around the court in *Wii Sports Tennis* — the game automatically makes them run to intercept the bouncing ball. All you have to worry about is hitting the ball when it reaches your Mii. Doing this is as simple as swinging the Wii Remote like a real tennis racquet. Bend your elbow slightly and swing your arm around your body in a wide arc, as shown in Figure 12-7.

Figure 12-7: Basic form for forehand (left) and backhand (right) shots for a right-handed player.

Correct form and swing speed are very important here. If you swing too fast, the game may detect your motion as multiple swings, which can throw off your game. If you swing too slowly, the game may not detect a swing at all. The key is a nice, smooth motion that pushes the virtual racquet through the ball.

Be sure to keep a tight grip on your Remote as you swing. Overenthusiastic swinging and sweaty palms can lead to broken Remotes, TVs, and/or priceless vases. Be sure all players are using the wrist strap and Wii Remote jacket, as discussed in Chapter 3.

Forehands and backhands

There are two basic types of swings in *Wii Sports Tennis*: the forehand (a shot that starts on the same side of your body as the Wii Remote) and the backhand (a shot that starts on the opposite side from the Wii Remote). Recognizing when to do each type of shot is the key to success. When the ball is coming toward your player, try to determine which side of your Mii it will end up on — as early as possible. When you've figured out if the shot will require a forehand or backhand, move the Wii Remote slowly back to that side, at about waist level, in preparation for your forehand or backhand shot. You're then ready to swing immediately forward as the ball reaches your Mii. Anticipating shots is vitally important to success at *Wii Sports Tennis.*

Lobs and spins

The way you swing the Wii Remote in your hand affects the way the ball flies from your Mii's racquet. Twisting the Remote toward the screen as you swing, for instance, can put speed-enhancing topspin on the ball. Swinging the Remote from low to high, on the other hand, lobs the ball high in the air, well over players at the front of the net. Experiment with different Remote motions to see how the ball reacts.

Strategy for tennis

The following list provides some helpful tips for improving your game in *Wii Sports Tennis:*

✔ Figuring out how to anticipate forehand and backhand shots is the first key to *Wii Sports Tennis* success. Pay attention to the direction and angle the ball is coming in at *before* it actually gets to your Mii, and cock the Remote back on the appropriate side as soon as possible. Getting into position before the ball gets to you makes timing and positioning your shots that much easier.

✔ After you know when to use a forehand and when to use a backhand, you need to learn how to direct shots left and right deliberately. Timing is the key, here. Hit the ball early, when it's slightly out in front of your Mii and it flies away from the racquet side (to the left for a right-handed forehand). Hit the ball late, when it's slightly behind your Mii, and the shot is angled toward the racquet side (to the right for a right-handed forehand). This might seem tough to remember at first, but keep practicing and eventually positioning your shots will become second nature. When you can direct the ball reliably, try to place it away from your opponents on the opposite side of the court.

✔ After you've mastered positioning your shots, start experimenting with putting spin on the ball, as described in the "Controls for tennis" section. A low shot with some nice topspin can slide by a tough defense, and using lob shots strategically can get you out of a lot of tight jams.

✔ If you're controlling a player that's standing close to the net, remember that you don't have to hit every ball that comes to you. The player behind you might be in a better position to return a devastating shot (even if that player is also controlled by you).

✔ As your skill level starts rising in the single-player game, mastering the high-speed serves is crucial to succeeding against the tougher computer opponents. Work on your timing until you can get that white smoke behind your ball reliably.

✔ If a ball looks like it might land out of bounds, wait for it to bounce before returning it. If it's out, you win the point. If it's in, you can always return it at that point.

Secrets and Easter eggs in tennis

You can find these secrets and Easter eggs in *Wii Sports Tennis:*

✔ Hold down the 2 button after you choose your Miis to play a match on a blue court with no spectators.

✔ If you're on the team that won the last point, you can skip the replays by pressing the A button. This can help keep things moving quickly (and if you're playing against me, it can help prevent me from throttling you with my bare hands).

✔ When you reach Pro status (with a skill level of over 1,000) you'll notice more Miis crowding the stands on the side of the court.

Baseball: Getting into the Swing of Things

The national pastime, baseball is American as Mom, apple pie, and (judging by recent sales data) the Wii itself. *Wii Sports Baseball* is a decent approximation of pitching and hitting, but it's unfortunately not a great replacement for the real game.

Gameplay basics for baseball

Wii Sports Baseball differs from real baseball in a number of important respects. For one thing, there are only three innings. For another thing, the fielders and base runners are controlled automatically by the game. There are no stolen bases, no double plays, and no tagging up in this extremely simplified version of the sport. Some things remain constant, though — for instance, three strikes still make an out and three outs make an inning.

For the pitcher, the goal is to strike out the batter by throwing the ball over the plate in a way that's hard to hit. For the batter, the goal is to hit the ball, putting it in play in fair territory (inside the angled white lines) so that it lands safely in the outfield (the grassy area) without getting caught in mid-air. This is a *base hit,* which puts a runner on base. Further hits can advance the base runners to home plate, which counts as a run. The team with the most runs at the end of three innings wins the game (and while there are no ties in baseball, there are unfortunately ties in *Wii Sports Baseball*).

Controls for baseball

In *Wii Sports Baseball,* the players are divided into two separate yet equally important parts: the batters who try to score runs, and the pitchers who try to strike them out. Their stories are described in the following sections.

Batting

Swinging the bat is as simple as, well, swinging the Wii Remote like a bat. First, make sure you're standing correctly, with your feet spread about shoulder-length apart, your knees slightly bent, and your body turned perpendicular to the screen. Hold the Wii Remote vertically, the way you would a baseball bat — and wrap both hands around it, as shown in Figure 12-8. Make sure the buttons on the Remote are facing toward you, not toward the screen. While waiting for the pitch, you can wiggle the Remote in your hands to make your on-screen batter wiggle the bat.

Figure 12-8:
The
correct
batting
stance.

When you're standing correctly, wait for the ball to cross the plate and swing the Remote smoothly in a sweeping motion around your body, parallel to the ground at about waist height. Don't swing too lightly or the game won't register your motion. Swinging hard can get some extra distance on the ball, but keep it within reason — there's no reason the Remote should be in danger of slipping from your hands.

Pitching

Before making your actual pitch, you can adjust your aim using the Wii Remote. Press the left and right buttons on the directional pad to make the pitch go to the left or right side of the plate, respectively. If the controller is set to rumble, you should feel it shake when you make these selections. To cancel a directional pitch, press up or down on the directional pad to choose a pitch that will go down the center of the plate.

You can also choose from four different varieties of pitch by pressing buttons on the Wii Remote before the actual throw:

- ✔ **Fastball:** Don't press any buttons when making your throwing motion to make a fast, straight throw to the plate.

- ✔ **Curveball:** Hold down the A button as you make your throwing motion to get a pitch that curves from right to left (for right-handed players).

- ✔ **Screwball:** Hold the B button as you make your throwing motion for a pitch that curves in from left to right (for right-handed players).

- ✔ **Splitter:** Hold both A and B as you make your throwing motion to throw a pitch that slows down and drops suddenly as it gets to the plate. This pitch is great for fooling overeager batters.

Occasionally, your pitcher messes up when trying to throw one of the curving pitches discussed in the preceding list, throwing a simple fastball instead. A red exclamation point appears over the pitcher's head when this happens. Fielders also occasionally make exclamation-point-inducing errors when trying to field the ball, turning what should be an out into a base hit. There's no way to control these frustratingly random effects — your best bet is to just learn to live with them when they happen.

After you've chosen your aim and pitch type, throwing a pitch is as simple as making a throwing motion with your arm. Just swing the Remote over your head and down in front of your body.

Don't let go of the Wii Remote. Yes, I know you'd let go of a real baseball, but I repeat: DO NOT let go of the Wii Remote — just flick it in your wrist while maintaining a tight grip around it.

The speed with which you whip the Remote around your body affects the speed of the in-game pitch, from a slow 60 mph floater to a 90+ mph fastball. Despite this, there's no reason to get crazy with your Remote flicking. Whipping the Remote too hard is how wrist straps and objects in the room get broken. Keep things within reason and you should be fine.

Strategy for baseball

The following list provides some helpful tips for improving your game in *Wii Sports Baseball:*

- ✔ When batting, timing is the key. Hit the ball when it's square over the plate and it flies straight. Hit it too early or late, and it flies off to the side and foul. The game tells you if you're swinging too early or too late. Pay attention and concentrate on swinging at the right time.

- ✔ Don't just swing at every pitch — wait for one that looks easy to hit. Don't go chasing balls that aren't going to go over the plate. Be careful, though — the strike zone is bigger than you might think. Watch out for crafty pitches such as the sinker (nearly impossible to hit well, but it's almost always a ball if you don't swing). Remember, four balls means a free base runner!

- Swing power also has an important role in batting. You should swing hard enough to get the ball out of the infield, but not so hard that the ball is easy to catch by the outfielders. When you've got the timing and power down, it should be pretty easy to get relatively reliable base hits.

- If you're tired of boring, reliable base hits, you can always try swinging for the fences to get some home runs. Be sure to swing as hard as possible and raise the Remote from low to high as you swing. Timing and pitch position are still important when going for homers, of course. Perfect your technique with the Hitting Home Runs training game (see the later section, "Baseball training games").

- While pitching, mix up your pitches. Don't always go for top speed fast-balls — throw in some off-speed pitches and curves, too. Don't be afraid to make the batter chase an outside pitch or a splitter on occasion.

Secrets and Easter eggs in baseball

You can find these secrets and Easter eggs in *Wii Sports Baseball*:

- If either team is winning by five runs or more at the end of an inning, a "mercy rule" kicks in and ends the game early.

- While pitching, you can change to a sidearm throwing style by pressing the 2 button on the Wii Remote. This doesn't affect the way the pitches actually fly, just the way the Mii's pitching motion looks on-screen. Press the 1 button to go back to an overhand pitching style.

Getting Bowled Over with Bowling

Everyone's favorite alley-based sport has been simulated by countless video games over the years. *Wii Sports Bowling* is the first such simulation that actually makes the player perform real bowling motions instead of just pressing some buttons on a controller. *Wii Sports Bowling* is great for mastering fine control of the Wii Remote, and is probably the most accurate representation of its real sport to be found on the *Wii Sports* disc.

General gameplay in bowling

The goal of bowling is to knock down all ten pins by rolling a ball down to the end of a lane. The game is divided into ten frames with two chances to knock down pins in each frame.

The score for each frame is equal to the number of total pins knocked down in that frame, unless all ten pins are knocked down. If all ten pins are knocked down in one throw, the total from the next two throws is added to that frame's score (this is called a *strike*). If it takes both throws to knock down all the pins in the frame, the total from the next throw is added to that frame's score (this is called a *spare*).

A perfect game is 12 strikes in a row (including two extra strikes for the bonus on the tenth frame) for a total of 300 points.

Controls for bowling

Throwing a ball down the lane is probably the most complex process in all of *Wii Sports,* so I've broken it down into its component parts. Follow these steps and you'll be hurling the ball down the lane in no time:

1. **Position your bowler.**

   Use the left and right buttons on the directional pad to align your bowler in relation to the pins.

2. **Aim your shot.**

   When your bowler is positioned, press the A button to switch from positioning mode to aiming mode. In aiming mode, use the left and right buttons on the directional pad to angle your shot, as represented by the red dotted line going down the lane, as shown in Figure 12-9. Press up on the directional pad to zoom in on the pins and get a better view of your aim — press up again to go back to the normal view. If you need to adjust your bowler's position again for any reason, press A to go back to positioning mode.

Figure 12-9:
Aiming a
shot.

3. **Stand in the ready position.**

   Stand up straight and hold the Wii Remote in the standard vertical position, as shown in the "a" part of Figure 12-10. Bring the Wii Remote up to your chest, making sure the tip of the Remote is pointing toward the ceiling. Your on-screen Mii raises the ball upwards to his or her chest when you do this.

4. **Begin your throw.**

   When you're ready to throw, press the B button on the Wii Remote. Your Mii immediately starts advancing toward the lane. As he advances, quickly swing your arm back and to the side, as if you were preparing to throw a real bowling ball as shown in the "b" part of Figure 12-10. Be sure to continue holding the B button through this process, or your Mii will drop the ball too early.

5. **Swing forward and release.**

   While still holding the B button, swing your arm forward in a smooth motion, as if you were throwing a real bowling ball. You may want to step forward with your opposite foot while doing this, as shown in the "c" part of Figure 12-10. Release the B button at any point during this forward motion to release the ball. Timing is important — if you release the B button too late or too early, the ball simply drops to the ground instead of rolling forward. *Do not* actually throw the Wii Remote, but *do* follow through with the Remote after releasing the B button.

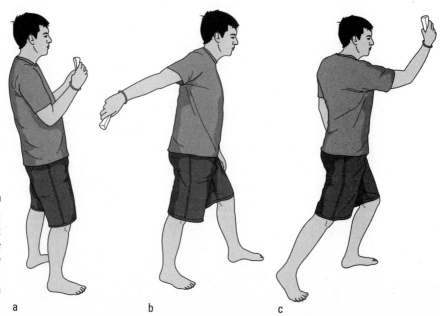

Figure 12-10:
Correct
*Wii Sports
Bowling*
form.

a   b   c

The speed of your forward swing at the time of release affects the speed of the ball in the game. You can also add spin to the ball by twisting the Remote in your hand just before releasing the B button (see the "Strategy for bowling" section for more on this).

The process in Steps 4 and 5 happen quite quickly, so you should start making your throwing motion as soon as you first press the B button. If you mess up or let go of the B button at the wrong time, don't panic — just press A and start again from Step 3.

If you're using a single Wii Remote for multiple players, you have to hand off the Remote between frames.

Strategy for bowling

The following list provides some helpful tips for improving your game in *Wii Sports Bowling*:

✔ Many beginners complain that their shots drift to one side for no reason. There is a reason behind this strange drift, though. Most people naturally twist their wrists slightly at the end of their throwing motion. If you're going for a straight shot, focus on really keeping the remote straight and level through the entire throwing motion. The smoother your throwing motion is, the better. Letting go of the B button early can also help limit this unintentional drift.

✔ When you're comfortable with straight throws, try adding some spin to the ball by deliberately twisting the Remote in the desired direction just before you release the B button. Don't twist the Remote too much (more than 90 degrees), or the game might not register the spin correctly. The ball starts out going straight, and then starts drifting in the direction of the twist as it goes down the lane. These curved shots get more "pin action" and have a much better chance of getting a strike than straight shots. Remember to adjust your curve according to your aim and throwing power — a slow-moving shot is much more affected by spin than a fast-moving one.

✔ In general, don't aim directly for the head pin. Instead, aim for what bowlers call "the pocket," a sweet spot just between the 1 and 3 pins for right-handed bowlers, or between the 1 and 2 pins for lefties (see the labeled pin diagram in the upper-left corner of Figure 12-9). Shots that hit the pocket have a better chance of being strikes and not leaving a *split,* where two or more pins are left standing far apart.

- ✔ After you find a combination of positioning, aiming, power, and curve that gets a strike, stick with it. Work on repeating that shot reliably over and over, with the same throwing speed and curve. It might not be very exciting, but maintaining this consistency is the key to getting a lot of strikes and really high scores.

- ✔ Even expert bowlers can't get a strike every time. What separates the good bowlers from the great ones is the ability to turn missed strikes into spares by picking up the last few pins on the second throw. Work hard on aiming and throwing accurately to pick up those spares to get consistently high scores.

Secrets and Easter eggs in bowling

You can find these secrets and Easter eggs in *Wii Sports Bowling:*

- ✔ Right after you choose your Miis (as the screen fades to black), hold down the following directions on the Remote's directional pad to change the color of your bowling ball:

  - **Up:** Blue

  - **Down:** Green

  - **Left:** Red

  - **Right:** Gold

- ✔ To shock the assembled audience of Miis in the bowling alley, release the B button at the very back of your backswing (see Step 4 in the "Controls for bowling" section). The ball flies backwards, causing the Miis in the alley to jump and scream in surprise.

- ✔ To make the audience of Miis laugh at you, maneuver your bowler to either side of the alley. Aim the shot as far as it will go to that same side, until the red aiming line goes into the adjacent lane. Throw the ball as normal, releasing B at the very end of your forward swing. The ball flies up and into the gutter of the next lane, causing the assembled Miis to burst into laughter at your ineptitude.

- ✔ Reach Pro level by earning a skill level over 1,000 and you can play with a special ball decorated with sparkling stars. This ball is slightly heavier than the normal ball and curves slightly differently as a result.

Golf: Hitting the Links

Golf has been called "a good walk spoiled." *Wii Sports Golf* is just like that, except without the good walk part (rim shot). Seriously, *Wii Sports Golf* is part of a long tradition of Nintendo golf games, dating back to the accurately named *Golf* on the Nintendo Entertainment System. All in all, *Wii Sports Golf* is a pretty good representation of the real thing, even though it only has one nine-hole course and a limited selection of clubs.

Gameplay basics for golf

Golf is a pretty simple game, when you get down to it. The goal is to get the ball in the hole using as few swings (*strokes*) of the club as possible. On-course hazards such as sand traps and high grass (the *rough*) can make it harder to hit the ball accurately and far. Be sure to avoid trees, which can block the ball's path, and water hazards, which can cost you a one-stroke penalty if your ball is unlucky enough to land in one.

Controls for golf

Grip the Wii Remote firmly but not too tightly, and be sure you have your wrist strap and Wii Remote jacket attached before starting. Make sure there's lots of room to maneuver without hitting other players or any objects in the room. I can't stress this last point enough — you need a lot of space to make sure you don't cause physical damage to anyone or anything around you.

Aiming

When starting your first hole, you see a screen much like the one shown in Figure 12-11. The blue line on the radar in the lower-right corner shows where your current shot is aimed (the ball could end up anywhere on that line, depending on the power you hit it with). You can change the direction of this line using the left and right buttons on the Wii Remote's directional pad. Try to aim for the hatched green fairway area or the light-green greens on the radar. Aim away from the tan sand traps, dark-green rough, and blue water. Note the direction and speed of the wind (as shown in the upper-right corner of Figure 12-11); take them into account when aiming your shot.

Figure 12-11:
The default
view in *Wii
Sports Golf*.

Club selection

Changing your club changes the length of the blue line on your radar and, thus, the maximum distance of your shot. To change clubs, use the up and down buttons on the Wii Remote's directional pad. Your club choices are

- **Driver:** The club with the potential to hit the ball farther than all the others. Use this club for your initial shot from the tee and for long shots from the fairway.

- **Iron:** Good for mid-distance shots from the fairway. Not so great for shots from the rough or sand traps.

- **Wedge:** Good for short, approach shots and for getting out of the rough and sand traps.

- **Putter:** Used to push the ball into the hole when it's already extremely close. Only recommended when you're already on the green.

Practice swings

After you've chosen your club and lined up your shot, it's time for some practice swings. First, hold the controller like a golf club, as shown in Figure 12-12, with the tip of the remote pointing down toward the ground. Place your feet shoulder length apart, and stand perpendicular to the TV, with your weak side facing toward the screen (mimic the stance of your Mii if you're confused). Make sure you're wearing the Wii Remote's wrist strap and have the Wii Remote jacket on.

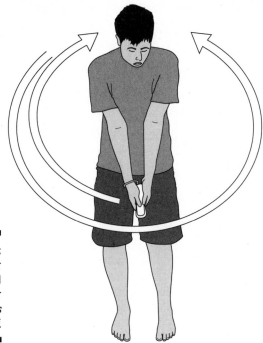

Figure 12-12:
The proper grip and stance for *Wii Sports Golf.*

When you have the grip down, it's time for a practice shot. Swing the Remote as you would a real golf club. First swing back and away from the screen — farther back for powerful shots, less far for weaker shots. You may want to twist your wrist at the very back of your backswing to raise the club higher. Then swing the club forward and across your body in a smooth motion, ending up with the Remote across your chest and up near your head. Don't worry too much about doing things wrong — this is just a practice shot.

As you swing, you'll notice that your Mii roughly replicates your swing motion. You'll also notice that the power meter on the left side of the screen (refer to Figure 12-11) will fill up briefly with a blue bar. This bar represents the power of your practice shot. The white dots on the bar correspond to the white dots on the blue line shot path on the radar. For example, a shot that filled the power meter up to the second white dot would fly roughly to the second white dot on the radar's blue line. A shot that filled the power meter to the yellow diamond at the top would fly to the yellow diamond at the end of the blue line on the radar. Note that these power markings are approximate and that your shot can be affected by the wind. Also remember that the ball bounces after landing, and could roll off into a hazard if you're not careful.

Note that it *is* possible to swing too hard. Try taking a practice swing as fast as possible and you'll probably notice the Power Bar turn red and start wobbling (you hear a truly awful sound come out of the Wii Remote speaker, too). Shots that turn the power meter red tend to drift off-center at random, often ending up quite far from their intended target. For accurate, powerful shots, keep practicing until you can get the power meter to fill up close to the yellow dot but not beyond it.

When your ball is sitting in the rough or a sand trap, the top portion of the power meter is grayed out. Any shot whose power goes into this grayed-out area turns red and be subject to the random wobble.

The swing

After you've practiced enough and feel you have a good handle on your power level, hold down the A button on the Remote to make your on-screen golfer approach the ball. While still holding A, repeat the shot you just practiced and the ball flies through the air with the greatest of ease. Be sure to hold A through the entire shot motion — if you let go early, your golfer backs up frustratingly at the last second.

Putting

When you reach the green (the small green area around the hole), you're forced to use the putter to push the ball toward the hole. Aiming and swinging the putter works just like aiming and swinging the other clubs, but it requires a much smaller and more restrained swing. Don't follow through too much on your putts or your power meter overfills every time. A light touch is the key.

While on the green, you can change the camera to a lower angle by pressing the 2 button. You can get a more detailed view of the elevation of various parts of the green by hitting the 1 button. Lighter colors in this view represent higher points than darker colors.

Strategy for golf

The following list provides some helpful tips for improving your game in *Wii Sports Golf:*

- ✔ Mastering shot power is the key to low scores. Don't focus too much on proper golfing form — the Wii doesn't care. Instead, focus on making a smooth and steady motion and controlling the speed of the Remote as it reaches the bottom of your swinging motion. Practice makes perfect, so keep trying those practice shots until you're confident you can get the desired distance. Don't let anybody rush you! Golf is a game of patience.

- ✔ While it's pretty easy to fill up the power meter with a little practice, pulling off weaker shots can be a little tough. If you swing the Remote too slowly, the game might not even detect that you made a swing at all (this is especially true on putts). Try flicking your wrist a little bit at the end of a slow swing to get the Wii to detect the weak shots.

✔ Remember to pay attention to the wind — it can easily guide a perfect shot into an errant hazard if you're not careful. Remember that the ball is going to bounce and roll after it lands too, so aiming your shot for the edge of that water hazard might be a little risky.

✔ Overpowered shots that turn the power meter red aren't always a bad thing. Yes, it's harder to predict where they'll end up, but if you really *need* a little extra oomph on a shot, it might be worth the risk. Use these overpowered shots sparingly.

✔ Learn how to read the greens when putting. Remember that the ball tends to drift downhill slightly as it rolls, so aim your shot toward the uphill side of the hole. Also remember that an uphill putt might need a little more oomph to get to the hole, while a downhill hole might need a little less. Don't use too much oomph, though, or the ball is liable to bounce over and past the hole.

✔ Be conservative to start. Don't go for the tricky shot that grazes right up against the edge of the sand trap unless you're sure you can get it. When you know the courses and the controls a little better, you can try getting fancy.

Secrets and Easter eggs in golf

True golf pros and/or purists can turn off the power meter and aiming radar by holding down the 2 button on the Wii Remote while selecting a course.

Boxing: The S-Wii-t Science

Whether you're a prizefighter or a pacifist in real life, *Wii Sports Boxing* is a great way to let out aggression without the risk of breaking a rib or losing teeth. Plus, it's almost as good a workout as real boxing. In fact, it's by far the most motion-intensive game in the *Wii Sports* library.

Gameplay basics for boxing

The basics of boxing are simple enough — just hit the other guy until he falls down. The other side of this strategy, which many boxers forget, is that you should really try to *avoid* being hit by the other guy so *you* don't fall down. This means blocking your opponent's punches by keeping your guard up and dodging sideways, backward, and generally away from his or her fists.

In *Wii Sports Boxing,* hitting an opponent takes away sections from the hexagonal health meter hovering next to his head (as seen in Figure 12-13). When a section of the meter is flashing, it means another solid hit will turn it black.

Figure 12-13:
*Wii Sports
Boxing.*

When all the sections of a player's health meter are removed, that player falls down and a count starts. If the count gets to ten before the player gets up, it's a knockout and the player left standing wins. If the player gets up before the count of ten, his health meter is partially filled and the fight continues. The more times a player is knocked down, the less energy that fighter tends to have after getting up (and the longer he or she tends to stay down on the mat next time).

While your opponent is knocked down, it's a great opportunity for you to wave the Remote and Nunchuk in your hands. Your on-screen Mii mimics your motions and taunts your fallen opponent. Boxing is not a sport for the magnanimous.

A *Wii Sports Boxing* match is divided into three three-minute rounds. If no player gets a decisive knockout by the end of the third round, the game goes to a point-based decision. Players are scored by punches landed, damage taken, and by who scored more knockdowns. Ties are possible, but rare.

Controls for boxing

Note that you need a Nunchuk hooked up to the Wii Remote to play this game. Two-player bouts require two Remotes and two Nunchuks. Hold the Remote in your dominant hand and the Nunchuk in your weaker hand, as shown in Figure 12-14. See Chapter 3 for more on the Nunchuk and how to hook it up to the Remote.

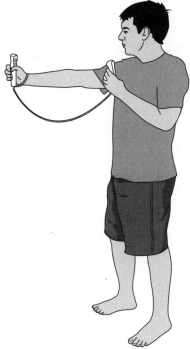

Figure 12-14:
Proper
form for
*Wii Sports
Boxing.*

The moves in *Wii Sports Boxing* can be broken down into three main categories:

- **Blocking:** Simply hold the Remote and Nunchuk up in front of your face to block high punches. Both the Remote and the Nunchuk should be pointing straight up toward the ceiling for this to work. To block low punches, move the Remote and Nunchuk down around your belly and point them toward the screen. The orientation of the Remote is more important than the actual height. Note that each hand can block independently, so you can have the Nunchuk put up a high left block while the Remote blocks low on the right.

- **Dodging:** Tilt the Remote and Nunchuk 45 degrees to either side to make your Mii quickly shimmy to that side. This is good for throwing off an opponent's aim and timing. You can also dodge backwards by leaning the Remote and Nunchuk 45 degrees away from the screen. While it's not strictly necessary to physically lean your body as you dodge with the controller, it's a lot more fun if you do (not to mention, it's a good workout). Note that you can throw punches while leaning as well.

✔ **Punching:** *Wii Sports Boxing* punches can be divided into a few categories:

- **Head shot:** Raise the Remote and/or Nunchuk in a high block, as described above, and then keep the Remote or Nunchuk at head level and jab forward quickly. The more speed you put into your punch the more powerful the on-screen punch will be.

- **Body blow:** Go into a low block and punch forward with the Wii Remote or Nunchuk tilted forward slightly and at the same waist level for a quick punch to the gut. Again, the speed of the punch affects the power.

- **The hook:** Move the Remote or Nunchuk sharply backwards and to the side sharply to pull off a powerful shot that comes in at the opponent from the side. It might be hard to get the Wii to recognize this punch, but keep practicing and you should get it. These punches are slightly slower and can leave you open to counterattack, but they're very hard to block and very powerful when they hit.

- **The uppercut:** Swing the Remote quickly from low to high in a wide arc, just like a real uppercut. These punches are notoriously hard to get the Wii to recognize, but they do work sometimes.

- **The 1-2 combination:** Timing is everything for this quick set of punches. As soon as you connect with a punch with one fist, follow up with a quick, powerful punch from the other hand. If you timed it right, the second punch should do a lot more damage than normal and be nearly impossible to block.

Strategy for boxing

The following list provides some helpful tips for improving your game in *Wii Sports Boxing:*

✔ Most beginners make the mistake of simply flailing away randomly with the Remote and Nunchuk, trying to get their on-screen punches to fly as fast as their real-life hands. The game doesn't work that way. Be quick but deliberate with your punches, and don't throw a new punch until your gloves come back to your Mii's body after the previous punch.

✔ The early computer opponents fall pretty easily to any quick barrage of punches. When you reach the Pro level, though, you need to remember to mix up your punches and use blocking and dodging to keep out of the opponent's reach. Look for openings in your opponent's guard and take advantage. Remember, hooks are a good way to get past the opposing guard.

✔ The more strong punches you use in reducing the opponent's health meter, the more likely he'll stay down for a long time. Put together a lot of 1-2 combination punches to get a quick knockout.

Secrets and Easter eggs in boxing

After beating Matt in the single-player game, you can unlock special, gold boxing gloves by holding down the 1 button during the fade to black before a match starts.

Training Mode

These mini-games are the hidden gems of *Wii Sports,* extending the basic experience of the actual sports into fun training vignettes. The games are found by clicking the dumbbell on the *Wii Sports* main menu (refer to Figure 12-1). This brings up the selection screen shown in Figure 12-15. At first, only the top row of training games are available, but simply trying a training game once unlocks the one below it.

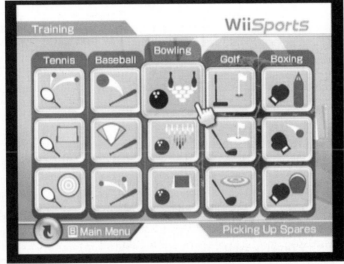

Figure 12-15: The Wii Sports Training selection screen.

Up to four players can compete at each training game by handing off the Wii Remote in between rounds. You can earn bronze, silver, gold, and platinum medals for especially good performances at each game. These achievements are noted with a message sent to your Wii Message Board.

The following sections provide a short description of each training game and some basic strategies for each.

Tennis training games

The three tennis training games are as follows:

- ✔ **Returning Balls:** Simply return the automatically hit balls to the other side of the net, making sure to land each shot in-bounds. Concentrate on your character's location on the court and watch the timing on your swings. Try to get the ball as close as possible to the center of the court so you have some margin for error.

- ✔ **Timing Your Swing:** Return the balls so that they go through an ever shrinking orange target area on the other side of the net. Timing is still the key to positioning the shots precisely. Remember, swinging early makes the ball go away from the racquet side; a late swing angles the ball toward the racquet side.

- ✔ **Target Practice:** Bounce a ball against a wall continuously, hitting a moving target as you go. Missing the targets weakens the bricks in the wall, until the ball eventually flies through the hole you create to the other side. Concentrate on slow, deliberate shots that are easy to reach when they bounce off the wall. If the ball starts drifting to one side, correct for it quickly.

Baseball training games

The three baseball training games are as follows:

- ✔ **Hitting Home Runs:** Just as it says on the tin, focus on hitting as many home runs as possible. Good timing and a quick, upward swing are key.

- ✔ **Swing Control:** Hit the pitches onto the specified area of the field. The dark blue area is worth the most, while the white area is worth the least. Timing is everything — late swings go away from the batter's side; early swings go toward the batter's side.

- ✔ **Batting Practice:** Simply hit the pitches into fair territory — field position doesn't matter. Be careful, as the pitches get a little fancier as the training session goes on.

Bowling training games

The three bowling training games are as follows:

- **Picking Up Spares:** Instead of trying to knock down all ten pins, in this mode you have to knock down only the pins set up in specially designed patterns. Five misses and you're out. Focus on aiming at pins from an angle so they get knocked into other pins when they're hit.

- **Power Throws:** A new row of pins is added to the lane every round, so that the initial set of ten pins has increased to 91 total pins by round ten. As the name implies, more powerful throws are more likely to get excessive "pin action" that knocks down those stray pins in the back. The pin count is doubled when you get a strike in this training game, so really focus on getting those last few stragglers for a super-high score.

- **Spin Control:** Use your Remote twisting abilities to curve the ball around the lane barriers and into the pins. Note that both leftward and rightward spins are required in this challenge. Some setups also require a late release to launch the ball over a seemingly impassable barrier.

Golf training games

The three golf training games are as follows:

- **Putting:** Sink a series of ever-lengthening putts. Five misses and you're out. Remember to read the hills on the green by pressing the 1 button on the Wii Remote. Be careful with your shot power — too much or too little can be fatal. Take your time and you should be fine.

- **Hitting the Green:** Use your wedge to chip the ball as close to the hole as possible. Despite the name, just getting on the green isn't necessarily enough — your score depends on the total distance the ball ends up from the hole. Shots that don't end up on the green is scored as "100 feet" from the hole, so make sure to at least end up on the green.

   Don't overshoot the hole — take into account the bounce after landing.

- **Target Practice:** Aim your shot for the two large targets sitting on this specially designed course. Scoring is based on where the ball lands, not where it bounces or rolls to. In general, aim for the back target, which is larger and has higher scoring values. Pay attention to the ever-changing wind conditions before each shot and adjust as needed.

Boxing training games

The three boxing training games are as follows:

- ✔ **Working the Bag:** Timing is the key as you throw 1-2 combos to take out a series of heavy punching bags. Throw your punches fast, but not too fast, and in time one after another for maximum speed and damage. Note that certain bags may require you to lean to one side to hit them.

- ✔ **Dodging:** Avoid the balls thrown by the trainer by leaning left and right. Watch the trainer's hands and dodge before the ball is thrown. The trainer sometimes throws two balls at once — dodge quickly to the opposite side to avoid them. The trainer gets craftier as he goes, messing with his usual timing, so watch out.

- ✔ **Throwing punches:** Hit the mitts the trainer puts up, not the trainer himself. Watch that your punches don't go too high or too low. Note that one glove sits a little higher than the other in this mode, so it might be easier to hit certain pads by leaning and hitting them with the opposite glove. Take your time and be careful not to hit the trainer.

Wii Fitness

Before there was *Wii Fit* (covered in Chapter 13) there was the Wii Fitness mode of *Wii Sports*. This mode randomly picks three of the training games and throws them at you one after another. Your results in these training games are used to determine your "Wii Fitness Age," an extremely unscientific measure of your "fitness" that has almost nothing to do with how fit you actually are. This age can range from 20 (the best) to 80 (the worst). Your age is graphed for every day you play, but can only be recorded once per day per Mii. This mode is good for getting a quick workout and adding some variety to your usual Wii Sports routine.

Chapter 13

Wii Fit

. . . .

In This Chapter

▶ Registering a Mii for a *Wii Fit* account

▶ Taking the Body Test and setting your goals

▶ Working out with the various *Wii Fit* exercises

. . . .

From its inception, the Wii has always been marketed as a system that would get gamers off the couch and moving around. It's hard not to work up a sweat swinging the boxing gloves in games such as *Wii Sports Boxing* or shaking the controller to the beat in *Rayman: Raving Rabbids*. But while these games are definitely a good way to get moving, the workout always felt like an incidental part of the gameplay. With most Wii games, the health effects seem more like a fringe benefit than the "real reason" you're playing the game.

Enter *Wii Fit,* a Wii game specifically designed to give you a workout. Using the included Wii Balance Board, *Wii Fit* measures your center of balance as you lean, shake, and twist your body into a wide variety of configurations. Suddenly, your entire body is the controller, not just your arms and hands. This chapter walks you through setting up the game and your Wii Balance Board, using the board for yoga poses and strength training, and playing aerobic and balance games.

Starting Wii Fit for the First Time

The first steps to setting up *Wii Fit* are the same as setting up any game — just put the disc in the system and start it up using the Disc Channel. The game creates a new save data file — press A on the Wii Remote to acknowledge this.

Registering the Balance Board

After the game starts, you have to sync the Balance Board so the Wii can recognize it. This process is similar to the one used to sync a new Wii Remote to your Wii, as described in Chapter 3. The specific method for syncing the Balance Board is described in the following steps:

1. **Open up the battery cover on the bottom of the Balance Board.**

   The specific location of this battery cover is shown in Figure 13-1.

2. **Place four AA batteries in the Balance Board, as shown in Figure 13-1.**

   Batteries are included inside the *Wii Fit* box. Make sure you insert the batteries in the correct direction, with the negative end near the springs. Note that each battery alternates direction.

3. **Press the red SYNC button on the Balance Board.**

   This button is right next to the battery housing. The light on the Balance Board's power button should begin flashing (refer to Figure 13-2). If it doesn't, check to make sure that the batteries are inserted correctly (see Step 2). Do not push the SYNC button again when the power light is flashing.

4. **Press the red SYNC button on the Wii.**

   This button is located on the front of the Wii, underneath a protective flap. (Refer to Chapter 3.)

After a few seconds, the light on the Wii Balance Board should stop blinking and remain on. This means your Balance Board is registered and ready to use with your Wii. Replace the battery cover and close the flap on the front of the system.

If the light stops blinking and turns off after 15 seconds or so, repeat Steps 3 and 4 in the preceding list. Make sure the Balance Board is close enough to the Wii to be recognized. If the problem persists, contact Nintendo at 1-800-255-3700 or www.nintendo.com/consumer.

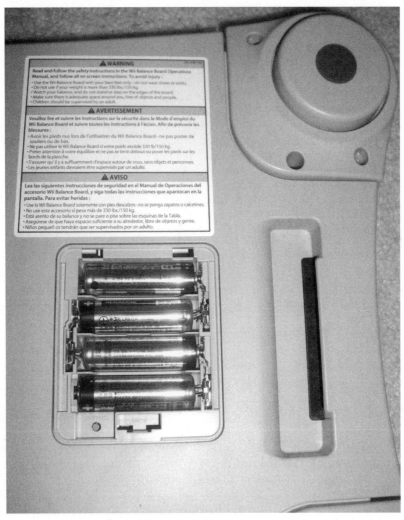

Figure 13-1:
The Balance
Board
battery
housing and
SYNC
button.

Placing the Balance Board

Playing *Wii Fit* means clearing a lot of space in front of your TV. I mean a
LOT of space. You may think you have enough space for just standing on the
board, but some strength tests require you to get down on the floor and lay
out your body horizontally. Other games may cause you to lose your balance
and fall into nearby furniture or appliances. Make sure you clear out a radius
of at least three feet around the Balance Board and that there are no sharp
corners nearby.

Note that the Balance Board should be placed with the power button sticking away from the TV screen, with the long end parallel to the screen. You don't have to stand on the Balance Board or turn it on yet — the game tells you when to do these things.

Registering your Mii

After the Balance Board is set up, you're ready to personalize your *Wii Fit* experience. An animated version of the Wii Balance Board jumps on-screen to walk you through this process. After a few pleasantries, the board asks you to confirm the date and time settings on the Wii system itself. If these are correct, click OK. If they're incorrect, click No to jump to the Wii System Settings menu, where you can correct them. (See Chapter 2 for more on setting the date and time.)

After the time is set, you're asked to choose which Mii you want to represent you on-screen as you play *Wii Fit*. The Miis from your Mii Channel's Mii Plaza appear on-screen in groups of ten. Click the arrows on the left and right sides of the screen to scroll through the list, or use the + and – buttons on the Wii Remote. When you see your preferred Mii, click him or her and then click OK to confirm your selection.

Your selected Mii drops down from the top of the screen and takes a small bow. The animated Balance Board uses this opportunity to lecture you and your Mii about proper posture and the effect it can have on your health. Feel free to read through this alarmist rant, or just keep hitting the A button on the Wii Remote to skip through it.

Eventually, the Balance Board asks you to enter your height by clicking the up and down arrows on-screen. Click OK when the height is correct. This is used to calculate your Body Mass Index (BMI) later on, so be as accurate as possible. You're then asked to enter the year you were born in a similar manner, and then the month and day of your birth. If the Mii you selected had a birthday set on the Mii Channel, it is automatically entered here. Neat!

Calibrating the Balance Board

After your personal data is confirmed, the game asks you to press the power button on the Balance Board. This button sticks out from the edge of the Balance Board, as shown in Figure 13-2. Give the button a quick tap with your toe and the light on the power button should blink and then turn solid. If it doesn't, check that the Balance Board is properly registered with the system as described in the earlier section, "Registering the Balance Board."

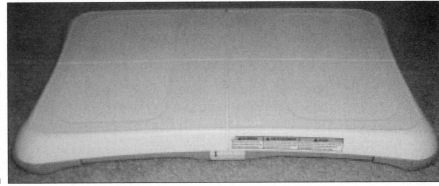

Figure 13-2:
The Wii
Balance
Board
power
button.

After the Balance Board is turned on, the game tells you that it is "Starting up" in a cute robotic voice. Don't stand on the Balance Board during this process — the Balance Board is calibrating. After a few seconds of this, the game tells you to "step on." Follow its instructions by placing your feet on the textured foot areas as shown Figure 13-3.

Make sure you're barefoot — shoes make it hard to make the fine movements needed in many games, and socks could cause you to slip and possibly fall off the board.

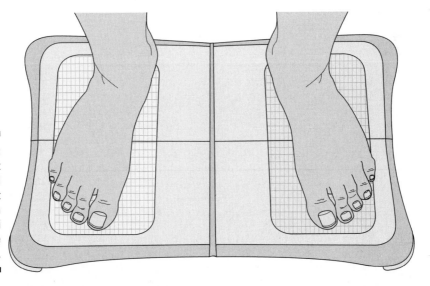

Figure 13-3:
Correct
initial
placement
of feet on
the Wii
Balance
Board.

After you step on the board, relax your shoulders and stand as still as possible as the Balance Board calibrates itself to your weight. If you fidget too much or take too much time getting on the Balance Board, the calibration fails and you have to step off and try gain. If you stand still correctly for five seconds or so, the game displays the message, "Confirmation complete! Ready to go!" So you are.

You may notice a ghostly, floating green dot appearing on the white background of the screen during this calibration process. This green dot is your center of balance as it relates to the Wii Balance Board. This can help you center yourself as the game is calibrating and make sure you're not fidgeting too much.

Note that you may have to recalibrate the Balance Board many times as you play *Wii Fit*. Just follow the on-screen directions when they tell you to step on and off the board and you should be fine.

After the initial calibration, the Wii asks you to input the weight of your clothes using the menu shown in Figure 13-4. This is to help the game estimate your true weight without requiring you to strip down to your underwear. Choose the light or heavy options to subtract two to four pounds from your in-game weight, respectively. You can also specify a specific weight for your clothes by hovering the pointer over the Other option (as shown in Figure 13-4) and pressing the up and down arrows on the Wii Remote's directional pad. You can subtract up to seven pounds worth of clothing, or even add seven pounds to your weight if you're wearing helium-based clothing or something. (You can even add zero pounds if you're exercising naked, but please make sure the blinds are closed tight if this is the case!)

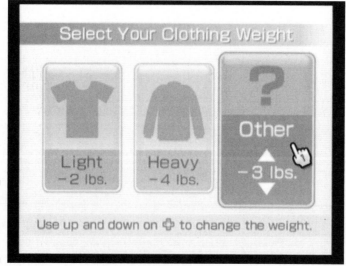

Figure 13-4:
The clothes-weight menu.

Try to wear the same or similar outfits each time you play *Wii Fit,* and choose the same clothing option each time you start the game up. This ensures that the game measures your weight consistently across many days' worth of play.

The Body Test

The Body Test is your daily measure of progress. The first time you start up your game, the Body Test is used as a baseline for your progress from here on in.

Center of Balance Test

When you're all set up, the game tests your posture using a Center of Balance Test. As the game instructs you, go ahead and stand on the Balance Board, as shown in Figure 13-3. Relax the tension in your shoulders and stand as still as possible over the center of the board. The game gives a three-second countdown and then begins measuring your center of balance. Don't tense up during this test — just relax and keep still. When the test is done, the game says "All done," and you can feel free to fidget and move about.

Your results are then shown as a moving red dot on the on-screen Balance Board, as shown in Figure 13-5. This red dot represents your center of balance. If it's moving around a lot, you have to work harder on standing still during the test. Your average center of balance is shown on the board, along with a percentage measure of your left and right balance. Take the results to heart, and try to correct for any natural tendency you might have to favor one side or the other. You may also want to shift your position on the Balance Board if the results show you too far to one side or the other.

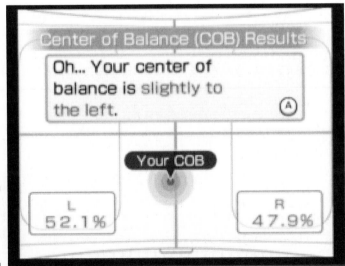

Figure 13-5: The center-of-balance screen.

Sometimes, after the Center of Balance test, the game asks you to "become more aware of your center of balance" by centering yourself on the board. A red dot representing your current center of balance appears on-screen. Lean your body forward and back and side to side to position this dot in the blue circle in the center of the screen. Hold this position for three seconds — tightening your abs can help.

Body Mass Index

The Wii Balance Board wasn't just evaluating your posture during that Center of Balance test — it was also weighing you. Yes, the Balance Board can also act as a high-tech scale, measuring your weight-loss progress as you play every day. The game also uses this weight to calculate your body mass index (BMI), as shown on the BMI Results screen in Figure 13-6. This basic measure of your health is based on your weight and the height you entered earlier (see the "Registering your Mii" section).

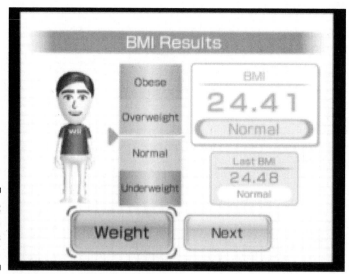

Figure 13-6:
The BMI
Results
screen.

Wii Fit puts a lot of stake in your BMI, even though it's not the end-all and be-all of health statistics (see the sidebar, "The limits of BMI"). The game even changes the shape of your Mii's body to correspond to your BMI/weight data. The game also places you in one of four categories based on your BMI: Underweight, Normal, Overweight, or Obese. These are technical medical terms, so don't be too offended if you end up somewhere you don't like. If you'd like to view your actual weight in pounds instead of your BMI, you can do this by clicking the Weight button. When you're done watching your weight, click Next to move on.

The limits of BMI

Even though *Wii Fit* puts a lot of stock in your Body Mass Index, the measure is generally a pretty bad measure of your overall health by itself. By only measuring your height and weight, BMI doesn't take into account blood pressure, cholesterol, heart rate, and many other factors that can affect your overall health. Even the weight measure can be misleading because the BMI rankings assume an average distribution of fat, muscle, and bone. Because muscle is denser than fat, a person with lots of lean muscle may be classified as overweight or obese despite being in perfect health.

You also should be wary of using the Body Mass Index for people 20 years of age or younger. Because children's bodies are constantly growing, the standard Body Mass Index used by *Wii Fit* can be wildly misleading about youth health. A BMI calculator for children and teens is available at `http://apps.nccd.cdc.gov/dnpabmi/Calculator.aspx`.

In short (once more with feeling), while the BMI is a useful tool for measuring general progress in a fitness regime, it's not the end-all and be-all measure of your health.

Body Control Test

The final part of your initial testing is a series of body control tests. These tests measure your ability to shift your center of balance quickly and precisely. The first time you play *Wii Fit,* you're confronted with the Basic Balance Test, as described in the following list. When doing the Body Test on subsequent days, you're tasked with two of the following tests at random:

- **Basic Balance Test:** This test measures your ability to shift your weight between your left and right legs. Two bar graphs are shown on the screen representing your relative left-right balance. As you put more weight on one side, the graph for that side gets shorter, while the graph for the other side gets longer. Your goal is to shift your weight so that both graphs stop in the highlighted blue area, and then hold that position for three seconds. If the graph slips outside the blue area the count resets, so focus on tightening your muscles and holding your position. Bend your knees and shift your upper body slightly to help you get into the correct position.

- **Steadiness Test:** This test measures your ability to hold still without fidgeting. As the countdown begins, straighten your shoulders and tighten your abs over the center of the Balance Board. A red dot appears on-screen, showing your moving center of balance against a black-and-white grid. After ten seconds, the grid starts moving behind the dot. Don't move along with it! Continue standing as still as possible. After 20 seconds, the grid and dot disappears completely, so you have to rely on your internal sense of balance to detect any movement.

  After thirty seconds, the test is done and your movements is displayed on the screen. If you're moving around a lot, try controlling your breathing — slowly in and out. (I find it helps to have my hands clasped behind my back.)

✔ **Agility Test:** This test measures your ability to shift your center of balance quickly. As usual, your center of balance appears as a red dot in the black-and-white grid. You have to shift your balance so that the red dot hits the blue boxes that appear on the grid. When you hit one box, more appears, until the timer finishes its countdown. After a few rounds, multiple boxes appear at once, and the boxes start moving.

The key to success here is control. Don't just flail your body around wildly — use small, controlled movements to hit those boxes. Be sure to bend your knees and move your lower body along with your upper body to get that fine control.

✔ **Walking Test:** This test measures your ability to distribute your weight equally as you walk in place. As the game instructs you, simply walk in place for twenty paces. Focus on keeping your back straight and centered over the middle of the Balance Board. Try not to favor one side over the other, but walk in an imaginary straight line. Be careful to place your feet on the textured areas of the Balance Board, or it may not work. The faster you walk, the better the results will be.

✔ **Single Leg Balance Test:** This test measures your ability to balance on one leg. Choose whichever leg you'd like and place it on the line in the middle of the Balance Board, with your toes facing toward the TV. Lift your other leg up and press the A button to start the test. Your side-to-side balance is shown as a line graph going up the screen. The blue borders on the edge of the graph get closer to the center as the timer counts down from thirty seconds — if your center of balance touches the blue area, it's game over. Try to last for the entire thirty seconds, but don't be afraid to put your foot out if you need to. No need to get hurt. It's very easy to cheat at this game by placing the other leg in front of you, but remember, the only person you're cheating is yourself!

If you do a body test more than once in a single day, you can override the initial results. It's not really useful for anything but bragging rights, but still, it is possible.

Wii Fit Age

After your Body Tests are complete, the game calculates a Wii Fit Age for you based on your results. This Age is an extremely unscientific measure of your body's age as it relates to your chronological age ("You have the body of a 20-year-old!"). Note that your Wii Fit Age has nothing to do with your BMI or weight and everything to do with your results of the body tests for that day. Your Wii Fit Age can vary from 2 to 99 day to day, depending how well you do on these tests.

After you get your Wii Fit Age for the day, you can put a stamp on an on-screen calendar to mark your progress. Point the Wii Remote at the date shown on the screen and press the A button to stamp down the stamper. As you continue playing, you unlock new stamps to stick on your calendar.

Setting a goal

It's a good idea to go into _Wii Fit_ knowing what you want to get out of it. To that end, the game asks you to set a weight-loss or weight-gain goal for yourself after your first body test. Use the up and down arrows to set a target weight and then click OK. You can hold down the A button to scroll quickly through the tenth-of-a-pound increments. A BMI of 22 is considered healthy, but remember: There are limits to what BMI can measure. Choose whatever you're comfortable with.

After you've set a target weight, give yourself a time limit to reach that weight. Use the on-screen arrows to choose between two weeks, one month, two months, three months, six months, or a year to reach your target.

It's generally considered unhealthy to lose more than two pounds a week, so be realistic in your expectations. Consult a doctor before going on any fitness regimen. Don't worry if you're not sure you can meet your goals — be optimistic. You can revise your goals later.

Using a password

If you're sensitive about other _Wii Fit_ users seeing your personal weight and weight-loss goal, you can protect them with a password. Click Yes and then use the on-screen keypad to enter a four-digit PIN, and then click OK. Re-enter the same PIN to lock your _Wii Fit_ data away from prying eyes. You need this PIN to access your data later, so make sure you pick one that you'll remember. (Your ATM PIN, perhaps?)

Navigating the Wii Fit Menus

After the initial personalization setup is done, you're free to explore the rest of _Wii Fit_ on your own. _Wii Fit_ is divided into three main areas: The Wii Fit Plaza, the Calendar screen, and the Training menu. The following sections explore all the various buttons and options available on these screens.

Wii Fit Plaza

When you start up _Wii Fit_ the first time, you have to go through the initial setup described earlier in this chapter. After that, you come straight to the Wii Fit Plaza screen, the starting point for your daily _Wii Fit_ training. After your registered Miis run in, you see the Wii Fit Plaza as shown in Figure 13-7. The various options on this screen are described in the following list:

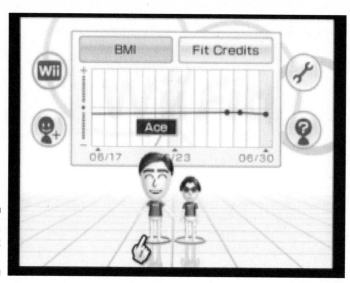

Figure 13-7:
The Wii Fit
Plaza.

✔ **Wii Menu:** Click the Wii icon to return to the Wii Menu. Remember, you can return to the Wii Menu at any time by clicking the Home button on the Wii Remote.

✔ **New Profile:** Click the face with a plus sign next to it to create a new user profile. The new user have to go through the entire setup process as described earlier in this chapter. After getting registered, the new Mii appears on the Wii Fit Plaza as a selectable profile.

✔ **Settings:** Click the wrench icon to bring up a submenu with the following configuration options:

• **Install Channel:** Installs a new Channel on your Wii Menu that lets you perform the basic Body Test without inserting the *Wii Fit* disc into the system. (See Chapter 10 for more on installing and using the Wii Fit Channel.)

• **Wii Balance Board Check:** Use this option to confirm that the Wii Balance Board is functioning properly. Lay the board flat on the ground and turn it on. Stand on the board when instructed by the game and the check commences. If all four sensors come up with check marks, your Balance Board is working properly. If the sensors aren't working properly, contact Nintendo at 1-800-255-3700 or www.nintendo.com/consumer.

• **Credits:** Click the *Wii Fit* logo in the lower-right corner of the screen to see a list of the people who helped make the game. Enjoy the pleasant music and the background exercise animation as you do. If you tire of reading, press the B button on the Wii Remote to go back to the Settings menu.

✔ **Trial:** Click the silhouette with a question mark on it to start up a trial version of the game that doesn't require the lengthy setup discussed earlier in this chapter. After choosing from a selection of five built-in, generic Miis, you can perform a basic Body Test (as described in "The Body Test" section) or choose from a selection of 12 training games (as described in the "Taking the Training Train" section). Note that weight and training data won't be saved in the Trial mode, so it's probably most useful for visiting friends or family who want to try out the game without going through all the bother of registering a new Mii. If you plan to play the game more than once, use the setup instructions described earlier in this chapter instead.

✔ **Graph:** This area displays the daily body mass index measurements for all the Miis currently registered with *Wii Fit.* Click the Fit Credits button to change to a daily bar graph view of how much time you've been putting into the game day after day. If you'd prefer to see data for only a single player, you can isolate that graph by hovering the Wii Remote over that player's Mii. Click anywhere on the graph and drag the Wii Remote pointer to view earlier dates.

✔ **Miis:** Click a Mii and then click Begin to advance to the Calendar screen, as discussed in the next section.

When left alone, the Miis on the Wii Fit Plaza screen show off some clever animations, doing basic calisthenics and looking back approvingly at the graph of their progress. If a specific Mii hasn't been weighed in for a few days, he or she may even fall asleep, complete with big cartoon Zs coming out of his or her mouth. Hover the Wii Remote pointer over a Mii to snap that little slacker out of the animation and back to attention.

Calendar screen

As shown in Figure 13-8, the Calendar screen is the first thing you see after registering a new Mii with *Wii Fit.* It's also the screen that comes up when you choose a Mii from the Wii Fit Plaza and the secondary gateway to daily training with *Wii Fit.* The various options on the Calendar screen are discussed in the following list:

✔ **Wii Fit Plaza:** Click the wavy arrow to go back to the Wii Fit Plaza.

✔ **Graph:** Click the button with a line graph on it to bring up a detailed chart of your daily progress. Use the buttons on the top row to toggle the graph's display between your BMI, daily weight measurement, Wii Fit Age, and Fit Credits. Hover over a dot on the graph with the Wii Remote pointer to view the specific value for that day.

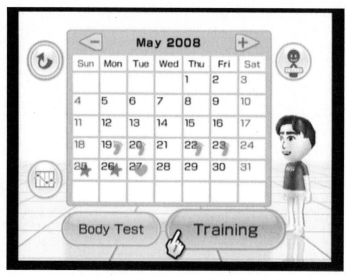

Figure 13-8:
The
Calendar
screen.

Use the + and – buttons in the lower-right corner to change the date range displayed on the graph (pressing the + and – buttons on the Wii Remote has the same effect). Note that the vertical range of the graph changes along with the horizontal time range. To scroll through the graph, click and drag the Wii Remote pointer anywhere on it. You can scroll further by letting go of A and grabbing again. Click the Back button to return to the Calendar screen.

✔ **User Settings:** Click the silhouette with the word balloon full of dots in the upper-right corner to bring up a submenu with the following configuration options:

• **Edit Profile:** Edit the height, date of birth, and password you set earlier. Click an option, and then use the on-screen arrows or keypad to edit it. Click OK when done or Back to back out.

• **Change Design:** Choose a new design for the stamp used to mark your daily progress on the Calendar screen. The more you play the game, the more stamps you unlock.

• **Change Trainer:** Toggle between the Male and Female trainers for the Yoga and Strength Training trials. (See the "General navigation" section, later in this chapter.)

• **Delete User Data:** Be careful! This option deletes all the stored data for your current Mii. If you choose Yes from the confirmation screen, all the evidence of your hard work and daily measurements will be gone, with no way to recover them.

- **Calendar:** The large calendar in the middle of the screen shows a stamp for every day you've checked in to *Wii Fit* with a Body Test. Click a day with a stamp to see the result of your BMI and Center of Balance tests for that day. Click the + and – buttons at the top of the calendar to scroll through the months (the + and – buttons on the Wii Remote have the same effect).

- **Body Test:** Perform the Body Test for the day, as described in "The Body Test" section, earlier in this chapter. You can perform more than one body test in a day, and replace the older results with the newer ones if you want. In general, though, you should only measure your progress once a day. Your weight tends to fluctuate throughout the day, so try to do your daily Body Test at the same time each day to keep the results consistent.

- **Training:** Open the Training menu to do some actual exercise, as described in the next section.

On the Calendar screen, click your Mii on the face, stomach, or feet to get a rather surprised reaction. Also, look closely for the Wii Balance Board running around in the background of the Calendar screen.

Training menu

After working your way through the Wii Fit Plaza and the Calendar screens, the Training menu is where you find the real meat of *Wii Fit*. I'm talking about the myriad training exercises designed to make you more flexible, stronger, and generally fitter. Initially, the Training menu looks as shown in Figure 13-9. The piggy bank on the left keeps track of how many Fit Credits you've earned through your training today — click on the bank to see the total number of Fit Credits you've earned throughout your training history. Click any of the training types to bring up a training submenu.

See that animated Balance Board running on a treadmill in the background of the training menu? Click it to unlock the super-secret Ultimate Balance Test. This brutally hard test is a lot like the regular balance test described in the earlier section, "The Body Test," but with much thinner blue bars. If you can pass all three of these challenges in sixty seconds, you're truly a balance master.

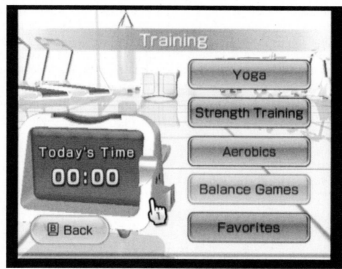

Figure 13-9: The Training main menu.

Taking the Training Train

While the Body Test is a nice, daily diversion, the training section is where you actually get fit with *Wii Fit*. Use the exercises and games described in the following sections regularly to burn calories and tone your muscles. Try to keep a balanced workout with tasks from all four menus for a well-rounded fitness regimen.

While some of the training exercises described in the following sections require the Wii Remote, most simply require you to stand on the Balance Board. You may want to put the Remote in a pocket or lay it on a nearby table when performing these exercises.

General navigation

From the Training menu (refer to Figure 13-9), click any of the options on the right-hand side to bring up the applicable training submenu. An example for the Yoga poses submenu is shown in Figure 13-10.

Initially, many of the exercises on these submenus are grayed out, but you can unlock them simply by playing more and earning more *Wii Fit* credits. Hover over an icon that's not grayed out to see the name of the exercise and how many times it's been attempted.

When viewing a training submenu, you can click the + and − arrows at the top of the screen to go directly to the other training submenus (the + and − buttons on the Wii Remote have the same effect). Click the Back button in the lower-left corner or press the B button on the Wii Remote to go back to the main Training menu. You can also use the Change Trainer button to toggle between the male and female trainers. In addition to the standard training types, the Favorites area is an easy place to access your top ten most-played training exercises.

Figure 13-10:
The Yoga
Poses
menu.

Click a pose or exercise icon to bring up an exercise description screen, much like the one seen in Figure 13-11.

Figure 13-11:
An exercise-
description
screen.

After attempting some workouts a few times, you can unlock more reps or harder difficulties. If you've done this, you can alter the difficulty or number of reps from the description screen by clicking the + and – buttons as seen in Figure 13-11 (the + and – buttons on the Wii Remote have the same effect).

For Yoga and Strength Training exercises, click Demo to watch a three-dimensional trainer demonstrate and explain how to do the chosen exercise (if you haven't done the exercise yet, this demo runs automatically before starting the exercise). Click the Skip button at any time during the demo to jump to the end, where you can view the trainer. From this screen, you can rotate around the trainer by clicking and moving the Wii Remote pointer around the screen. Use the 1 and 2 buttons to zoom in and out, respectively. Click the Pause button on the screen to stop the trainer's movement and study a pose, or click Restart to have the demonstration explained to you again. When you're confident you understand the moves required, click Start Workout to try it for yourself. While you're actually performing the exercise, press up or down on the directional pad on the Wii Remote to toggle the camera angle between front and back angles.

At any time during training, you can push the + button on the Wii Remote to bring up the pause menu. This menu lets you restart the exercise or quit back to the training menu. Note that if you quit, you won't get any Fit Credits for the current exercise.

Yoga

Yoga exercises are all about balance, both physical and mental. While many of them require strength and flexibility to perform, the emphasis is on stability and calm. It's all about holding poses, not speed or agility. Yoga exercises are great for stretching and strengthening your muscles and can be very relaxing. The yoga exercises in *Wii Fit* are generally less intense than those found in the other sections, and are a good starting point for a daily workout.

During most of the yoga exercises, your center of balance is shown as a red dot in a small square on the right side of the screen. Try to keep your center of balance in the yellow area as you do each pose, but don't focus so much on your balance that you mess up the form. Remember, you're only competing with yourself. That said, the better your balance, the more points and stars you get.

The in-game demonstrations do a pretty good job explaining each yoga exercise, but the following list gives you some tips and more information about each:

✔ **Deep Breathing:** By far the easiest exercise in the game, this pose requires you to stand still and breathe deeply. Really, that's it. Good for a basic warm-up, but not really a great workout.

✔ **Half-Moon:** Raise your arms above you as you bend to your side. You can really feel how this exercise stretches the muscles going up and down your hips and torso.

✔ **Warrior:** This pose requires taking one foot off the Balance Board and placing it well behind you, so make sure you have a lot of space around your play area. Keep your front knee bent and make sure to keep enough weight on the foot that remains on the Balance Board. If you're finding it hard to keep your balance steady in the blue area on screen, try changing your stance by putting your back foot farther back. This pose is great for strengthening your hips and thighs, as well as for improving balance.

✔ **Tree:** Place the base of your foot on your inner thigh as you stretch your hands high above your head, like a tree. If you're having trouble keeping your balance on one foot, try placing your other foot lower on the leg you're standing on (just don't put too much pressure on your knee). This pose strengthens your legs and back.

✔ **Sun Salutation:** A bit trickier than the others, this pose involves repeatedly holding your arms back above your head, and then bending down and touching your toes. Follow the on-screen trainer and you should be fine. This pose tones your arms and thighs.

✔ **Standing Knee:** While standing on one leg, raise one knee in front of you, wrap both arms around it, and then pull it in and out of your chest rhythmically. Helps your thighs become more flexible.

✔ **Palm Tree:** Stand on your toes and throw your arms behind you while arching your back forward. If you're having trouble balancing, lower your heels and inch forward on the Balance Board. Strengthens your ankles and back.

✔ **Chair:** Bend your knees at a 30-degree angle and stick your hands in front of you, like the armrests on a chair. A good all-body workout that strengthens your back, legs, and abs.

✔ **Triangle:** This one's a bit tricky to figure out mechanically, but well worth it. First, take one leg off the Balance Board and put it behind you, with the foot turned parallel to the board. Then twist your body to bring the opposite hand down to grab the ankle that's still on the Balance board. Point your free arm toward the ceiling and look up toward the tips of your fingers. Don't overdo it — this pose should be uncomfortable but not painful. A great way to tone your lower body and waist.

✔ **Downward-facing Dog:** Get on your hands and knees in a doggy-style position, with your hands on the Balance Board, and then straighten out your legs and arms to form a triangle with the ground. Good for your back and whole-body strength.

✔ **Dance:** A very tough pose to balance, this one involves standing on one leg and pulling the other leg up and behind you with one hand, while reaching the other hand and arm straight in front of you for counterbalance. Take it slow and don't pull your leg any farther than it can go. A great way to tone your hips and align your spine.

The remaining yoga poses in this section do NOT require the use of the Balance Board, so you're on your honor to follow the on-screen trainer. Using a soft surface such as a rug or a yoga mat helps make these poses more comfortable, especially if you have hard, noncarpeted floors.

✔ **Cobra:** Lie face down on the floor and push your upper body up with your arms. Hold the pose and breathe naturally. Strengthens your back and helps improve your posture.

✔ **Bridge:** Another pose that doesn't require the Balance Board. Lie face up with your feet flat and your knees bent, and then put your arms to your side and press your hips upward. Great for your torso and hips.

✔ **Spinal Twist:** While lying flat on the ground, grab your knee with one hand and twist it across your body. Stretches your lower back and helps align your pelvis.

✔ **Shoulder Stand:** Another tricky one, you can do this if you take your time and do each step. Lie flat on the ground and bend your back to place your legs on the floor above your head. Grab your back with your hands, placing your elbows on the floor for support. Straighten your back and stick your legs as high in the air as possible. Strengthens your abs and back.

Strength Training

The exercises in the Strength Training menu help tone your muscles and increase your endurance. For an added challenge, grab some ankle and wrist weights to make your muscles work that much harder. Follow the whistle and try to go in time with the on-screen trainer. Remember, it's more important to focus on the correct form than your balance on the board.

The Strength Training exercises are as follows:

✔ **Single-Leg Extension:** Stand on one leg while raising the knee of the other leg in front of you. Kick your leg back and thrust the opposite arm forward for balance, and then come back to the original pose. Repeat this motion for the set number of reps. Be careful to move your leg and arm at the same time and speed.

✔ **Push-Up and Side Plank:** For this exercise, place both hands on the Balance Board and extend your legs behind you in a push-up pose. After doing a basic push-up, cross one leg over the other and twist your body to the side, lifting one arm straight overhead as you do. If you're having trouble keeping your balance or supporting yourself during this exercise, keep your knees on the floor instead of extending your legs all the way out.

✔ **Torso Twists:** Stretch your arms out to your sides and twist in place, turning 90 degrees in each direction. Then twist diagonally by turning while simultaneously leaning forward. Focus on keeping in time with the on-screen trainer.

✔ **Jackknife:** Note that you should not sit on the Balance Board for this exercise. Instead, lie down on the floor with your knees bent and your heels resting lightly on the Balance Board. Then, with your arms stretched above you, clench your ab muscles to raise your legs off the ground and your arms toward your toes. Make sure to touch your heels to the Balance Board in between each rep. Use the whistle sounds coming from your speakers to keep time, as it can be hard to see the screen while you're lying on the floor.

✔ **Lunge:** Take one foot off the Balance Board and put it behind you for this exercise. With your hands clasped behind your head, lower your back knee so it almost touches the ground, and then raise up to your original position. Keeping your abs tight is the key to succeeding at this exercise.

✔ **Rowing Squat:** Stand with your arms in fists directly in front of you, and then pull your elbows in and behind you as you bend your knees approximately 30 degrees. Focus on moving in a smooth, fluid motion and keeping your upper body as straight as possible.

✔ **Single-Leg Twist:** Standing on one leg, stick the other leg out to the side, putting the opposite arm up at the same time to maintain your balance. Then raise the knee of your free leg, and bring your arm down in a chopping motion to meet it. Focus on moving your leg and arm at the same time and speed; the idea is to keep your balance steady.

✔ **Sideways Leg Lift:** Lean to one side, raising one leg slightly off the ground. Kick that leg up to the side while raising the opposite arm simultaneously for balance. Take it slow to start, and then kick your leg out more dramatically as you go. Make sure you're moving both your arm and leg at the same time and speed.

✔ **Plank:** Place your forearms on the Balance Board for this exercise, extending your legs back in a push-up style pose. Then raise your butt in the air and hold the position as steady as you can for thirty seconds. Focus on keeping your abs clenched and your form tight.

The next three exercises in this section do not use the Wii Balance Board, but instead use a Wii Remote held in your hand to detect your motion and form. Trying to use the Balance Board for these exercises can result in slipping and injury. Move the Balance Board to the side and use a yoga mat or rug for better support.

- ✔ **Tricep Extension:** Hold the Wii Remote in one hand and extend it toward the ceiling. Grab the elbow of your outstretched arm with your other hand and bend the arm with the Remote down to your shoulder, and then back up. Focus on keeping your arm as vertical as possible and really stretching those tricep muscles. Switch the hand holding the Wii Remote in the middle of the exercise and press the A button to continue.

- ✔ **Arm and Leg Lift:** Holding the Wii Remote in one palm, get down on all fours in a doggy-style position. At the same time, raise the arm with the Remote and the opposite leg so they're parallel to the ground. Keep the Remote as flat and stable as possible until you hear the whistle. Switch the hand holding the Remote in the middle of this exercise and press the A button to continue.

- ✔ **Single-Arm Stand:** Lie down on the ground and stick the arm holding the Wii Remote straight up toward the ceiling. Use your other arm to pick yourself up into a standing position. Focus on performing this exercise in one clean, fluid motion. Remember to keep the Remote as vertical as possible through the entire exercise to get a good score.

- ✔ **Challenges:** Instead of following the trainer, these three challenges ask you to compete with the trainer to see who can do more of the indicated exercise. The number of reps increases each time you're able to beat the trainer.

Aerobics

Great for burning fat and working up a sweat, aerobic exercise is what many people think of when they think of a traditional workout. The games in this section raise your heart rate and make your body a lean, mean, fat-burning machine:

- ✔ **Hula Hoop:** Shake your hips in a circular motion as quickly as possible to keep the on-screen Hula Hoop spinning around your Mii's waist. The only catch is, er, catching the Hula Hoops thrown by the Miis in the background. I find the best strategy is to stop spinning and lean my entire body to the appropriate side as soon as a Hula Hoop is thrown. Raising your arms above your head can help the Wii detect that you're actually leaning instead of hulaing. The more Hula Hoops you catch, the more rotations you earn for every shake of your hips.

- ✔ **Super Hula Hoop:** Earn a three-star ranking in the Hula Hoop game to unlock this more intense version. It plays just like a longer version of the original game, only you have to change between clockwise and counter-clockwise rotation halfway through.

- ✔ **Basic Step:** Step on to and off of the Balance Board in time with the music and the on-screen instructions. Note that the directions with blue feet mean you should step off the Balance Board to the side, rather than backwards. If you find the step notation confusing, try watching the Miis in the background and mimicking their moves. Timing your steps with the beat of the music is key to getting a good ranking.

✔ **Advanced Step:** Much faster than the basic step, this more difficult program also introduces two new steps — one that requires you to kick your leg in front of you and another that asks you to turn sideways before stepping on the Balance Board. Again, watch the Miis in the background if you get confused, and work hard to stay in time with the music.

✔ **Free Step:** Rather than following specific instructions, this exercise asks you to repetitively step on and off the Balance Board for the set period of time. You don't even have to watch the screen during this time — you can switch the TV input over to your favorite program while you step on and off in rhythm. The Wii Remote speaker makes sure you stay at the right rhythm. The Remote keeps you up to date on the time remaining, and updates your number of steps periodically as well.

   You can press up and down on the Wii Remote's directional pads to change the tempo of the stepping. You can also press the A button to change the sound of the rhythmic tones on the Wii Remote, or get rid of them entirely.

✔ **Basic Run:** This exercise doesn't use the Balance Board, instead using the Wii Remote to detect your movement. Simply hold the Remote in your hand or place it in a pocket as you run in place. As you bounce up and down, your on-screen Mii runs through an elaborate island setting. Try to keep an even pace with the Mii running just ahead of you on the screen.

✔ **2-P Run:** This exercise is identical to the Basic Run, only now you can use two Remotes to have two Miis running at the same time. Note that this is the only two-player game in all of *Wii Fit*.

✔ **Free Run:** Run in place again, this time using the Wii Remote's speaker as a guide as you watch your favorite TV show. The Wii Remote tells you if you're going too fast or too slowly.

✔ **Rhythm Boxing:** Use the Balance Board, the Wii Remote, and the Nunchuk in this complicated game. First watch and listen as the Mii trainer shows off a basic pattern of steps and punches with the Remote/Nunchuk. You may also have to dodge to one side or the other by tilting the Wii Remote and Nunchuk in that direction. When the game tells you to, repeat the pattern in the same order and timing as the trainer just did. Perfectly timed punches are worth two points, while steps and badly timed punches are worth just one.

Balance Games

While everyone knows that exercise is good for you, it can be hard to keep up with an exercise regimen that involves the same boring, repetitive steps over and over again. These games try to alleviate this problem by working the exercise into skill-based games that use your entire body as the controller. The games might be a little simple, but they're a heck of a lot more interesting than riding an exercise bike for an hour!

✔ **Soccer Heading:** Lean left and right to head the soccer balls flying at you. Avoid the occasional flying cleats and panda-bear heads (which look remarkably and infuriatingly like the soccer balls). Note that you don't have to thrust your head forward the way the Mii on-screen does — just lean left and right to position the Mii. Hitting multiple balls in a row without a miss (or a bonk from an obstacle) activates a combo multiplier to your score.

Focus on leaning slightly and moving into position as soon as the ball or obstacle is kicked. If you want to cheat a bit, lift one leg to immediately make the Mii jump to the opposite side.

✔ **Ski Slalom:** Lean left and right to guide your skier through the slalom gates. Note that you can also lean forward and backward to control your speed. While a higher speed obviously gets your through the course faster, you might want to hang back on your heels for some of the tighter turns.

Each missed gate is worth a penalty of seven seconds, so really focus on making it in between those gates. As a rule, don't lean too far to either side; it slows you down and makes it harder to change directions quickly.

✔ **Ski Jump:** To start, bend your knees and lean forward, *slightly* like the on-screen Mii. Look in the upper-right corner of the screen and try to keep the red dot representing your center of balance in the blue dot (indicating the perfect aerodynamic pose).

When the on-screen Mii gets to the red jump area, unbend your knees and stand up straight and centered as quickly as possible. Don't actually jump off the board — the game gets mad and yells at you if you do. Don't wait too long either, or you'll fall off the ramp. When your Mii is airborne, stay as still and centered as possible to extend your hangtime. The total distance of your two combined jumps is your final score.

✔ **Table Tilt:** Lean forward, backward, and side to side to tilt a floating table and guide the balls toward the holes. Be careful to keep the balls on the table — if a ball falls off, the table spins around and a few precious seconds tick away before that ball is dropped back on the playing field. Pay attention to the hills and grooves on each table and adjust your leaning accordingly. Don't be afraid to go up on your toes or back on your heels for that final little push to the hole.

✔ **Tightrope Walk:** A rather difficult-to-control game. Walk in place to make the on-screen Mii advance forward on the tightrope. Your Mii leans left and right depending on your center of balance. If the Mii starts leaning too far to one side, you have to lean hard to the other side to center him or her again before continuing your advance. To jump over the advancing metal munchers, first make sure your Mii is centered, and then bend and quickly extend your legs to jump over it.

Don't actually jump off the board or the game stops and yells at you.

- **Balance Bubble:** Lean forward, backward, and side to side to control a Mii suspended in a floating bubble as it floats down a river. Avoid touching the buzzing bees or the edges of the riverbank as you try to make it to the delta as quickly as possible.

- **Penguin Slide:** Lean left and right to control the iceberg underneath the sliding penguin. Aim for the fish that jump up from the water underneath you. The bouncing green fish are worth two points each; the rare red fish that hover over the edges are worth ten — you have to change your center of balance quickly to flick the iceberg and grab them. Be careful not to let the penguin fall off the edge of the iceberg; it takes a few precious seconds for him to climb back out again.

- **Snowboard Slalom:** Turn the Balance Board 90 degrees clockwise for this game. The controls and goals are similar to the skiing slalom mentioned earlier, except now everything is turned to the side. Most players find this game more difficult to control than skiing, but with some practice it does get easier.

- **Lotus Focus:** By far the oddest game on the *Wii Fit* disc. Sit as still as possible in a cross-legged position on the Balance Board as you watch the flickering flame. Don't get distracted by the fly that flies by after a few seconds — just continue to hold your position, breathing gently and maintaining focus on the flame. If you move too much, the candle goes out and the game ends abruptly. Weird.

Chapter 14

Recommended Wii Games

With over two hundred titles on store shelves as of this writing, and more coming out every week, there's a Wii game for practically every taste. Unless you're independently wealthy, though, you probably can't afford to purchase every one of them to figure out which ones are good. Somehow, you're going to have to decide on just a few of those games for your personal library.

Chapter 11 has some general recommendations for picking out games, but let's face it — sorting through all the reviews and information on a game can be a lot of work. Sometimes you just want a friend to recommend a few games that he or she thinks you'll like.

Well, consider me that friend, and consider this chapter a big box of those friendly recommendations. Each of the fifteen games detailed here comes personally approved as one of the best currently available for the Wii. These recommendations are broken down into categories so you have a handy gaming pick for a variety of situations.

One more word of warning: Just because I like a game doesn't mean you'll necessarily share my tastes. Be sure to read the descriptions for the game to figure out if it sounds like it will be up your alley. Wiley Publishing and its partners are not responsible if your tastes do not match the tastes of the author. No liability is implied or expressed. All rights reserved. Void where prohibited.

Five Games for the Non-Gamer

Nintendo has had great success in marketing the Wii to people who don't usually consider themselves gamers. Sure, these new Wii owners might play the occasional game of computer solitaire, or a quick game of *Bejeweled* on their cell phones, but before the Wii, they weren't generally the type to spend hundreds of dollars on a game console. These players are looking for simple games with intuitive controls and designs that don't require a lot of previous gaming experience from the get-go. The games listed in the following sections are for them.

Wii Sports and *Wii Fit* are also great games for the non-gamer. They're discussed in much more detail in Chapters 12 and 13, respectively.

How to get a non-gamer into the Wii

After you've been up-and-running with your Wii for a little while, you've probably told all your friends how much fun it is and how much you're enjoying your purchase (and how helpful this book as been in that regard . . . hint, hint!). But maybe you have one recalcitrant friend who just refuses to believe in the appeal of the Wii. This friend is adamant — never played a video game before, isn't about to start now, yada, yada, no matter how revolutionary or amazing you say it is.

I find that the best way to win these stubborn people over is to just put a Wii Remote in their hands. Really. When skeptics see how simple and natural it is to convert their real-world motions into on-screen actions with the Wii, they'll more than likely be hooked. *Wii Sports* is probably the best game for this initial demonstration, as it doesn't require much explanation to get a new player started ("Swing the Remote like a tennis racquet," usually suffices).

If your stubborn friend won't even deign to pick up the controller, you may have more luck

just getting him or her to watch. So invite your favorite wet blanket over to the house (see the "Planning a Wii party" sidebar), and offer him or her a seat on the couch, with a view of you and your less-wary friends enjoying the system. Be sure to put some energy into your play, and make it apparent by your face and your actions how much fun you're having. Don't be pushy — chances are your friend will ask to join in after a while. Again, when the controller's in that ex-non-gamer's hand, you're probably good to go.

Of course, if your friend won't even agree to come and watch the Wii, there's not much you can do short of the old tie"em-up-and-drag-'em-to-your-entertainment-center approach. Of course, I would never endorse such a rash action. Let me be clear, you definitely should *not* tie up your video-game-hating friends, throw them in your trunk, drive them to your house, and hold them captive until they agree to try the Wii. That is definitely something you should *not* do. Are we clear? Good.

MySims

Developer: Electronic Arts Redwood
Publisher: Electronic Arts
Release Date: Sept. 18, 2008
Number of Players: 1
ESRB Rating: E — Comic Mischief, Mild Cartoon Violence

MySims, shown in Figure 14-1, falls into the simulation genre. Use the following list to decide if *MySims* is a game you'll enjoy:

Figure 14-1:
A screen-shot from EA's *MySims.*

- ✔ **The game in a nutshell:** A super-cute dollhouse for your Wii.

- ✔ **Gameplay description:** On the PC, the original *Sims* proved a game could be a success without the casual violence and non-stop action that characterize most video games. This "game" didn't even have a goal per se, letting players build a virtual house and manipulate the family inside it however they wanted. This simple concept led the series to become one of the most popular in all of gaming, with over 100 million copies sold across the franchise so far.

  MySims takes these basic *Sims* ideals and makes them slightly more Wii-friendly. Instead of controlling a tight-knit family unit, you create and control a new citizen in a dilapidated town full of cute, super-deformed characters that resemble nothing so much as Playskool toys. You and your avatar are quickly tasked with restoring the run-down town to its former glory by redesigning buildings, repairing bridges, and the like. To do this, you need to gather magical, emotional "essences" that get dropped when you perform everyday activities such as gardening, fishing, or simply splashing around in a fountain. The endearing character designs are so full of life that it's easy to get sucked in for hours, doing nothing more substantial than just running around and interacting with the various townspeople.

✔ **You'll like it if:** You loved playing with dolls/action figures but were never too crazy about cleaning them up.

✔ **You won't like it if:** You have a strong allergic reaction to cute things.

✔ **My favorite in-game moment:** Socking a virtual hotel bellhop in the nose and watching the huge, cartoony, dust-cloud brawl that ensues. Why? Just because!

Endless Ocean

Developer: Arika
Publisher: Nintendo
Release Date: Jan. 21, 2008
Number of Players: 1
ESRB Rating: E

Endless Ocean, shown in Figure 14-2, falls into the simulation genre. Use the following list to decide if *Endless Ocean* is a game you'll enjoy:

Figure 14-2:
A screenshot from Nintendo's *Endless Ocean.*

- ✔ **The game in a nutshell:** A relaxing, interactive aquarium.

- ✔ **Gameplay description:** What better way to explore the unspoiled beauty of the sea than scuba diving? Of course, before you dive into the ocean in real life, you have to drive to the beach, rent some bulky, expensive scuba equipment, sign up for lessons, get your diving certification, pick a dive spot, rent a boat . . . it's all a real hassle. For those who don't want to go to all that trouble, there's *Endless Ocean*.

  As the newest marine biologist with the Manoa Lai Oceanic Research Society, your "job" (if you can call such a relaxing task a job) is to explore the ocean and identify the wide variety of sea life swimming around down there. The game occasionally gives you specific objectives to complete, such as guiding a tourist or looking for a specific fish, but for the most part it's just you and the open water. The slow pace and soothing underwater scenes make it easy to just swim around aimlessly and feel the stress melt away. Ahhhh.

- ✔ **You'll like it if:** You enjoy relaxing underwater scenes.

- ✔ **You won't like it if:** You're looking for an action-packed thrill-fest.

- ✔ **My favorite in-game moment:** Swimming over a ridge and seeing a huge underwater valley, teeming with life, open up before me.

Cooking Mama: Cook Off

Developer: Office Create
Publisher: Majesco
Release Date: March 20, 2007
Number of Players: 1-2 (simultaneous)
ESRB Rating: E — Alcohol Reference

Cooking Mama: Cook Off, shown in Figure 14-3, falls into the simulation genre. Use the following list to decide if *Cooking Mama: Cook Off* is a game you'll enjoy:

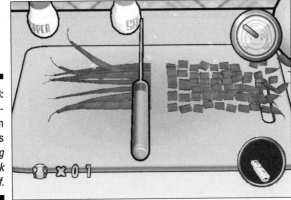

Figure 14-3: A screenshot from Majesco's *Cooking Mama: Cook Off.*

✔ **The game in a nutshell:** All the fun of cooking with none of the mess.

✔ **Gameplay description:** Of all the exciting, real-world items you can emulate with the Wii Remote — golf clubs, bow and arrows, steel swords, and so on — you wouldn't think that "chef's knife" would rank very high on the list. You'd be wrong, though, as *Cooking Mama* proves that even a mundane, everyday task such as preparing a meal can be made more engaging with the Wii.

Cooking Mama walks you through the preparation of gourmet meals, using simple Wii Remote motions to chop onions, peel potatoes, mince meat, drizzle sauce, stir ingredients, and much more. You're judged on your timing and speed by Mama, a cartoon cooking expert whose exacting standards keep you on your toes as the meals get more and more elaborate. The quest for the perfect meal keeps you happily shaking the Wii Remote until you collect every last cooking medal. Heck, it might even make you want to go into the kitchen and make a real meal!

✔ **You'll like it if:** You're a demon in the kitchen, or wish you were.

✔ **You won't like it if:** Most of your food comes from the microwave, and you're fine with that.

✔ **My favorite in-game moment:** Hearing Mama judge my recipe as "Wonderful! Better than Mama!" in her endearing, faux-French accent.

Big Brain Academy: Wii Degree

Developer: Nintendo
Publisher: Nintendo
Release Date: June 11, 2007
Number of Players: 1-2 (simultaneous)
ESRB Rating: E

Big Brain Academy: Wii Degree, shown in Figure 14-4, falls into the puzzle genre. Use the following list to decide if *Big Brain Academy: Wii Degree* is a game you'll enjoy:

Figure 14-4:
A screen-
shot from
Nintendo's
*Big Brain
Academy:
Wii Degree.*

✔ **The game in a nutshell:** Learning gets competitive.

✔ **Gameplay description:** The large majority of games are designed as an escape — a mindless respite from the mental toil of school or work. And then there's *Big Brain Academy,* a game designed specifically to tax your brain in interesting ways.

Big Brain Academy is, at its core, a collection of 20 or so mini-games, each centered on a basic mental task. One minute, you're looking for differences in two similar pictures, the next, you're counting colored balls as they quickly fall into a basket or memorizing and repeating a complicated series of musical notes. On their own, these games aren't especially compelling, but when combined together, the game transforms into a high-intensity bout of mental gymnastics, requiring quick switching between many different skills to succeed.

In the end, the game rates your mental prowess using a unique (if highly unscientific) ranking system that estimates your brain's weight and judges your competence in areas such as memorization and analysis. While self-betterment is all well and good, it's even more fun to compete with friends in alternating or split-screen duels. The game even automatically adjusts the difficulty level as you go, ensuring that everyone can compete together fairly.

✔ **You'll like it if:** You like a little mental exercise mixed in with your entertainment.

✔ **You won't like it if:** You play games specifically so you can turn your brain off.

✔ **My favorite in-game moment:** Proving once and for all that I'm smarter than my wife . . . at least when it comes to the tests in this game.

Bust-a-Move Bash!

Developer: Happy Happening
Publisher: Majesco
Release Date: April 17, 2007
Number of Players: 1-8 (simultaneous)
ESRB Rating: E

Bust-a-Move Bash!, shown in Figure 14-5, falls into the puzzle genre. Use the following list to decide if *Bust-a-Move Bash!* is a game you'll enjoy:

Figure 14-5:
A screen-
shot from
Majesco's
*Bust-a-
Move Bash!*

✔ **The game in a nutshell:** Follow the colored, bouncing balls.

✔ **Gameplay description:** At first glance, *Bust-a-Move Bash!* seems ridiculously simple: Just fire the colored balls from the bottom of the screen toward the same colored balls at the top of the screen to clear them away. This initial simplicity makes the game incredibly easy to pick up and play for anyone who isn't color blind. But as the game speeds up and the balls on the ceiling begin encroaching closer and closer to the floor, it takes quick reflexes and a steady hand to stay on top of things.

Bust-a-Move Bash! is the kind of game you think you'll play for five minutes, but when you look at the clock, you realize you've been blissfully bursting bubbles for five hours without noticing the time pass. A complex puzzle mode with 500 unique challenges and a multiplayer bash that supports up to eight players (each holding one-half of a Remote/Nunchuk pairing) help extend the experience past the relatively basic bubble-bursting main game.

✔ **You'll like it if:** You like games that are easy to pick up but hard to put down.

✔ **You won't like it if:** You like your games to have endearing characters and storylines.

✔ **My favorite in-game moment:** Causing a screen-clearing cascade of explosions with a single shot.

Five Games for a Party

Look at the face of your Wii Remote. See the four lights across the bottom? Those lights are the Wii's way of reminding you that you can play many Wii games with up to four people at a time. If you're only using that left-most light for one-player games, you're not really getting the most out of your Wii.

Sure, the Wii itself can be your play partner when there's no one else around to play with, and plenty of games let you play against friends and strangers on the Internet. But some of the most fun you can have with a Wii involves getting four people in the same room, laughing and flailing around as they all try to control the on-screen action. The following sections discuss some of the best games for creating that party atmosphere.

The five games listed in the following sections are just the tip of the iceberg when it comes to multiplayer gaming on the Wii. Check the "Number of players" description on the game boxes (or game reviews) to find more multiplayer games.

Some multiplayer games require more than one Remote for simultaneous play, while others allow you to hand off the Remote in between rounds for alternating multiplayer fun. Be sure you know which type of multiplayer experience you're getting before you purchase a game (check out Chapter 11 for help picking out games). Also be sure that you have the correct type and number of controllers before you get started. There's nothing more embarrassing than inviting your friends over for a night of Wii fun and then finding they can't all play because you don't have enough Wii Remotes, Nunchuks, or other accessories.

In addition to the following games, *Wii Sports* (which came with your system) is also a great game to play at a Wii party. (See Chapter 12 for more on enjoying that game with a group of your closest friends.)

Rock Band

Developer: Harmonix
Publisher: Electronic Arts
Release Date: June 22, 2008
Number of Players: 1-4 (simultaneous)
ESRB Rating: T — Lyrics, Mild Suggestive Themes

Rock Band, shown in Figure 14-6, falls into the simulation genre. Use the following list to decide if *Rock Band* is a game you'll enjoy:

Figure 14-6:
A screen-shot from Electronic Arts' *Rock Band.*

- ✔ **The game in a nutshell:** 'Cause we all just want to be big rock stars.

- ✔ **Gameplay description:** While the Wii Remote has a wide variety of uses, it just isn't quite versatile enough to accurately simulate the workings of an entire rock quartet on its own. That's why Harmonix decided to package *Rock Band* with a simplified plastic guitar, a microphone, and a full-size drum kit that connect to the Wii wirelessly. These extra controllers let you play along with simple, scrolling on-screen instructions that tell you when to bang the drum, where to grip the neck of the guitar, and what note to sing on the microphone (the game even detects and judges your rhythm and pitch as you go). Your performance on these plastic faux instruments actually controls the music coming out of the TV speakers; the better you play, the better it all sounds, just like a real rock band!

Four adjustable difficulty levels means everyone from rock neophytes to rock superstars can play together, and with 63 songs from the past four decades included on the disc, all are bound to find something they like (if they don't, an optional track-pack disc can add 20 more songs to the mix). The only potential downside is the package's high price — $170 as of this writing (add on another $50 if you want a second guitar for a bass player). If you can't swing it on your own, recruit some friends to chip in. Tell them it's an investment in regular *Rock Band* parties. They'll be glad they did when they find themselves coming over to rock and roll all night and party ev-er-y day.

Note: As of this writing, *Rock Band 2* is in development for the Wii.

✔ **You'll like it if:** You want to be a rock superstar.

✔ **You won't like it if:** You're tone deaf and have no rhythm. (Actually, the game might help with these problems.)

✔ **My favorite in-game moment:** Having everyone in the band come together to hit that final note with perfect timing.

Planning a Wii party

What better way to celebrate your shiny new game console than getting a few dozen of your closest friends together for some Wii-themed revelry? Here are some tips for making sure your Wii-themed bash goes off without a hitch:

✔ **Clear out lots of space:** Wii players tend to move around the room as they play, sometimes more than they actually have to. Move the coffee table to the side and move anything breakable to another room before the guests come over. Also be sure to set up plenty of seating for spectators on the periphery of the room.

✔ **Prepare some snacks:** Remember, players can eat with one hand while grasping a Wii Remote with the other. Just be sure to keep plenty of napkins handy to keep the Remotes from getting too greasy.

✔ **Set up a tournament:** Nothing gets the competitive juices flowing like a tournament, complete with a giant bracket/scoring sheet set up on the wall. Start off with *Wii Sports* to get everyone warmed up, and then mix it

up with an assortment of games that test a variety of skills (see the list of games in the "Five Games for a Party" section).

✔ **Make sure everyone plays:** No one wants to be a wallflower, so encourage everyone to try out the system at least once. Set up a system to rotate players off the system after a set number of attempts. Pair newcomers against each other so they won't be scared off by that one guy who's already an expert at every video game ever made. (You know the one I'm talking about. Yeah . . . that one.)

✔ **Wii drinking games:** For attendees over 21, a little lubrication is a great way to loosen players up and make the Wii-inspired flailing even funnier. Have players take a drink every time they win a game, or every time they win a point. If you do break out the alcohol, be sure to have a "designated gamer" (as well as a designated driver) who can be on wrist-strap watch. Having a tipsy friend break your TV is no fun.

WarioWare: Smooth Moves

Developer: Nintendo
Publisher: Nintendo
Release Date: Jan. 15, 2007
Number of Players: 1-12 (alternating)
ESRB Rating: E10+ — Crude Humor, Mild Cartoon Violence

WarioWare: Smooth Moves, shown in Figure 14-7, falls into the puzzle genre. Use the following list to decide if *WarioWare: Smooth Moves* is a game you'll enjoy:

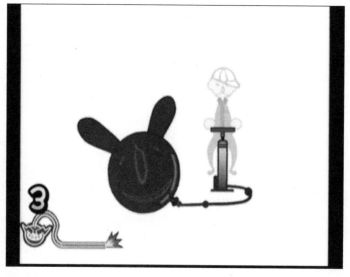

Figure 14-7:
A screen-shot from Nintendo's *WarioWare: Smooth Moves.*

✔ **The game in a nutshell:** ADHD: The game.

✔ **Gameplay description:** Many video games are actually just collections of smaller mini-games — simple, five-minute tasks that aren't quite deep enough to sustain an entire game on their own. *WarioWare: Smooth Moves* takes this trend to a logical extreme, splitting itself into hundreds and hundreds of micro-games that give the player a simple, one-word instruction and five seconds to perform it using the Wii Remote.

The frenetic pace and surreal micro-game design forces you to adjust your strategies — and your grip on the Wii Remote — constantly in preparation for the next challenge. One moment you're inserting dentures into a grand-mother's mouth, the next you're shaking your hips to rotate an on-screen Hula Hoop, the moment after that you're using the Remote as a virtual fire hose.

You can take on these myriad challenges alone, but the game really comes together when you get a group of up to eleven friends together, handing off the controller frantically between micro-games. The game does require some quick reactions, so players who aren't familiar with video game standards might be at a disadvantage. They should still have a great time, though, as long as they don't mind making fools of themselves in front of friends.

✔ **You'll like it if:** You get bored easily.

✔ **You won't like it if:** You want a game that stays on one subject for more than five seconds at a time.

✔ **My favorite in-game moment:** Watching friends put the Wii Remote up to their noses to imitate an elephant, and taking pictures of same.

Super Monkey Ball: Banana Blitz

Developer: Totally Games
Publisher: Sega
Release Date: Nov. 14, 2006
Number of Players: 1-4
ESRB Rating: E — Cartoon Violence

Super Monkey Ball: Banana Blitz, shown in Figure 14-8, falls into the puzzle/ party genre. Use the following list to decide if *Super Monkey Ball: Banana Blitz* is a game you'll enjoy:

Figure 14-8: A screenshot from Sega's *Super Monkey Ball: Banana Blitz.*

✓ **The game in a nutshell:** Every mini-game you could possibly think of . . . and then some!

✓ **Gameplay description:** If you remember the wooden tabletop game labyrinth, then you pretty much know what to expect from *Super Monkey Ball's* single-player mode. You tilt the Remote to tilt the playfield, guiding the titular ball-encased monkeys through wacky obstacles and toward the goal. It's a fine game on its own, but the single-player mode isn't nearly as important for our purposes as the collection of 50 multiplayer-focused mini-games.

No, that's not a misprint . . . there are *FIFTY* unique (if somewhat simplistic) games included in addition to the full-fledged single-player mode. With that much variety, some of the games are bound to be clunkers, and indeed there are a few you're liable to try once and never touch again. But the variety also means there's bound to be something that you and your friends come back to time and time again. For my friends and me, the Snowboard Racing mini-game provided a simple yet engaging experience for gamers of all skill levels. You might get the same effect with Monkey Darts, or Monkey Rock-'em Sock'em Robots, or Monkey Disc Golf, or the Monkey Jigsaw Puzzle, or Monkey Mini Golf, or Monkey Whack-a-Mole. (Remember: If none of those sound compelling, there are still over forty more to choose from!)

✓ **You'll like it if:** You like keeping your options open.

✓ **You won't like it if:** You have something against monkeys.

✓ **My favorite in-game moment:** Discovering the unexpectedly deep Monkey Target game, which involves navigating hang-gliding monkeys onto an island in the middle of the water.

Mario Kart Wii

Developer: Nintendo
Publisher: Nintendo
Release Date: April 27, 2008
Number of Players: 1-4
ESRB Rating: E — Comic Mischief

Mario Kart Wii, shown in Figure 14-9, falls into the racing genre. Use the following list to decide if *Mario Kart Wii* is a game you'll enjoy:

Figure 14-9:
A screen-
shot from
Nintendo's
*Mario Kart
Wii.*

- ✔ **The game in a nutshell:** The fun of go-kart racing mixed with the fun of projectile weapons.

- ✔ **Gameplay description:** Since its debut on the Super Nintendo in 1992, the *Mario Kart* series has been a simple, cartoon-like bastion against the increasing focus on realism in the racing game market. *Realistic* is the last word you'd use to describe *Mario Kart Wii,* with its fantastical characters in go-karts racing around courses with hazards such as fireballs, moving walkways, and car-crushing cement blocks.

  The basic gameplay is simple enough for anyone who's ever driven a car, thanks in large part to the packaged Wii Wheel, which turns the Wii Remote into a stylized steering wheel. Becoming an expert, though, means learning how to utilize the many course shortcuts and items that grant bonuses such as speed boosts, invincibility, and the ability to fire projectile weapons at other racers. These items add a lot to the multiplayer mode by letting inexperienced drivers stay competitive with expert racers. There's even a battle mode that focuses exclusively on using these items to take out opposing karts in an enclosed arena.

- ✔ **You'll like it if:** You've always wanted to throw a banana peel in front of that guy who cut you off on the highway.

- ✔ **You won't like it if:** You're already a racing expert who doesn't like getting blindsided.

- ✔ **My favorite in-game moment:** Watching an opponent who's been in first for the whole race get hit over and over again just before the finish line, ending up in eleventh place.

Rayman Raving Rabbids

Developer: Ubisoft Montpelier
Publisher: Ubisoft
Release Date: Nov. 19, 2006
Number of Players: 1-4
ESRB Rating: E — Cartoon Violence, Comic Mischief

Rayman Raving Rabbids, shown in Figure 14-10, falls into the party genre. Use the following list to decide if *Rayman Raving Rabbids* is a game you'll enjoy:

Figure 14-10:
A screen-shot from Ubisoft's *Rayman Raving Rabbids.*

✔ **The game in a nutshell:** Silly rabbit tricks, for kids and adults.

✔ **Gameplay description:** The real star here is the titular Raving Rabbids — crazed white bunnies prone to violent attacks and random, high-pitched screaming. Through over 70 mini-games, these "rabbids" get thrown into increasingly ridiculous situations that involve blowing up cows, shooting plungers from specially designed guns, and even shaking your booty on a disco-themed dance floor. The ridiculous situations are sure to pull a few belly laughs out of people with a little bit of wackiness in them.

The sequel, *Rayman Raving Rabbids 2,* released a year later, continues the antics and is even friendlier to multiplayer play. Another sequel, *Rayman Raving Rabbids TV Party,* will take advantage of the Wii Balance Board as a controller, and is in development as of this writing.

✔ **You'll like it if:** You're a fan of absurd humor.

✔ **You won't like it if:** You're not a fan of absurd humor.

> ✔ **My favorite in-game moment:** Pulling off some freelance dance moves during the booty-shaking mini-games.

Five Games for a Family-Friendly Adventure

Legendary game designer Shigeru Miyamoto said he was inspired to create the original *The Legend of Zelda* partly by the time he spent during his youth exploring the caves in the Japanese countryside. Of course, most kids don't have access to caves (even if their parents would let them explore caves unattended). It's much safer letting children explore virtual caves and countrysides from the comfort of the living room. Mom and Dad can even join in on the virtual adventuring. And best of all, no one has to get dirty!

Super Mario Galaxy

Developer: Nintendo
Publisher: Nintendo
Release Date: Nov. 12, 2007
Number of Players: 1-2
ESRB Rating: E — Mild Cartoon Violence

Super Mario Galaxy, shown in Figure 14-11, falls into the platform game genre. Use the following list to decide if *Super Mario Galaxy* is a game you'll enjoy:

Figure 14-11: A screen-shot from Nintendo's *Super Mario Galaxy.*

- ✔ **The game in a nutshell:** An adventure that's equal parts mind-bending and gravity-bending.

- ✔ **Gameplay description:** Back in 1996, *Super Mario 64* practically created an entire genre of three-dimensional run-and-jump gameplay on the Nintendo 64. Over a decade later, *Super Mario Galaxy* reinvents that genre by throwing it onto a series of increasingly odd three-dimensional planetoids of all shapes and sizes. Some are so large that they feel like an entire planet, while others are so small that Mario can orbit them with a running leap. Gravity plays an important role, constantly changing direction and intensity as Mario runs around the worlds searching for hidden power stars.

 Super Mario Galaxy might be the perfect family adventure, as it even includes some basic support for a second player to join in the fun. The second player doesn't have quite as much to do as the first, but he or she can shoot star bits at enemies using the Remote pointer, and even help Mario jump over some of the tougher bits. The game's gentle transition from easy tasks to nail-bitingly frustrating challenges draws in players of all skill levels.

- ✔ **You'll like it if:** You like bright colors and childlike joy.

- ✔ **You won't like it if:** You're in the mood for a slightly more serious game.

- ✔ **My favorite in-game moment:** Taking a long jump around an ever-shrinking planet and getting sent into orbit.

Family Wii night

Most of the games in the "Five Games for a Family-Friendly Adventure" section are designed for only one player, seemingly making the *family-friendly* part of the title a bit unnecessary. After all, what's there for the rest of the family to do while junior is off on his virtual adventure?

Well, a lot, actually. Surprising as it may sound, watching a skillful adventurer on the Wii can be just as fun as playing the system yourself.

Spectators can help out with the solutions to puzzles, often picking out hidden details that the focused player might have missed. If you get bored sitting fallow on the couch, you can set up a system to alternate with your child every 15 minutes or so (or just when you get to a section that's too tough for you to complete). Even if you're not helping out, it's still plenty of fun to live vicariously through the vicarious life of the player. It's just good, quality bonding time, plain and simple.

Zack & Wiki: The Quest for Barbaros' Treasure

Developer: Capcom
Publisher: Capcom
Release Date: Oct. 23, 2007
Number of Players: 1
ESRB Rating: E — Cartoon Violence

Zack & Wiki: The Quest for Barbaros' Treasure, shown in Figure 14-12, falls into the puzzle genre. Use the following list to decide if *Zack & Wiki: The Quest for Barbaros' Treasure* is a game you'll enjoy:

Figure 14-12:
A screen-shot from Capcom's *Zack & Wiki: The Quest for Barbaros' Treasure.*

 ✔ **The game in a nutshell:** A pirate's life for me.

 ✔ **Gameplay description:** The past few years have seen a steady decline in the popularity of the pure adventure game. These are the kinds of games where you point-and-click to explore elaborate environments and find items that work together to provide some non-intuitive, yet strangely sensible, solutions to the obstacles blocking your progress. If there's any justice in the world, *Zack & Wiki* will lead this fading genre to its glorious resurgence.

You control Zack, a young, towheaded pirate wannabe, and his transforming, flying monkey Wiki, on a quest to recover the golden skeleton of a pirate legend. Along the way you have to guess-and-check your way through a wide variety of inventive traps, many of which require you to convert the local wildlife into useful tools with the ring of a magical bell. The old-school brain-teasers can sometimes be frustratingly obtuse, but the game's lighthearted tone and super-cute animation keeps you scratching your head — or running for the strategy guide.

✔ **You'll like it if:** You love banging your head against some tough puzzles.

✔ **You won't like it if:** You're looking for a game with a lot of action.

✔ **My favorite in-game moment:** Finally figuring out that the solution to a puzzle was staring me in the face all along, if only I had realized it.

The Legend of Zelda: Twilight Princess

Developer: Nintendo
Publisher: Nintendo
Release Date: Nov. 19, 2006
Number of Players: 1
ESRB Rating: T — Animated Blood, Fantasy Violence

The Legend of Zelda: Twilight Princess, shown in Figure 14-13, falls into the adventure genre. Use the following list to decide if *The Legend of Zelda: Twilight Princess* is a game you'll enjoy:

Figure 14-13:
A screen-shot from Nintendo's *The Legend of Zelda: Twilight Princess.*

✔ **The game in a nutshell:** Your standard boy-meets-girl, girl-gets-captured, boy-turns-into-wolf, boy/wolf-saves-girl-with-help-of-mystical-dark-world-entity story.

✔ **Gameplay description:** The series that practically invented the action-adventure game is back with this Wii launch title. As usual, you control Link, an elvish boy who has greatness thrust upon him when he becomes the one and only being who can stop the world from being engulfed in an encroaching, permanent twilight. Oh, did I mention the twilight turns him into a wolf? Or that a strange creature from the Twilight realm named Midna is helping him out? That's all kind of important.

Link starts out relatively weak, but true to the series, he periodically gains new items and abilities to advance past various obstacles as the game goes on. The game makes rather satisfying use of the Wii's motion controls to swing Link's sword, aim his bow and arrow, and more. But the real stars here are the elegantly designed dungeons, which cap off a series of intriguing puzzles with massive bosses that really show off the Wii's graphical chops.

✔ **You'll like it if:** You've always wanted to save an entire fantasy realm.

✔ **You won't like it if:** You prefer games that are more grounded in reality.

✔ **My favorite in-game moment:** A thrilling horseback swordfight atop a crumbling bridge.

Lego Star Wars: The Complete Saga

Developer: Traveller's Tales
Publisher: LucasArts
Release Date: Nov. 6, 2007
Number of Players: 1-2
ESRB Rating: E10+ — Cartoon Violence

Lego Star Wars: The Complete Saga, shown in Figure 14-14, falls into the adventure genre. Use the following list to decide if *Lego Star Wars: The Complete Saga* is a game you'll enjoy:

Figure 14-14:
A screen-
shot from
LucasArts'
*Lego Star
Wars: The
Complete
Saga.*

- **The game in a nutshell:** It's *Star Wars* . . . in Lego form. The title really says it all. . . .

- **Gameplay description:** Seeing the familiar universe of the *Star Wars* movies recast as a series of battles between super-cute and largely silent Lego mini-figures does take some getting used to. When you do get used to it, though, you're in for one of the most mindlessly fun action experiences you can have with your Wii.

  Simple action is the name of the game here, with the familiar stories of all six *Star Wars* movies boiled down to endless waves of attacking aliens, robots, and storm troopers. The game is tuned for simplicity, meaning even gaming neophytes can take out large swathes of enemies using blasters, light sabers, and the Jedi's signature force powers. It gets even more fun when you add a second player to join in the plastic-brick-based carnage.

  Lego Star Wars is also one of the rare games that enables you to play cooperatively with another player, and fighting the galactic empire with a partner is delightful. It's all a little repetitive, but it's hard to care when blasting enemies into their component bricks is such an endearing experience. You'll want to keep playing just to see the next familiar *Star Wars* character or locale done up in the inimitable Lego style.

- **You'll like it if:** You acted out the Death Star run with action figures as a child.

- **You won't like it if:** You've never seen a *Star Wars* movie.

- **My favorite in-game moment:** Destroying a room full of storm troopers and then collecting up the Lego pieces they drop to buy new Lego vehicles.

Super Paper Mario

Developer: Intelligent Systems
Publisher: Nintendo
Release Date: April 9, 2007
Number of Players: 1
ESRB Rating: E — Comic Mischief, Mild Cartoon Violence

Super Paper Mario, shown in Figure 14-15, falls into the role-playing genre. Use the following list to decide if *Super Paper Mario* is a game you'll enjoy:

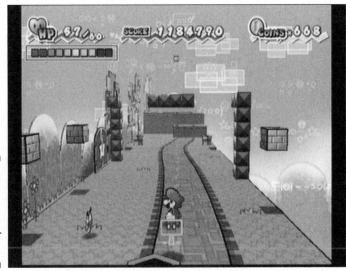

Figure 14-15:
A screen-shot from Nintendo's *Super Paper Mario.*

✔ **The game in a nutshell:** A two-dimensional plumber in a three-dimensional world.

✔ **Gameplay description:** While Mario is best known for run-and-jump action games, more recently he's starred in a series of successful, albeit slower-paced, role-playing games where the focus is on turn-based battles rather than quick reflex action. *Super Paper Mario* mixes these two distinct Mario game styles into a delightful blend that captures the best of both genres.

The story, which revolves around a quest to collect some powerful stars and save the universe, isn't really important. What's important is the gameplay, which sees Mario switching between a flat, two-dimensional side-scrolling quest to a full three-dimensional open world with the touch of a button. This quick-switch in perspective is the key to solving some mind-bending puzzles that change the way you look at the world for hours after you put down the controller. Add in the basic jump-on-enemies-heads action of the original Mario series, and it's like mixing peanut butter and chocolate.

- ✔ **You'll like it if:** You want a new perspective on the world.

- ✔ **You won't like it if:** Your current perspective on the world is just fine, thank you very much.

- ✔ **My favorite in-game moment:** The first time you turn the world on its axis and find you can easily walk around a previously impassable wall.

Part IV
The Part of Tens

In this part . . .

Did you ever get to the end of a major project and realize you have a bunch of pieces that just don't seem to fit anywhere in the finished thing? That's what this part is for — a place for those leftover pieces — and what better way to organize them than to put 'em in simple lists of ten? First you find out about ten games to download from the Wii Shop Channel. Then you discover ten of the most common accessories for blinging out your Wii. These two topics might not seem to have much to do with each other, but neither does the meatloaf and tuna casserole that land on your plate on leftover night, and I don't hear you complaining about that!

Chapter 15

Ten Games to Download

. . . .

*A*s the video-game medium gets older, gamers who grew up with classic systems might find themselves nostalgic for the simple games of yester-year. Similarly, new gamers might be curious about the decades of gaming they missed. Luckily, the Wii lets both groups relive the golden age of gaming through the Wii Shop Channel and its library of hundreds of downloadable classics. Not only that, but the service has recently added original WiiWare games designed specifically for the Wii system. This chapter details some games that are well worth your hard-earned Wii Shop Points.

Note that this chapter barely scratches the surface of the selection of great games available for download on the Wii. I've tried to highlight games that range from a wide variety of developers, systems, and franchises on offer. A complete list of the true classics available on the Wii Shop Channel could fill up a whole separate book.

To download any of the games listed here, you need to have your Wii hooked up to the Internet and purchase them using the Wii Shop Channel. Many of these games require extra controllers besides the original Wii Remote and Nunchuk included with your system.

Super Mario 64

Developer: Nintendo
Publisher: Nintendo
Release Date/System: 1996, Nintendo 64
Number of Players: 1
ESRB Rating: E
Cost: 1,000 Wii Shop Points

Super Mario 64, shown in Figure 15-1, falls into the platform game genre. Use the following list to decide whether *Super Mario 64* is a game you want to download:

> ✔ **The game in a nutshell:** The original three-dimensional platformer, and still the greatest.

Figure 15-1:
A screen-shot from *Super Mario 64.*

✔ **Gameplay description:** Eleven years after *Super Mario Bros.* practically invented the two-dimensional run-and-jump platform game, *Super Mario 64* reinvented the concept for a new generation and a new dimension. The story hasn't evolved much — it's still a tale of a captured princess and the high-jumping plumber who has to save her — but you don't play a game like this for the riveting storyline. You play it for the sense of exploration, the thrill of finding one of the 120 secret power stars hidden in some remote corner of one the game's 15 sprawling, beautifully designed levels. Heck, it's a delight just to run around the castle court-yard, whiling away the time simply climbing trees, swimming in the moat, or even flying around the spires.

✔ **You'll like it if:** You're a fan of joy.

✔ **You won't like it if:** Your heart is a black, withered shell.

✔ **My favorite in-game moment:** Shooting Mario from a cannon and flying around the bright blue sky.

Toe Jam and Earl

Developer: Sega
Publisher: Sega
Release Date/System: 1992, Genesis
Number of Players: 1-2
ESRB Rating: E - Comic Mischief
Cost: 800 Wii Shop Points

Toe Jam and Earl, shown in Figure 15-2, falls into the platform game genre. Use the following list to decide if *Toe Jam and Earl* is a game you want to download:

- ✔ **The game in a nutshell:** The funkiest game on this side of the galaxy.

- ✔ **Gameplay description:** Saying *Toe Jam & Earl* is unique is like saying the Parthenon is kind of old. You control either a three-legged red tongue-shaped creature named Toe Jam or his large, orange buddy Earl as they wander around Earth looking for the pieces of their wrecked ship. This isn't a normal conception of Earth, though — this world is a randomly generated maze of hazards including sadistic, prancing dentists, shopping-cart-pushing soccer moms, and pitchfork-wielding red devils, among other distractions. Luckily, Toe Jam and Earl have access to items such as tomato-launching slingshots, high-jumping spring shoes, and zippy rocket boots to help them get around and away from these hazards.

  Traipsing around by your lonesome is all right, but the search becomes much more fun with a second player who can navigate on a split-screen. You can work together to cover more ground, or just cover each other's back as the hazards get more numerous.

- ✔ **You'll like it if:** You're looking for something different.

- ✔ **You won't like it if:** You like your game straightforward and fast-paced.

- ✔ **My favorite in-game moment:** Using the Rocket Skates to fly across the ocean to the secret hot-tub island.

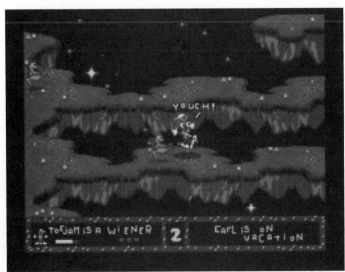

Figure 15-2: A screen-shot from *Toe Jam and Earl.*

The Legend of Zelda: A Link to the Past

Developer: Nintendo
Publisher: Nintendo
Release Date/System: 1992, Super NES
Number of Players: 1
ESRB Rating: E - Mild Animated Violence
Cost: 800 Wii Shop Points

The Legend of Zelda: A Link to the Past, shown in Figure 15-3, falls into the adventure genre. Use the following list to decide whether *The Legend of Zelda: A Link to the Past* is a game you want to download:

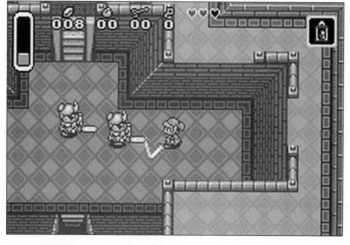

Figure 15-3:
A screen-shot from *The Legend of Zelda: A Link to the Past.*

- ✔ **The game in a nutshell:** The pinnacle of two-dimensional adventuring.

- ✔ **Gameplay description:** While the original *Legend of Zelda* helped create the two-dimensional action-adventure genre, *A Link to the Past* perfected it. The story starts with an unexpectedly touching opening vignette wherein young hero Link ventures out in the rainy night to receive a sword from his betrayed, dying uncle. From there the tale expands to include a captured princess, evil wizard, a mystical sword, and a magic mirror that transports Link to a dark world that mirrors his own in strange and disturbing ways.

    It's this magic mirror that is the key to many of *Link to the Past*'s clever puzzles, which involve manipulating items in one world to gain an advantage in the other. It's not all about brain-teasers, though — there are plenty of monsters to swing your sword at, including some impressive, screen-filling bosses. By the time you reach the end of this epic, you'll find its intricate dungeons and touching moments permanently stuck in your consciousness.

✔ **You'll like it if:** You like a good mix of fantasy, action, and puzzles.

✔ **You won't like it if:** You're looking for a quick, straightforward game.

✔ **My favorite in-game moment:** Navigating my way through the Lost Woods and finally lifting the fabled Master Sword from its hidden pedestal.

Sonic the Hedgehog 2

Developer: Sega
Publisher: Sega
Release Date/System: 1994, Genesis
Number of Players: 1
ESRB Rating: E - Comic Mischief
Cost: 800 Wii Shop Points

Sonic the Hedgehog 2, shown in Figure 15-4, falls into the platform game genre. Use the following list to decide whether *Sonic the Hedgehog 2* is a game you want to download:

✔ **The game in a nutshell:** He's the fastest thing alive.

✔ **Gameplay description:** In the early 90s, Sega was looking for a new mascot to make its Genesis system stand out from the Super Nintendo and its dominant Super Mario franchise. That mascot was Sonic, a spiky blue hedgehog with big red high-tops and an attitude. Where Mario games stressed exploration and puzzle solving, Sonic games emphasized speedy dashes through thrilling loops, sky-high jumps, and tumbles. *Sonic 2* was the pinnacle of this design, sending Sonic and new companion Tails the fox through levels that resemble a Vegas casino, a massive oil rig, and a flying super-fortress. The imaginative level design and fast-paced, white-knuckle gameplay turn the game into a day at the theme park.

✔ **You'll like it if:** You like your games to resemble the roller coasters at a theme park.

✔ **You won't like it if:** You prefer your games to resemble the spinning teacups at a theme park.

✔ **My favorite in-game moment:** Transforming into the golden, invincible, flying Super Sonic and blazing through the rest of the level.

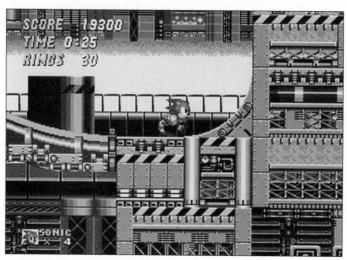

Figure 15-4:
A screen-
shot from
*Sonic the
Hedgehog 2.*

Super Mario Bros. 3

Developer: Nintendo
Publisher: Nintendo
Release Date/System: 1990, NES
Number of Players: 2 (alternating)
ESRB Rating: E
Cost: 500 Wii Shop Points

Super Mario Bros. 3, shown in Figure 15-5, falls into the platform game genre. Use the following list to decide whether *Super Mario Bros. 3* is a game you want to download:

✔ **The game in a nutshell:** The height of 2-D platform game design.

✔ **Gameplay description:** If you were fifteen or younger in 1990, chances are good that you owned this game, or were at least exposed to it through one of the roughly ten million or so kids who did. If you weren't so lucky, then you missed out on a game that improved on the seminal run-and-jump gameplay of the original *Super Mario Bros.* in a variety of ways. For one, you could now choose which level to play next through a simple map screen. For another, you now had access to a variety of transformational suits that helped Mario deal with dozens of new enemies. But the most relevant advance of *Super Mario Bros. 3* was probably the ability to send Mario skyward for the first time by using a magic raccoon tail. To this day, the 88 levels of this game represent some of the finest design in the history of the medium.

✔ **You'll like it if:** You like simple yet fun design.

Figure 15-5:
A screen-
shot from
*Super Mario
Bros. 3.*

✔ **You won't like it if:** You enjoy kicking puppies and setting fires.

✔ **My favorite in-game moment:** That first sprint and take-off into the sky as Raccoon Mario.

Bomberman '93

Developer: Hudson
Publisher: Hudson
Release Date/System: 1992, TurboGrafx-16
Number of Players: 5
ESRB Rating: E - Comic Mischief
Cost: 600 Wii Shop Points

Bomberman '93, shown in Figure 15-6, falls into the puzzle/party genre. Use the following list to decide whether *Bomberman '93* is a game you want to download:

✔ **The game in a nutshell:** The golden rule: Blow up others as they would blow up you.

✔ **Gameplay description:** While the Wii is a great system for multiplayer party gaming, the folks at Nintendo didn't single-handedly invent the idea in 2006. Multiplayer action has been a part of video games for a long time, as proved by the excellent *Bomberman '93.*

As the name suggests, Bomberman uses his bomb-laying abilities to destroy both enemies and the obstacles that prevent him from getting to those enemies. The single-player mode in this game is eminently forgettable — a slow-paced, uninteresting trek through nondescript, sparsely populated levels. That all turns around in multiplayer, where up to five players rush around the gridlike levels trying to blow each other up. Items can increase your bombing strength and the number of bombs you can lay at once, but be careful — the same bombs that can destroy your opponents can also be your undoing.

✔ **You'll like it if:** You have some friends to play it with.

✔ **You won't like it if:** You're playing the slow-paced single-player mode.

✔ **My favorite in-game moment:** When one bomb destroys all the remaining players, ending a tense duel in a draw.

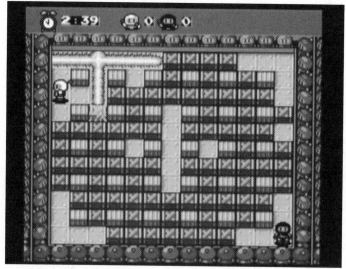

Figure 15-6:
A screen-shot of *Bomberman '93.*

Kirby's Adventure

Developer: HAL Laboratory
Publisher: Nintendo
Release Date/System: 1993, NES
Number of Players: 1
ESRB Rating: E - Comic Mischief
Cost: 500 Wii Shop Points

Kirby's Adventure, shown in Figure 15-7, falls into the platform game genre. Use the following list to decide whether *Kirby's Adventure* is a game you want to download:

- ✔ **The game in a nutshell:** Kirby see, Kirby do.

- ✔ **Gameplay description:** By the early 90s, it seemed every other game that came out was a simple run-and-jump platform game that asked some generic character or other to run from one side of the world to the other. Kirby stood out from the crowd thanks to a unique design that allowed him to swallow and steal the abilities of a wide variety of interesting enemies. With a quick inhale and gulp Kirby can throw bombs, wield a sword, transform into a fireball, perform karate moves, and much, much more as the situation dictates. A massive selection of levels makes this one a bargain for platform game fans.

- ✔ **You'll like it if:** You're never quite comfortable in your own skin.

- ✔ **You won't like it if:** You like characters with small, easy-to-remember sets of abilities.

- ✔ **My favorite in-game moment:** The first time Kirby turns into a hovering, laser-spitting UFO.

Figure 15-7:
A screen-shot of
*Kirby's
Adventure.*

Pokémon Snap

Developer: Nintendo
Publisher: Nintendo
Release Date/System: 1999, N64
Number of Players: 1
ESRB Rating: E
Cost: 1,000 Wii Shop Points

Pokémon Snap, shown in Figure 15-8, falls into the simulation genre. Use the following list to decide whether *Pokémon Snap* is a game you want to download:

Figure 15-8:
A screen-shot of *Pokémon Snap.*

- ✔ **The game in a nutshell:** Your ticket to a career in the cute-critter-photography biz.

- ✔ **Gameplay description:** An under-appreciated gem from the end of the last millennium, *Pokémon Snap* sits lonely in the relatively small photography simulator genre. As the name implies, you're tasked with taking Safari-style pictures of the animal-like Pokémon in their natural habitats (and yes, these are the same Pokémon that briefly took over practically every facet of children's marketing and culture in the late 90s). A motorized cart pushes you along as you pan and zoom your viewfinder to look for the cute critters, which are often hiding in the last place you'd think to look.

If you're a Pokémon fan, you'll enjoy at seeing your favorite critters cavorting in the wild in full three-dimensional glory. Even if you don't know who or what these things are supposed to be, you'll enjoy the challenge of correctly framing and angling your pictures of the cute little beasts. Some are pretty shy, requiring you to throw lures to get them out into the open.

✔ **You'll like it if:** You're a shutterbug.

✔ **You won't like it if:** You like being in direct control of the experience.

✔ **My favorite in-game moment:** Completing a complicated set of moves to lure a rare Pokémon out of hiding and into the frame.

Defend Your Castle

Publisher: XGen Studios
Release Date/System: 2008, Wii
Number of Players: 1-4
ESRB Rating: E - Cartoon Violence
Cost: 500 Wii Shop Points

Defend Your Castle, shown in Figure 15-9, falls into the action genre. Use the following list to decide whether *Defend Your Castle* is a game you want to download:

Figure 15-9:
A screen-shot of
*Defend Your
Castle.*

- ✔ **The game in a nutshell:** Er, defend your castle.

- ✔ **Gameplay description:** Sometimes the simplest games are the most effective. Case in point: *Defend Your Castle,* a game in which you defend a cardboard castle from hordes of rampaging stick figures by picking them up and flinging them to the side. It's hard to undersell how satisfying it is to point at a stick figure intruder, pick him up, and send him careening to the ground with a satisfying splat.

  As the stick figure flow increases from a trickle to a flood, you can purchase new allies to help squelch the invasion, ranging from archers to disturbingly cute suicide bombers. Strategy isn't as important as rampant clicking and flicking, though. It's a great way to let off some stress — just picture each stick figure as a person or thing that's causing you aggravation and SPLAT.

- ✔ **You'll like it if:** You need to let out some aggression.

- ✔ **You won't like it if:** You have trouble keeping track of a lot of things at once.

- ✔ **My favorite in-game moment:** Letting the stick figure soldiers amass for a few seconds, and then sending a bomber out to destroy them en masse.

Dr. Mario Online Rx

Developer: Nintendo
Publisher: Nintendo
Release Date/System: 2008, Wii
Number of Players: 1-4
ESRB Rating: E
Cost: 1,000 Wii Shop Points

Dr. Mario Online Rx, shown in Figure 15-10, falls into the puzzle genre. Use the following list to decide whether *Dr. Mario Online Rx* is a game you want to download:

- ✔ **The game in a nutshell:** The prescription for online puzzle fun.

- ✔ **Gameplay description:** Nintendo's answer to *Tetris* involved colored pills that have to be lined up to match four colored sections in a row. This WiiWare version of the classic game updates the timeless puzzle gameplay with online play and a mode that uses the Wii Remote pointer to navigate the pills into place.

- ✔ **You'll like it if:** You're a fan of puzzles.

Figure 15-10:
A screen-
shot of
*Dr. Mario
Online Rx.*

✔ **You won't like it if:** You're not a fan of puzzles?

✔ **My favorite in-game moment:** Causing a chain reaction that clears
a bunch of pills at once.

Chapter 16

Ten Types of Accessories

*T*ime for a riddle: How is the Wii like a little black dress? Give up? Neither one is complete without the right accessories supporting it! Also, they both look great on a supermodel.

Seriously, while the Wii technically comes with everything you need to get gaming, you can buy a variety of accessories to make your Wii experience a more enjoyable one. This chapter takes you through ten of the most popular types of Wii accessories, walks you through the pros and cons of each, and recommends some specific brands that you might enjoy.

This chapter does not talk about the various optional controllers that you might need to play certain games on the Wii. For more on these controllers, see Chapter 3.

The accessories in this chapter are listed in descending order of how much use the average Wii user will get out of them — the most useful accessories are first, with the least useful accessories at the end.

SmartDigital Card

A SmartDigital (SD) card is definitely an item you'll want to buy for your Wii.

- ✔ **What is it?** These small, thin, plastic cards (also known as *SD cards*) actually contain thousands of microscopic memory cells that can hold computer data. This includes Wii data, in the form of saved games, Channel data, and Message Board messages. (For more on the Wii's internal memory and how to back it up to an SD card, see Chapter 5.)

- ✔ **Why you need it:** If your Wii should fail for any reason, an SD backup is often the only way to recover the game save data and downloaded Channels on your system. You also need a SmartDigital card to transfer photos from your digital camera on to the Wii's Photo Channel (see Chapter 8).

✔ **Why you might be able to get by without it:** If you're willing to risk losing all the data stored on your Wii in case of a hardware failure, that's your business. Don't come crying to me when a power surge causes you to lose the 30 hours of progress you've put in to *The Legend of Zelda: Twilight Princess* though.

✔ **Which one to get:** SD cards come in a wide variety of sizes. A 512 Megabyte (512 MB) card is big enough to back up literally everything on your Wii's internal memory. If you plan to use the card for digital photos as well, or if you're planning on using the card for temporary storage of data that won't fit on the Wii's internal memory, you might want to splurge for a bigger card.

Any brand of SD card will work equally well with your Wii, so it's not necessary to pay extra for a card with official Wii branding.

Note that some cell phones and cameras use mini- or microSD cards rather than the standard-size SD cards. These cards will work with the Wii, but you need a special adapter to fit them in the slot in the front of the system. These adapters are sold at any major electronics retailer for about $10.

GameCube Memory Card

If you play GameCube games on your Wii, you'll want to buy a GameCube Memory Card.

✔ **What is it?** These proprietary digital data-storage cards, originally designed for Nintendo's GameCube system, can also be used to save GameCube games played on the Wii. (See Chapter 5 for more on playing GameCube games on the Wii and using GameCube Memory cards on the Wii. Note that you also need a GameCube Controller if you're planning on playing GameCube games on your Wii.)

✔ **Why you need it:** If you're going to be playing any GameCube games on your Wii, you absolutely need a GameCube Memory Card to save your progress. Otherwise, you have to start over from the beginning of the game every time you turn the system off. (For games that can take dozens and dozens of hours to complete, this doesn't seem like such a great plan.)

✔ **Why you can get by without it:** If you plan to never, *ever* buy a GameCube game to play on your Wii, then you don't need to invest in a GameCube Memory Card. You're missing out on hundreds of great games, though — many of which can be bought used very cheaply these days (see Chapter 11 for more on finding cheap used games).

✔ **Which one to get:** While Nintendo no longer manufactures new GameCube memory cards, you can find unopened and used cards at gaming retailers and online at sites such as Amazon and eBay. An official, 251-block, Nintendo-made card should run anywhere from $5 to $15, roughly. Stay away from any competing cards made by a company other than Nintendo; they have a tendency to fail much more often.

Controller Charger

A controller charger is an item you'll find useful for your Wii.

✔ **What is it?** For all the great features of the Wii Remote, long-lasting battery life is not among them. Nintendo claims a fresh set of alkaline AA batteries will last up to 35 hours in your Remote, but in practice the batteries tend to die out around the ten- to fifteen-hour mark. A specially designed controller charger is the most cost-efficient and environmentally friendly way to make sure your Remote always has juice.

✔ **Why you need it:** Not only will a battery charger save you money and help reduce toxic waste from disposable batteries, but it's also a lot more convenient. A charger makes sure your Wii Remote is always ready to use at a moment's notice, without the need to swap out batteries in the middle of an intense play session.

✔ **Why you can get by without it:** If you don't use the Wii that often, you might not find much of a need for a Remote charger. That said, you should be using your Wii more often. This book is full of fun and useful things to do with your system. Pick up your Remote and give them a try, for goodness sakes!

✔ **Which one to get:** I personally use the Nyko Charge Station, which comes with two Nickel-Metal Hydride battery packs and a stylish charging base station that charges both of them at once. The base station also has convenient LED lights to show when your Remotes are fully charged. Not bad for $30.

There are a wide variety of competing Remote chargers from a wide variety of companies. Some plug into the wall, while others plug into the USB port in the back of the Wii, drawing power from the system to charge the Remotes. Of course, you could always just buy some plain old, rechargeable AA batteries for your Remote, but then you have to constantly swap them in and out of the Remote. And who wants to do that?

Decorative System Skins

While the Wii is pretty stylish by itself, some people find the system's sleek white exterior too boring. If you're one of these people, you can buy a decorative skin for your system.

- ✔ **What is it?** Tired of that plain, white Wii clashing with the rest of your entertainment center? Dress up that drab facade with some decorative plastic skins. These high-quality stickers go right on top of the Wii casing, turning your basic system into a work of art. Some even come with matching stickers for your Wii Remote and Nunchuk so you can keep everything color-coordinated. (Now, that's what I call fashion-forward.)

- ✔ **Why you need it:** If you feel a deep, abiding need to jazz up your electronics.

- ✔ **Why you can get by without it:** If you enjoy the simple, clean look of the basic Wii system.

- ✔ **Which one to get:** You can order skins from `www.DecalGirl.com` and `www.PimpMyWii.com` — both have an excellent selection of Wii system and controller skins in the $5 to $15 range.

Travel Cases

If you want to take your Wii with you when you visit friends or when you travel, you may want to buy a travel case.

- ✔ **What is it?** Kind of like a suitcase for your Wii, a specially designed travel case makes it much easier to bring your new system over to a friend's house for some multiplayer fun.

- ✔ **Why you need it:** If you're the only one of your friends who owns a Wii, and you find yourself constantly asked to bring the system over for cookouts, parties, Bar Mitzvahs, and so on.

- ✔ **Why you can get by without it:** If all your friends have Wiis of their own to play. Or if none of your friends are very interested in having you bring your system over to their place. Or if you have no friends.

- ✔ **Which one to get:** You can find a wide variety of Wii travel cases that vary greatly in design and price. Intec's Pro Gamer case is probably the top of the line, with a hard, metal case that includes compartments for controllers, cables, and games for about $30. If you're looking for something a little less pricey, the DreamGear Wii Game Bag is a soft mesh alternative that can hold your Wii and all its accessories for about $15.

Classic Controller Shells

You might find a Classic Controller shell useful if you play a lot of download-able classics on the Wii's Virtual Console.

- ✔ **What is it?** These plastic controller shells snap on to the Wii Classic Controller or Wii Remote, making them easier to hold and use for big-handed players.

- ✔ **Why you need it:** If you play a lot of games on the Virtual Console or a lot of games that require you to hold the Wii Remote in the horizontal position.

- ✔ **Why you can get by without it:** If you can comfortably hold the Wii Remote and/or Wii Classic Controller in your hands without any attachments.

- ✔ **Which one to get:** There are really only two choices here: Nyko's Classic Controller Grip adds more room for your palms and a convenient holder for the dangling wire and attached Wii Remote, all for only roughly $10. For players using the Wii Remote in the horizontal position, CTA Digital's Wii Remote Grip adds a similar palm-friendly area to the edges of the Remote, also for $10.

Controller Sleeves

A variety of controller sleeves in various colors, such as pink and blue, are available for your Wii Remote and Nunchuk.

- ✔ **What is it?** Controller sleeves are silicone shells that cover the Wii Remote and Nunchuk. The hard, plastic shells of the Wii Remote and Nunchuk not only make the controllers prone to breaking in serious impacts, but they also make the controllers hurt when they inevitably bonk someone in the head during gameplay. Controller sleeves can help alleviate both these problems by adding a squishy layer that protects the controllers from both breaking and bonking. These sleeves also make the controllers easier to grip and less prone to slipping out of sweaty hands.

- ✔ **Why you need it:** If you're concerned with the health and safety of your Wii Remote and its owner.

- ✔ **Why you can get by without it:** If you're the kind of devil-may-care rebel that willingly wears the same pair of underwear two days in a row.

✔ **Which one to get:** Nintendo's free, official Wii Remote sleeve has cut into the market for non-free sleeves somewhat, but plenty of companies still market sleeves of their own. While they're infinitely more expensive, these sleeves have the advantage of being much less bulky than Nintendo's free Wii Remote sleeves and come in a wide variety of stylish colors. One brand is largely like all the others, truth be told; prices range from $1 to $5 per sleeve.

For something a little different, Nerf makes a controller shell from its trademark foam. It's a little bulkier than its plain silicone counterparts and more expensive, but it might be worth it just for the coolness factor alone.

Wireless Sensor Bar

A wireless sensor bar might be useful if your entertainment setup requires you to put the sensor bar too far away from the Wii system.

✔ **What is it?** While the Sensor Bar that comes with the Wii plugs into the back of the system, it doesn't actually send any data to the system directly. The only reason for that overly long plug is to draw power for the Wii Sensor Bar's infrared lights, which are detected by a simple digital camera in the Wii Remote.

What all this technical mumbo-jumbo means is that there's no reason a wireless, battery powered sensor bar couldn't work just as well as the official wired version included in the Wii box. Given the tangled mess of cable behind most TVs these days, one less wire to snag is likely to be a welcome development.

✔ **Why you need it:** If you want one less wire snaking around your entertainment center. The wireless sensor bar can also be placed much farther from the system, which is useful for some entertainment setups that use a projector and screen.

✔ **Why you can get by without it:** If your default Wii Sensor Bar is working just fine, wires and all.

✔ **Which one to get:** Intec, Nyko, and DreamGear all make wireless sensor bars that are relatively hard to distinguish from one another. All three cost about $15 at retail.

Cooling Fans

A cooling fan is probably not necessary for your Wii (unless you really like to crank up the heat in your play area).

✔ **What is it?** Somewhere along the way, someone must have gotten the idea that Wiis the world over are overheating at a tremendous rate. While the outside of the Wii does indeed get hot if left on for an extended period, the natural ventilation provided by the included stand and the slots throughout the case are generally enough to keep the system running properly. Still, for those nervous nellies out there, you can find a variety of attachable, USB-powered fans and stands to blow that heated air away from the system at a much faster rate.

✔ **Why you need it:** If you routinely play your Wii in 140-degree heat.

✔ **Why you can get by without it:** If your Wii is set up in a cool, well-ventilated area.

✔ **Which one to avoid:** While all Wii cooling fans are pretty much equally useless, Ascend's $30 attachment packs the double punch of being more expensive than its competitors and much, much cheaper-looking. Stay away.

Plastic Remote Attachments

Other accessories that you probably can do without are plastic remote attachments.

✔ **What are they?** It seems some people just aren't satisfied with having their Wii Remote act like a virtual version of a sword, golf club, tennis racquet, baseball bat, or other real-world device. No, these people won't be happy unless their Wii Remote actually *looks* like a cheap, plastic version of the handheld tool it's emulating. Plenty of accessory makers are willing to take these people's money by making and marketing plastic attachments that attach to the Wii Remote, transforming it from a well-designed piece of electronics to something that looks like a cheap children's toy. These attachments don't add any functionality to the Remote, and they don't even make the games easier to play. They're just a waste of space, time, and money, really.

✔ **Why you need it:** If you always wanted a toy sword as a child but your non-violent parents wouldn't let you have one.

✔ **Why you can get by without it:** If you have an imagination.

✔ **Which one to avoid:** Of all the Wii Remote attachments currently on the market, the Wii Billiards cue is probably the most ostentatious and useless. Even if you're one of the few fans of the Billiards mini-game in *Wii Play,* you can probably get by without this attachment.

Index

• *N* •

Notes

Notes

BUSINESS, CAREERS & PERSONAL FINANCE

Accounting For Dummies, 4th Edition*
978-0-470-24600-9

Bookkeeping Workbook For Dummies†
978-0-470-16983-4

Commodities For Dummies
978-0-470-04928-0

Doing Business in China For Dummies
978-0-470-04929-7

E-Mail Marketing For Dummies
978-0-470-19087-6

Job Interviews For Dummies, 3rd Edition*†
978-0-470-17748-8

Personal Finance Workbook For Dummies*†
978-0-470-09933-9

Real Estate License Exams For Dummies
978-0-7645-7623-2

Six Sigma For Dummies
978-0-7645-6798-8

Small Business Kit For Dummies, 2nd Edition*†
978-0-7645-5984-6

Telephone Sales For Dummies
978-0-470-16836-3

BUSINESS PRODUCTIVITY & MICROSOFT OFFICE

Access 2007 For Dummies
978-0-470-03649-5

Excel 2007 For Dummies
978-0-470-03737-9

Office 2007 For Dummies
978-0-470-00923-9

Outlook 2007 For Dummies
978-0-470-03830-7

PowerPoint 2007 For Dummies
978-0-470-04059-1

Project 2007 For Dummies
978-0-470-03651-8

QuickBooks 2008 For Dummies
978-0-470-18470-7

Quicken 2008 For Dummies
978-0-470-17473-9

Salesforce.com For Dummies, 2nd Edition
978-0-470-04893-1

Word 2007 For Dummies
978-0-470-03658-7

EDUCATION, HISTORY, REFERENCE & TEST PREPARATION

African American History For Dummies
978-0-7645-5469-8

Algebra For Dummies
978-0-7645-5325-7

Algebra Workbook For Dummies
978-0-7645-8467-1

Art History For Dummies
978-0-470-09910-0

ASVAB For Dummies, 2nd Edition
978-0-470-10671-6

British Military History For Dummies
978-0-470-03213-8

Calculus For Dummies
978-0-7645-2498-1

Canadian History For Dummies, 2nd Edition
978-0-470-83656-9

Geometry Workbook For Dummies
978-0-471-79940-5

The SAT I For Dummies, 6th Edition
978-0-7645-7193-0

Series 7 Exam For Dummies
978-0-470-09932-2

World History For Dummies
978-0-7645-5242-7

FOOD, GARDEN, HOBBIES & HOME

Bridge For Dummies, 2nd Edition
978-0-471-92426-5

Coin Collecting For Dummies, 2nd Edition
978-0-470-22275-1

Cooking Basics For Dummies, 3rd Edition
978-0-7645-7206-7

Drawing For Dummies
978-0-7645-5476-6

Etiquette For Dummies, 2nd Edition
978-0-470-10672-3

Gardening Basics For Dummies*†
978-0-470-03749-2

Knitting Patterns For Dummies
978-0-470-04556-5

Living Gluten-Free For Dummies†
978-0-471-77383-2

Painting Do-It-Yourself For Dummies
978-0-470-17533-0

HEALTH, SELF HELP, PARENTING & PETS

Anger Management For Dummies
978-0-470-03715-7

Anxiety & Depression Workbook For Dummies
978-0-7645-9793-0

Dieting For Dummies, 2nd Edition
978-0-7645-4149-0

Dog Training For Dummies, 2nd Edition
978-0-7645-8418-3

Horseback Riding For Dummies
978-0-470-09719-9

Infertility For Dummies†
978-0-470-11518-3

Meditation For Dummies with CD-ROM, 2nd Edition
978-0-471-77774-8

Post-Traumatic Stress Disorder For Dummies
978-0-470-04922-8

Puppies For Dummies, 2nd Edition
978-0-470-03717-1

Thyroid For Dummies, 2nd Edition†
978-0-471-78755-6

Type 1 Diabetes For Dummies*†
978-0-470-17811-9

---

* Separate Canadian edition also available
† Separate U.K. edition also available

Available wherever books are sold. For more information or to order direct: U.S. customers visit www.dummies.com or call 1-877-762-2974.
U.K. customers visit www.wileyeurope.com or call (0)1243 843291. Canadian customers visit www.wiley.ca or call 1-800-567-4797.

INTERNET & DIGITAL MEDIA

AdWords For Dummies
978-0-470-15252-2

Blogging For Dummies, 2nd Edition
978-0-470-23017-6

Digital Photography All-in-One Desk Reference For Dummies, 3rd Edition
978-0-470-03743-0

Digital Photography For Dummies, 5th Edition
978-0-7645-9802-9

Digital SLR Cameras & Photography For Dummies, 2nd Edition
978-0-470-14927-0

eBay Business All-in-One Desk Reference For Dummies
978-0-7645-8438-1

eBay For Dummies, 5th Edition*
978-0-470-04529-9

eBay Listings That Sell For Dummies
978-0-471-78912-3

Facebook For Dummies
978-0-470-26273-3

The Internet For Dummies, 11th Edition
978-0-470-12174-0

Investing Online For Dummies, 5th Edition
978-0-7645-8456-5

iPod & iTunes For Dummies, 5th Editio
978-0-470-17474-6

MySpace For Dummies
978-0-470-09529-4

Podcasting For Dummies
978-0-471-74898-4

Search Engine Optimization For Dummies, 2nd Edition
978-0-471-97998-2

Second Life For Dummies
978-0-470-18025-9

Starting an eBay Business For Dummie 3rd Edition†
978-0-470-14924-9

GRAPHICS, DESIGN & WEB DEVELOPMENT

Adobe Creative Suite 3 Design Premium All-in-One Desk Reference For Dummies
978-0-470-11724-8

Adobe Web Suite CS3 All-in-One Desk Reference For Dummies
978-0-470-12099-6

AutoCAD 2008 For Dummies
978-0-470-11650-0

Building a Web Site For Dummies, 3rd Edition
978-0-470-14928-7

Creating Web Pages All-in-One Desk Reference For Dummies, 3rd Edition
978-0-470-09629-1

Creating Web Pages For Dummies, 8th Edition
978-0-470-08030-6

Dreamweaver CS3 For Dummies
978-0-470-11490-2

Flash CS3 For Dummies
978-0-470-12100-9

Google SketchUp For Dummies
978-0-470-13744-4

InDesign CS3 For Dummies
978-0-470-11865-8

Photoshop CS3 All-in-One Desk Reference For Dummies
978-0-470-11195-6

Photoshop CS3 For Dummies
978-0-470-11193-2

Photoshop Elements 5 For Dummies
978-0-470-09810-3

SolidWorks For Dummies
978-0-7645-9555-4

Visio 2007 For Dummies
978-0-470-08983-5

Web Design For Dummies, 2nd Editio
978-0-471-78117-2

Web Sites Do-It-Yourself For Dummie
978-0-470-16903-2

Web Stores Do-It-Yourself For Dummie
978-0-470-17443-2

LANGUAGES, RELIGION & SPIRITUALITY

Arabic For Dummies
978-0-471-77270-5

Chinese For Dummies, Audio Set
978-0-470-12766-7

French For Dummies
978-0-7645-5193-2

German For Dummies
978-0-7645-5195-6

Hebrew For Dummies
978-0-7645-5489-6

Ingles Para Dummies
978-0-7645-5427-8

Italian For Dummies, Audio Set
978-0-470-09586-7

Italian Verbs For Dummies
978-0-471-77389-4

Japanese For Dummies
978-0-7645-5429-2

Latin For Dummies
978-0-7645-5431-5

Portuguese For Dummies
978-0-471-78738-9

Russian For Dummies
978-0-471-78001-4

Spanish Phrases For Dummies
978-0-7645-7204-3

Spanish For Dummies
978-0-7645-5194-9

Spanish For Dummies, Audio Set
978-0-470-09585-0

The Bible For Dummies
978-0-7645-5296-0

Catholicism For Dummies
978-0-7645-5391-2

The Historical Jesus For Dummies
978-0-470-16785-4

Islam For Dummies
978-0-7645-5503-9

Spirituality For Dummies, 2nd Edition
978-0-470-19142-2

NETWORKING AND PROGRAMMING

ASP.NET 3.5 For Dummies
978-0-470-19592-5

C# 2008 For Dummies
978-0-470-19109-5

Hacking For Dummies, 2nd Edition
978-0-470-05235-8

Home Networking For Dummies, 4th Edition
978-0-470-11806-1

Java For Dummies, 4th Edition
978-0-470-08716-9

Microsoft® SQL Server™ 2008 All-in-One Desk Reference For Dummies
978-0-470-17954-3

Networking All-in-One Desk Reference For Dummies, 2nd Edition
978-0-7645-9939-2

Networking For Dummies, 8th Edition
978-0-470-05620-2

SharePoint 2007 For Dummies
978-0-470-09941-4

Wireless Home Networking For Dummies, 2nd Edition
978-0-471-74940-0

OPERATING SYSTEMS & COMPUTER BASICS

Mac For Dummies, 5th Edition
978-0-7645-8458-9

Laptops For Dummies, 2nd Edition
978-0-470-05432-1

Linux For Dummies, 8th Edition
978-0-470-11649-4

MacBook For Dummies
978-0-470-04859-7

Mac OS X Leopard All-in-One
Desk Reference For Dummies
978-0-470-05434-5

Mac OS X Leopard For Dummies
978-0-470-05433-8

Macs For Dummies, 9th Edition
978-0-470-04849-8

PCs For Dummies, 11th Edition
978-0-470-13728-4

Windows® Home Server For Dummies
978-0-470-18592-6

Windows Server 2008 For Dummies
978-0-470-18043-3

Windows Vista All-in-One
Desk Reference For Dummies
978-0-471-74941-7

Windows Vista For Dummies
978-0-471-75421-3

Windows Vista Security For Dummies
978-0-470-11805-4

SPORTS, FITNESS & MUSIC

Coaching Hockey For Dummies
978-0-470-83685-9

Coaching Soccer For Dummies
978-0-471-77381-8

Fitness For Dummies, 3rd Edition
978-0-7645-7851-9

Football For Dummies, 3rd Edition
978-0-470-12536-6

GarageBand For Dummies
978-0-7645-7323-1

Golf For Dummies, 3rd Edition
978-0-471-76871-5

Guitar For Dummies, 2nd Edition
978-0-7645-9904-0

Home Recording For Musicians
For Dummies, 2nd Edition
978-0-7645-8884-6

iPod & iTunes For Dummies,
5th Edition
978-0-470-17474-6

Music Theory For Dummies
978-0-7645-7838-0

Stretching For Dummies
978-0-470-06741-3

Get smart @ dummies.com®

- **Find a full list of Dummies titles**
- **Look into loads of FREE on-site articles**
- **Sign up for FREE eTips e-mailed to you weekly**
- **See what other products carry the Dummies name**
- **Shop directly from the Dummies bookstore**
- **Enter to win new prizes every month!**

* Separate Canadian edition also available
† Separate U.K. edition also available